D0800173

HOMESCHOOLING
in America

To the Premier Equestrian Person

HOMESCHOOLING
in America

Capturing and Assessing the Movement

Joseph Murphy

CORWIN
A SAGE Company

CORWIN
A SAGE Company

FOR INFORMATION:

Corwin
A SAGE Company
2455 Teller Road
Thousand Oaks, California 91320
(800) 233-9936
www.corwin.com

SAGE Publications Ltd.
1 Oliver's Yard
55 City Road
London, EC1Y 1SP
United Kingdom

SAGE Publications India Pvt. Ltd.
B 1/I 1 Mohan Cooperative Industrial Area
Mathura Road, New Delhi
India 110 044

SAGE Publications Asia-Pacific Pte. Ltd.
3 Church Street
#10-04 Samsung Hub
Singapore 049483

Acquisitions Editors: Hudson Perigo and
   Arnis Burvikovs
Associate Editors: Allison Scott and
   Desirée A. Bartlett
Editorial Assistants: Lisa Whitney and
   Kimberly Greenberg
Permissions Editor: Adele Hutchinson
Project Editors: Amy Schroller and
   Veronica Stapleton
Copy Editor: Sarah J. Duffy
Typesetter: Hurix Systems Pvt. Ltd.
Proofreader: Talia Greenberg
Indexer: Molly Hall
Cover Designer: Michael Dubowe

Printed in the United States of America

Library of Congress Cataloging-in-Publication Data

Murphy, Joseph, 1949-
Homeschooling in America : capturing and assessing the movement/Joseph Murphy.
p. cm.
Includes bibliographical references and index.
ISBN 978-1-4522-0523-6 (pbk. : alk. paper)
1. Home schooling—United States—History. 2. Home schooling—Social aspects—United States. I. Title.

LC40.M87 2012

371.04'20973—dc23

2012023419

This book is printed on acid-free paper.

12 13 14 15 16 10 9 8 7 6 5 4 3 2 1

Contents

About the Author   vii

1. **Staying Home: Definitions and Estimates**   1
    Why a Book on Homeschooling?   1
    An Overview   3
    Definition   4
    Prevalence of Homeschooling   7
    The State of Knowledge   12
    Conclusion   14

2. **A Portrait: The Demographics of Homeschooling**   15
    Parent Education Levels   16
    Family Income   18
    Occupational Status   19
    Race and Ethnicity   20
    Marital Status   21
    Parental Age and Religious Affiliation   22
    Political Viewpoints   24
    Geographical Location   24
    Family Size   25
    Schooling-Related Demographics for Students   26
    Conclusion   27

3. **Riding History: The Origins and Development
   of Homeschooling**   29
    Foundations of Homeschooling   30
    Toward the Mainstream   35
    The DNA of Normalization   39
    Evolving Homeschooling Models   47
    Conclusion   51

4. **Seismic Shifts: Exploring Environmental Conditions That Foster Homeschooling** 53
    The Essential Hypothesis 53
    Social Context: Before Homeschool (1800–1890) 55
    Social Context: Before Homeschool (1890–1970) 56
    Social Context: Homeschooling (1970 on) 58
    Conclusion 73

5. **The Calculus of Departure: Parent Motivations for Homeschooling** 75
    Motivational Dynamics 76
    Motivational Frameworks 83
    Conclusion 104

6. **A Ball in Play: Homeschooling in Action** 105
    Introduction 106
    Instructional Methods 107
    Curricular Programs 110
    Conclusion 120

7. **The End Game: The Impact of Homeschooling** 121
    The Quality of the Existing Research Base 122
    Homeschooling Effects: Broad Measures 126
    Homeschooling Effects on Children 133
    Conclusion 151

8. **Hunches: Explanations for Positive Effects** 153
    The Context 153
    A Theory of Action 155
    Conclusion 160

References 161

Index 179

About the Author

 **Joseph Murphy** is the Frank W. Mayborn Chair and associate dean at Vanderbilt University's Peabody College of Education. He has also been a faculty member at the University of Illinois and The Ohio State University, where he was the William Ray Flesher Professor of Education.

In the public schools, he has served as an administrator at the school, district, and state levels. His most recent appointment was as the founding president of the Ohio Principals Leadership Academy.

He is past vice president of the American Educational Research Association (AERA) and was the founding chair of the Interstate School Leaders Licensure Consortium (ISLLC). He is coeditor of the AERA *Handbook on Educational Administration* (1999) and editor of the National Society for the Study of Education yearbook, *The Educational Leadership Challenge* (2002).

His work is in the area of school improvement, with special emphasis on leadership and policy. He has authored or coauthored 20 books in this area and edited another 12. His most recent authored volumes include *Turning Around Failing Schools: Leadership Lessons from the Organizational Sciences* (2008), *The Educator's Handbook for Understanding and Closing Achievement Gaps* (2010), *Homelessness Comes to School* (2011), and *Leadership Lessons for School Leaders* (2011).

The rise of homeschooling is one of the most significant social trends of the last half century. (Lines, 2000a, p. 74)

Home schooling is both a means of educating children and an alternative social movement. (Collom & Mitchell, 2005, p. 274)

There is no question that home schooling is one of the most formidable educational causes of its time. (M. L. Stevens, 2001, p. 11)

Homeschooling has been and continues to be a controversial issue in the United States. (Green & Hoover-Dempsey, 2007, p. 283)

The time has come for in-depth study and critical analysis of this movement, its lessons, and its future. (Nemer, 2002, p. 21)

1

Staying Home

Definitions and Estimates

There is no single, accepted definition of homeschooling.
(Wenger & Hodari, 2004, p. 4)

~∽∾∿∼~

Although estimates vary widely and the question has been debated by
many, the number of children being home educated in the United States
has clearly risen over the past 30 years. (Ray, 2011, p. 1)

~∽∾∿∼~

❖ WHY A BOOK ON HOMESCHOOLING?

Throughout this volume we compile considerable information on the homeschooling movement in the United States. We begin with a rationale, statements about the wisdom of studying homeschooling. In the beginning of the book, we review the tremendous expansion in the number of homeschooled children, growth that clearly justifies an investigation of homeschooling. We also examine the data on family demographics, issues such as the income, education, and occupation of homeschooling parents. These data and those on the children being homeschooled merit attention for what they convey about the social fabric of the nation.

In later chapters we argue that homeschooling warrants our interest because of its unique place in the cascading privatization movement in the United States in general and the rapidly expanding school choice movement in education specifically. We also maintain that a study of homeschooling provides important insights on the conservative mosaic that has been formed in the United States over the last 30 years. It reveals a good deal about the tensions between individualism and community as well as new ways to think about these social constructs. It allows us to peer more thoroughly into the place of religion in the United States at the turn of the 21st century. Even more important, an examination of homeschooling provides significant insights into the nature of American families. Perhaps most centrally, we can discover the possibilities of movements that attempt to reverse the segmentation of life in America, of how homeschooling is both an animating force for and an exemplar of efforts to provide an integrated frame for life in the postmodern world.

As with most social movements of significance, analysis of homeschooling reveals much about the battle for the moral high ground in the country. While we attend to the history and development of homeschooling itself, we learn as much about the ebb and flow of waves of influence and the shifting pendulum in the area of social ideas and tastes in general. In a similar vein, homeschooling reveals how history is both a product of as well as a platform for powerful figures to push and pull ideas onto society's central stage. In the process of analysis, considerable insights about the legal workings of the nation are exposed. So too dynamics about social organizing become visible, especially in getting society to embrace ideas that once seemed anathema. By studying homeschooling we accumulate a good deal of knowledge about the evolving role of government in the affairs of its owners. We track an evolution from government as the unquestioned mechanism to produce a better society to government as a self-forged and confining manacle that also has the potential to hinder improvement. In short, a study of homeschooling permits us to peer deeply into social dynamics that transcend the content of the topic at hand.

At the same time, homeschooling merits examination for what it reveals about education and schooling in America. Ongoing and dilemma-based questions about governance and control play out across its pages in new ways. There is much to be learned here about possible forms of schooling in the 21st century, new conceptions and models that were unimaginable to the previous generation. Issues of funding and costs lurk in the background of the homeschooling play but nonetheless offer important insights into financing the nation's most costly and critical state and local service—and other services as well. Labor issues are prevalent in the homeschooling literature but usually cast obliquely. Even at this, it is difficult to overlook the implications for the traditional and deeply rooted notions of civil service in the nation, especially in light of the prevalence of parallel trends in education (e.g., vouchers, tax credits, privately managed charter schools) and the larger society. Although rarely underscored in homeschool analyses, a careful study of homeschooling produces considerable wisdom on the role of markets and profits in the education sector. Much can also be gleaned about the linkages between schooling and social justice by examining homeschooling, about how we frame this essential construct and how we actualize efforts to achieve progress in this domain through our educational system.

We are also well advised to study homeschooling because of the potential costs and benefits to the 2 million youngsters who are educated at home—and to the 96%–97% of their peers who continue to be educated in public and private schools. We need to know if the goals of homeschool families (e.g., healthier, more cohesive families) are being met. We also need to explore whether progress on goals set by society for its children is being made (e.g., appropriate socialization).

❖ AN OVERVIEW

The balance of this volume explores all the issues surfaced above in the rationale section. In accomplishing this, we follow the logic of the homeschool movement itself as well as the hallmark research questions that have been engaged over the last three decades to develop a portrait of homeschooling in America. Since this is a review of all the work available to date, we rely heavily on the studies and theoretical analyses of those who have helped demarcate homeschooling. In this chapter, we look at definitions and estimates of the scope of homeschooling. We also provide a note on the state of knowledge in the homeschooling arena. In Chapter 2, we investigate the demographics of homeschooling, looking at families and homeschool settings. In Chapter 3, we examine the history and development of homeschooling, with special emphasis on the contemporary homeschooling movement. In Chapter 4, we explore the reasons for the rapid growth of homeschooling at this particular time in history. There we attend to both the favorability of the larger context in which schooling is nested (e.g., the pushback against government in general) and the motivations of homeschooling families (e.g., a desire to use religion as the curriculum architecture for learning). In Chapter 6, we unpack the homeschooling experience, looking at home education in action. In Chapter 7, we examine what is known in terms of the impact of homeschooling, mostly on homeschooled youngsters but on schooling in general as well.

Before we proceed, however, a word or two explaining what this volume is not about is in order. As we document later in this chapter and in Chapter 7, there is not an overabundance of solid empirical work on homeschooling. Much of the literature in this area comprises testimonials and pieces that explain how to successfully start and conduct a homeschool.

This is important material. But it is not the focus of this volume. Nor is this book a resource guide in which readers can locate support organizations and vendors who can assist them in their quest to homeschool (Leppert & Leppert, 2001, and Ray, 2008, are excellent sources in this area). We also know that homeschooling is found in many other nations (Basham, Merrifield, & Hepburn, 2007; Ray, 1997b; Wright, 1988). But the international landscape is not the focus of this volume; our attention is directed exclusively to homeschooling in the United States. Finally, a body of knowledge is developing around homeschooling for specific types of children, especially youngsters who would traditionally be in special education programs in public and private schools (see, for example, Dowity & Cowlishaw, 2002; Hartnett, 2005; Holland, 2005; Pyles, 2004). While we include information on children in special populations in our analysis, no specific groups are highlighted herein.

❖ DEFINITION

Homeschooling is not easy to describe. (Belfield, 2005, p. 168)

⟿⟆⟆⟵

There are many variations in the definitions of what constitutes "homeschooling." (Mirochnik & McIntire, 1991, p. 8)

⟿⟆⟆⟵

Homeschooling is an umbrella term that is used to describe the choice and the activities of thousands of families. (Sheffer, 1995, p. 8)

⟿⟆⟆⟵

A comprehensive analysis of the homeschooling literature leads us to conclude that the concept is not quite as simple as it appears on the surface. Indeed, if anything, the concept has become fuzzier over recent years as hybrid models of homeschooling and public schools have emerged. Below, we present core definitions provided by scholars over the last quarter century. Homeschooling is:

- The administration of an education program of instruction offered in the home setting in lieu of attendance in the public or private school. (Schemmer, 1985, p. 7)
- A teaching situation wherein children learn in the home in lieu of a conventional school. The parents, tutors, or guardians assume the direct responsibility for the education of their children. (J. Taylor, 1986a, p. 14)
- A school conducted in the home by a parent primarily for the education of the children in that home. (Gladin, 1987, p. 12)

- Instruction and learning, at least some of which is through planned activity, taking place *primarily* at home in a family setting with a parent acting as teacher or supervisor of the activity, and with one or more pupils who are members of the same family and who are doing grade K–12 work. (Lines, 1991, p. 10)
- The education of school-aged children under their parents' general monitoring, and it replaces full-time attendance at a campus school. (Lines, 1999, p. 1)
- The education of school-aged children at home rather than at a school. (Lyman, 2000, p. 18)
- Education received in the home, usually administered by the parent. (Perry & Perry, 2000, p. 7)
- The practice of educating children and youth during what most people call the elementary and secondary school years, in a learning environment that is home-based and parent-led (or, at least, clearly under the authority of the parent rather than under the authority of a state-run public school system or a private school). (Ray, 2004a, p. 3)
- An alternative form of education in which children are instructed at home rather than at a traditional public or private school. Children who are homeschooled are instructed by parents, guardians, or other tutors. (Lips & Feinberg, 2008, p. 2)

Evident in these definitions are two linked components, the "decision by parents not to educate their children in an institutionalized setting and the decision by parents to educate their children in a home setting" (Hadeed, 1991, p. 1).

It is "a deliberate rejection of and alternative to government schooling" (Gaither, 2008, p. 219). Thus, in one sense, a homeschooler is "best defined by what he does not do as opposed to what he does" (Guterson, 1992, p. 5); "these children and youth do not spend the societally conventional school days and hours in institutional classroom schools with specialized or state-certified teachers" (Ray, 2004a, p. 3).

Homeschooling is also known by a variety of synonyms such as *home-based education, home education, unschooling, home-centered learning, home instruction,* and *deschooling* (Luebke, 1999; J. Taylor, 1986b), with a growing sense that *home-based education* may be a particularly appropriate term for this phenomenon (Ray, 2000a).

It is also helpful to consider what does not fit into the homeschooling portfolio besides traditional public and private school education, especially situations that may resemble homeschooling but are not. As the definitions above reveal, homeschooling implies both a voluntariness and a rejection of conventional schooling (Allie-Carson, 1990; Lubienski, 2000). Therefore, actions that are not voluntary do not count as homeschooling in our definition. Teaching at home because a youngster is unable to go to school is not considered to be homeschooling (Aurini & Davies, 2005).

Children who are being educated at home because of a medical condition, for example, do not show up in the homeschooling ledger (Belfield, 2004a; Princiotta, Bielick, & Chapman, 2004). Nor would we count children who have no real option to attend public school—for example, those in remote places with no access to school. Likewise, children who are not in regular schools because of their parents' itinerant lifestyles would not be defined as homeschooled students (Knowles & Muchmore, 1995).

Also, as Roach (1988) reminds us, instruction by a parent of other children for compensation would be defined as an example of a private school operated in a home, not homeschooling. Children who are taught at home before the option of formal schooling is available (i.e., prekindergarten children) are not considered homeschoolers, either.

For the first 15 to 20 years or so of the modern homeschooling movement, youngsters were educated almost exclusively in either one setting (the home) or another (public or private school). With the advent of more mixed models of schooling, with students spending some portion of the day or week at home and some portion in a formal school environment, the variable of time has been added to the definition of homeschooling. The National Center for Educational Statistics (NCES) sets a fairly low bar to claim homeschooling status (Belfield, 2004a; Bielick, Chandler, & Broughman, 2001; Princiotta et al., 2004). According to NCES, if regular school enrollment of a student learning at home does not exceed 25 hours per week, the student is still considered to be homeschooled. Since the average K–12 student is at school about 30 to 35 hours a week, under this definition a student can be at home for as little as 17%–30% of the week and still count as homeschooled. According to Kunzman (2009b), the Home School Legal Defense Association (HSLDA) uses a higher bar, holding that for students to be considered homeschooled parents must direct at least 51% of the education of those youngsters (see also Boyer, 2002). In an early seminal study, Wartes (1990) suggested a still higher standard, holding that 75% of a child's education needed to be provided in the home to be considered a case of homeschooling. While there is no universally accepted answer on the time issue, it does seem reasonable to assume that for counting purposes, homeschooled children should spend the majority of time outside the traditional school.

It is also instructive to tease out the core elements of homeschooling, what makes homeschooling homeschooling. We have already presented a framework with two ingredients: the rejection of public (and private) schooling and the use of the home as the center of educational gravity. A second framework that is also rooted in the privatization literature underscores criteria in the three dimensions of funding, provision, and regulation (Duvall, 2005; Murphy, 1996; Murphy, Gilmer, Weise, & Page, 1998). Using this framework, a student is homeschooled when (1) funding for the student's education comes from the family, not the government; (2) the service is provided by the parents, not state-funded (or privately financed) employees; and (3) regulation of the enterprise is internal to the family, not the responsibility of the government (or another entity such as a religious body). The closer one is to the family/parent end of the continuum on each of these three dimensions, the more robust is homeschooling (Guterson, 1992; Reich, 2005).

❖ PREVALENCE OF HOMESCHOOLING

Home schooling has been observed to be a rapidly growing movement.
(J. Taylor, 1986a, p. 23)

⁓◠⋮◠⁓

Homeschooling is one of the fastest growing initiatives in America's educational options. (Pearson, 1996, p. 1)

⁓◠⋮◠⁓

The homeschool population has grown remarkably for 30 years, and most indications are that it will continue to grow into at least the near future. (Ray, 2009a, p. 7)

⁓◠⋮◠⁓

Expanding Number of Students

Home schooling has been built almost entirely since the end of the era called the Sixties. (M. L. Stevens, 2001, p. 16)

⁓◠⋮◠⁓

1970s

Before 1980, very few children were homeschooled (Ray & Weller, 2003). Ray (2000a, p. 274) argues, in fact, that homeschooling had "waned to near extinction by the late 1970s." Analysts estimate the total number of children being homeschooled in the 1970s in the 10,000–15,000 range: 10,000 (Divoky, 1983; Glanzer, 2008); 10,000–12,000 (Houston, 1999); 10,000–15,000 (Holt, 1983; Lines, 1991); 13,000 (Cogan, 2010; Ray & Eagleson, 2008). (See Table 1.1)

1980s

By the mid-1980s, the number of homeschooled children had jumped considerably, while because of the weak methodologies available at the time the estimates had become even less reliable (Knowles, Marlow, & Muchmore, 1992). On the high end, some homeschool advocates suggested enrollments as high as 1 million youngsters. More scientifically anchored estimates reported something in the neighborhood of an eighth to a quarter of that projection (Lines, 1999, 2000b; Reich, 2002): 60,000–125,000 in 1983; 122,000–244,000 in 1985; and 150,000–300,000 in 1988 (Lines, 1991). (See also Houston, 1999; Knowles et al., 1992.) (See Table 1.1)

Table 1.1   Enrollment Growth in Homeschooling

	Current Population Survey and National Home Education Survey (Princiotta & Bielick, 2006)	U.S. Department of Education (Lines, all publications)	National Home Education Research Institute (Ray, all publications)	Other
1970		10,000–15,000		
1980				
1981				
1982				
1983		60,000–125,000		
1984				
1985		122,000–244,000		50,000[a]
1986				
1987				
1988		147,000–294,000		
1989				
1990		250,000–355,000		300,000[b]
1991				
1992		375,000		
1993			450,000–800,000	
1994	356,000 (0.8%)	450,000–800,000 (1.09%)		400,000[c]
1995		700,000–750,000		
1996	636,000 (1.4%)		1,230,000	
1997				
1998				
1999	850,000 (1.7%)	850,000		1,200,000[c]
2000				
2001				2,000,000[d]
2002				

Table 1.1 (Continued)

	Current Population Survey and National Home Education Survey (Princiotta & Bielick, 2006)	U.S. Department of Education (Lines, all publications)	National Home Education Research Institute (Ray, all publications)	Other
2003	1,096,000 (2.2%)		2,000,000	
2004				
2005				
2006			1,900,000–2,400,000	
2007	1,508,000 (2.9%)			
2008			2,000,000	
2009				
2010			2,040,000 (3.8%)	

[a] Aurini & Davies (2005).
[b] Collom (2005).
[c] Nemer (2002).
[d] Reich (2002).

1990s

During the 1990s, the number of homeschooled children continued its rapid ascent. In 1990, the U.S. Department of Education put the number between 248,500 and 353,500 (Houston, 1999). The HSLDA produced a higher estimate of 474,165 (Houston, 1999). Lines's (1999) studies suggested that in 1991 between 250,000 and 350,000 youngsters were being homeschooled. The next year 300,000 children were on the homeschool rolls according to Basham and colleagues (2007). Two years later, in 1994, the Current Population Survey documented 356,000 homeschoolers (K. Bauman, 2002). In 1995, the National Home Education Research Institute (NHERI) produced an estimate of nearly half a million (Houston, 1999; Pearson, 1996)—about 1% of the U.S. school-age population. In 1996, the National Household Education Survey (NHES) provided an estimate of 636,000 (K. Bauman, 2002), while Lines (1999) pegged the number at 750,000, or about 1.4% of the total school-age population. The HSLDA suggested an enrollment of around 1.23 million homeschooled students (Ray 1997b). Similar numbers have been offered for 1997 enrollments. By 1998, almost everyone was in agreement that there were in the neighborhood of 1 million youngsters being educated at home (M. L. Stevens, 2001), although considerable variation remained in the estimates.

By the end of the 1990s, with the advent of better data collection mechanisms and refinements to those already in use, the data on homeschooling began to firm up somewhat; it became more reliable. Data from the NHES revealed the presence of about 850,000 homeschoolers in the United States in 1999, about 1.7% of the total school-age population (Bielick et al., 2001; Princiotta et al., 2004). Numbers provided by homeschool advocates trended higher. For example, Perry and Perry (2000) noted an enrollment of 1.7 million. (See Table 1.1)

2000s

Wenger and Hodari (2004) provided these data for 2001: 1 million homeschooled students, representing 2% of the school-age population. Isenberg (2002) concurs, suggesting an enrollment of 1.04 million homeschooled children, representing 2.1% of their peer group. Again, estimates provided by advocacy groups tended to be higher: 2 million students according to the HSLDA, or roughly 3% of all school-age children (Wenger & Hodari, 2004). Data from a second NHES set enrollment at nearly 1.1 million homeschooled students in 2003 (Aurini & Davies, 2005; Princiotta et al., 2004), fully 2.2% of all youngsters of school age. The NHERI estimated that between 1.9 and 2.4 million students were homeschooled during the 2005–2006 school year (Ray, 2009b). Data from another NHES put enrollment at 1.5 million students in 2007, or 2.9% of the school-age population (Bielick, 2008). Ray (2011) pegged enrollment at 2.04 million in 2010, or 3.8% of the school-age population. (See Table 1.1)

Growth Rates

More children are homeschooled than attend charter schools. More children are homeschooled than attend conservative Christian academies.
(Reich, 2002, p. 56)

The growth of homeschooling in the United States has been nothing short of remarkable, even using the most conservative estimates available. Remember that only 10,000–15,000 children were being homeschooled in the 1970s. By 2010, somewhere in the neighborhood of 2 million students were part of this group. Growth rates have been calculated on the low end of the scale as in the range of 7%–12% per annum (Basham et al., 2007; Ray, 2005, 2011). Less conservatively, they have been measured at 15% over that time period (K. Bauman, 2002; Houston & Toma, 2003; McKeon, 2007; Nemer, 2002). We also learn that among education alternatives, homeschooling has the steepest line of ascent (K. Bauman, 2002). Since 2000, a time by which the movement was fairly well established, the number of homeschoolers has increased at a rate 10 times that of public school students (Kunzman, 2005).

There is also evidence that the startling rate of homeschool growth, especially between 1980 and 2000, may be slowing down (Bielick, 2008; Gaither, 2008; Isenberg, 2007; Ray, 2011). Analysts explore the reason for this slowing pattern and examine forces that could help cap homeschool enrollment in the years ahead. They note, for example, that while homeschool opponents and skeptics have been largely pushed to the sidelines in recent years, they have the potential to reassert themselves if the country's political and social climate changes (Kunzman, 2009a). These reviewers remind us that the pool of parents with the commitment to educate their children at home is hardly limitless (Gorder, 1990; Lines, 1987). Neither is the pool with the resources to do so completely elastic (Hill, 2000; Muntes, 2006), although scholars argue that there is still considerable room below the resource cap (K. Bauman, 2002; Houston & Toma, 2003). Finally, analysts suggest that the recent economic downturn might put pressure on parents to select employment over homeschooling (Ray, 2011). Analysts also remind us that the "publication" of the private endeavor of homeschooling could occur through the growth of public charter schools that cater to traditional homeschool parents (Gaither, 2008; Murphy, 1996).

Comparisons with other forms of schooling help put the enrollment and growth figures in perspective. We have already seen that homeschooling enrollment as a percentage of total school-age children jumped from almost nothing to around 3% in the span of 40 years. Scholars confirm that homeschool enrollment is now about one-fifth the size of private school enrollment, up from zero 40 years ago (Belfield, 2004b; Isenberg, 2007). We find that almost twice as many youngsters are schooled at home as are educated in conservative Christian schools (Glanzer, 2008). In addition, more children are taught at home (2 million) than attend charter schools (1.5 million) and receive vouchers combined (Apple, 2007; Belfield, 2004b; Hill, 2000). Remember also that percentage enrollment figures are for any given year— that is, they are point-in-time estimates. When life cycle numbers are compiled, we discover that fully 6%–12% of all students will have been educated at home at some time in their K–12 educational careers (Houston, 1999; Isenberg, 2007; Lines, 1999).

Compiling the Data

As with many social movements, counting members is difficult. (Bates, 1991, p. 6)

Pinpointing the number of homeschoolers in the United States is a difficult task. (Guterson, 1992, p. 227)

Homeschoolers have been a difficult population to identify. (Collom, 2005, p. 315)

As we have seen, there is some variability in estimates of the number of homeschooled children in the United States (Mayberry, 1992). Some of this can be attributed to the phenomenon described by Lotto (1983) as "believing is seeing." That is, there is likely an upward bias on the part of some homeschooling advocates. Some can also be linked to practical and methodological difficulties in counting these children (Belfield, 2004a; Lines, 1991). To begin with, as Reich (2005) reports, in many places (e.g., 10 states) registration of homeschooled children, a prerequisite to being counted, is not required. In other places, homeschool families simply neglect to register when they are required to do so (Bates, 1991; Kleist-Tesch, 1998; Lines, 1999). In still other cases, parents are so opposed to governmental oversight of their families, they refuse to participate in data collection activities, both census and research efforts (Bates, 1991; Collom, 2005; Kunzman, 2005). Others fail to register because they lack trust in government agencies (Wartes, 1988). Still others fall under provisions that do not require religious-based homeschoolers to register (Lines, 1999). Some families operate as "private schools," thus again eliminating the registration requirement (Aurini & Davies, 2005; Lines, 1999). Finally, problems stemming from the nature of the intervention itself— a small population, definitional issues, geographical dispersion, and decentralization to hundreds of thousands of sites (homes)—make counting (and studying) homeschoolers a difficult task (Belfield, 2004a; Collom & Mitchell, 2005). All of these conditions lead to production of less-than-satisfying estimates, ones that are biased downward.

Counting problems also arise from the methods used to arrive at estimates (Mirochnik & McIntire, 1991). For example, researchers often turn to lists of families who have joined homeschool associations to draw estimates. At other times, they rely on lists of those who purchase materials from homeschool curriculum providers. However, since some families do not join support groups and/or purchase from homeschool providers, these sources are likely to undercount homeschoolers (Lines, 1999). It is also important to remember that there is a lack of uniformity among states in how and when they collect data on this population (Lines, 1999).

More recently, researchers have employed household surveys to arrive at the number of homeschoolers in the United States. While this approach overcomes many of the problems inherent in the previously discussed methods, it is not free of problems (Bielick, Chandler, & Broughman, 2001). In particular, because they are often such a small percentage of school-age children, very few of them are likely to be included in national household surveys (Wenger & Hodari, 2004).

❖ THE STATE OF KNOWLEDGE

Homeschoolers are a difficult population to study and much of the existing research is limited. (Collom, 2005, p. 307)

~◠✦◠~

More than anything else, more—and better—research is needed.
(Medlin, 2000, p. 118)

~ᴖᵛᴖ~

One of the most stark conclusions one draws when reviewing the schol-arly literature on homeschooling is just how thin the empirical knowledge base is on this social phenomenon and educational movement. To be sure, there is a good deal of ideological bantering as well as some solid conceptual modeling. There is also a trace of good reports on how to engage the work of educating a child at home and fine collections of resources to assist in those efforts. But the research cupboard is not well stocked. This assessment first surfaced as the homeschool movement reached early adolescence. It was revealed that the entire domain was largely uncharted in a scientific sense (see Delahooke, 1986; Gladin, 1987; Groover & Endsley, 1988; Knowles, 1989; Mayberry, 1989a; Schemmer, 1985; J. Taylor, 1986a; Wartes, 1987; Williams, Arnoldson, & Reynolds, 1984; Wright, 1988). More troubling, this same con-clusion was consistently reached by scholars, analysts, and policymakers throughout the 1990s as well (see Dalaimo, 1996; Duvall, Ward, Delquadri, & Greenwood, 1997; Hertzel, 1997; Houston, 1999; Kelley, 1991; Knowles et al., 1992; Luebke, 1999; Mirochnik & McIntire, 1991; Rudner, 1999; Van Galen, 1991). Even more disheartening is that the next generation of reviewers has uncovered little evidence that the limited empirical evidence deficiency was addressed with much sense of robustness during the first half (see K. Bauman, 2002; Houston & Toma, 2003; Isenberg, 2002; Kunzman, 2005; Nemer, 2002; M. L. Stevens, 2003) or the second half of the first decade of the 21st century (see Cogan, 2010; Green & Hoover-Dempsey, 2007; Ice & Hoover-Dempsey, 2011; Isenberg, 2007; Kunzman, 2009a; Muntes, 2006; Taylor-Hough, 2010).

Not surprisingly, then, there is a nearly universal call for more research on homeschooling in the scholarly community, and increasingly for more sophis-ticated and stronger research designs (Basham et al., 2007)—with the occa-sional reminder of progress to date (McKeon, 2007; Ray, 2004b). To some extent, this can be traced to the newness of the field of homeschooling (Medlin, 2000; Ray & Eagleson, 2008). Nearly every domain of social science has expe-rienced the same problem during its formative era. But deeper analysis reveals that the problem is more pronounced here, a condition that will become clearer as we explore the research issue in more depth in Chapter 7.

The logical question is, of course, why has so little scientific evidence been generated on the contemporary homeschooling movement? Newness of the field cannot explain everything. After all, it is more prevalent than charter schools and roughly 15 years longer in its development (1975 versus 1990); yet the research on homeschooling can only be characterized as immature and poorly formed in comparison to the large-scale, sophisticated work on charter schools. We need to expand the quest for answers. Certainly there are many difficulties in conducting studies of homeschooling, and many unique ones at that (Knowles & Muchmore, 1995). All of the problems we detailed earlier in the discussion of counting homeschoolers come into play here, too, thus making research problematic as well (Hill, 2000). Even when they agree to be counted, resistance on the part of some of the homeschool community to engage with researchers is legendary (Kunzman, 2009b; Ray, 2011).

The well-developed practice of concentrating research on public schools probably explains some of the dearth of research. In addition, funding streams are not routinely devoted to the study of white, middle-class youngsters, which as we will see in Chapter 2 comprise the overwhelming bulk of homeschool students. Resources are devoted much more aggressively to understanding and ameliorating the plight of students placed at risk of school failure. The unregulated nature of homeschooling comes into play here as well. The decentralized nature of homeschooling, the fact that it unfolds in hundreds of thousands of "mini schools" with only a few "students," also causes considerable problems for researchers (Lips & Feinberg, 2008).

All of this is complicated by the limited availability of data sets on homeschooling. For example, unlike in public schools there are few representative databases on the academic performance of homeschooled children (Isenberg, 2007). State and district databases leave much to be desired (Houston, 1999). Records from individual families are even less valuable. At the national level, homeschooled youngsters are often not included in many important databases (e.g., NAEP; Nemer, 2002). The end game is that the study of homeschooling is made problematic by less-than-ideal data (Isenberg, 2007; Lines, 2000a).

❖ CONCLUSION

In this first chapter, we laid the groundwork for the balance of the volume. We began with a point often overlooked in the general literature on privatization, the mid-level research on choice, and the specific research on homeschooling. That is, homeschooling provides a window into understanding a great deal about how the political, cultural, and social fabric of the nation is being rewoven—probably more than any other educational intervention since the creation of the modern school system a century ago. We noted that homeschooling is both a powerful social and educational phenomenon. We also tracked the prevalence of home education in America since the beginning of the modern homeschooling movement around 1975, documenting rather startling growth from around 10,000–15,000 to roughly 2,000,000 children, something between 3% and 4% of the school-age population. At the same time, we reviewed problems that have confronted analysts in their efforts to count the number of homeschooled students. We examined the definition of homeschooling, culling critical criteria to be used to place the divide between homeschooling and regular public education. We closed the chapter with a brief advance organizer on the state of empirical knowledge in the area of homeschooling. In Chapter 2, we turn the analytic lens on the demographics of homeschooling.

2

A Portrait

The Demographics of Homeschooling

The recent increase in the popularity of home schooling has increased the demand for research on what these families look like. (Houston, 1999, p. 48)

⌒◦⌒

Homeschoolers are predominantly white and middle class; many espouse conservative Protestant faiths; their households have full-time or nearly full-time moms. (M. L. Stevens, 2001, pp. 17–18)

⌒◦⌒

Home school students and their families are in some ways a select population. (Ray, 2010, p. 23)

⌒◦⌒

We know that over the last 30 years a good deal of effort has been invested in exploring the demographic characteristics of homeschool children and their families, their religious affiliations, income, education, geographical locations, and so forth. Important early studies were conducted at the state level, for example Wartes (1987) in Washington and Mayberry (1989a, 1989b) in Oregon. The National Home Education

Research Institute (NHERI) in 1990 completed the first comprehensive survey at the national level, with subsequent reports released by Ray in 1997b, 2004, and 2010. The National Center for Educational Statistics began systematic surveying of households in the 1990s. Many other scholars have added to our knowledge about the demographics of homeschoolers and their families, often via their dissertations. Because of all this effort, a fairly good body of data is available for review. Although because of the counting problems and problems conducting research that we discussed in Chapter 1, there is still a sense that we need more reliable data on homeschool demographics (Kunzman, 2005; Nemer, 2002).

The conclusions scholars draw from looking at the demographic portrait have a good deal to do with where they focus within the homeschooling picture. When they direct their gaze to the most distinct elements of the portrait, similarities (measures of central tendency) are highlighted. As we discuss in this chapter, commonalities around income, race, marital status, religious affiliation, and education levels are routinely reported (Mayberry, Knowles, Ray, & Marlow, 1995; Ray, 2010). We learn that, indeed, homeschoolers are a select population (Lines, 2000b; Ray, 2010). When analysts step back to examine the entire homeschooling portrait, they are more likely to treat the diversity within the movement, the fact that there is considerable variability in homeschool demographics (Boone, 2000; Kunzman, 2009a; Ray, 2009b). In short, as Mayberry and colleagues (1995) remind us, demographic trends do not mean that there is a monolithic homeschool population. These later analysts also contend that the homeschool movement is becoming more diverse as it matures (Gaither, 2008; Ray, 2010).

❖ PARENT EDUCATION LEVELS

Well Educated

There is nearly universal agreement among scholars across time that homeschooling parents are generally well educated (Bielick, Chandler, & Broughman, 2001; Gustavsen, 1981; Sutton & Bogan, 2005). They tend to have moderate to high levels of education, without being heavily represented at the very highest levels of schooling completed (Belfield, 2004a). The typical homeschool mother and father have attended and often graduated from college (Ray, 2005). Reviewers report average education levels (i.e., years of schooling completed) for parents within a narrow band—14.3 for both (J. Taylor, 1986a), 14.7 for fathers and 14.1 for mothers (Wartes, 1990), and 15.6 for fathers and 14.7 for mothers (Ray, 1997b).

Documentation of education in terms of degrees has been a consistent line of investigation throughout the modern homeschool era. In the first important study of homeschooling, Gustavsen (1981) reported that 44.0% of parents had graduated from college. Gladin (1987) found that 38% of mothers and 52% of fathers in his study had a college degree or higher.

John Wesley Taylor (1986a) documented that homeschool parents generally had 1–3 years of college, with 41% having earned a degree. Wartes (1990) discovered that 28.6% of homeschool mothers and 40.7% of homeschool fathers were college graduates. Steven Gray (1993) pegged college completion of homeschool mothers at 50.0%. Ray's (1997b) nationally based numbers are 34.0% for mothers and 31.0% for fathers. Parker (1992) recorded a college completion rate of 36.0% for mothers and 34.0% for fathers. The most recent national data provide higher estimates of college completion: 62.5% of mothers and 66.3% of fathers (Ray, 2010).

Better Educated

Comparative data also consistently reveal that homeschool parents fall somewhere between "somewhat better educated" (S. Gray, 1993; Kelley, 1991; Lines, 1991; Mayberry, 1989a; Muntes, 2006; Wartes, 1987) and "considerably better educated" (Mayberry et al., 1995; J. Taylor, 1986a) than do non-homeschool parents. John Wesley Taylor (1986a) found that while nationally 66.5% of individuals 25 years of age or older had earned a high school degree, fully 94.6% of homeschool parents had done so. Bielick and colleagues (2001), in a later, more systematic study, concluded that only 19% of homeschool parents did not complete any schooling beyond high school, compared to 37% of non-homeschool parents. Rudner (1999) discovered that 88% of homeschool parents pursued their education beyond high school, compared to 50% for the nation as a whole. Basham and colleagues (2007) arrived at roughly similar numbers, 75% versus 56%. In his most recent comprehensive investigation, Ray (2010) reported that while 29.5% of all adult males and 78.0% of females over the age of 25 had completed college, fully 66.3% of homeschool fathers and 62.5% of homeschool mothers had done so.

Data from the National Home Education Survey over the last dozen years reinforce these conclusions. For example, in 1999, 33.3% of the parents of all students had a college degree, while 47.4% of homeschool parents had earned a 4-year college degree (Bielick et al., 2001). By 2003, those percentages had narrowed a bit, to 36.5% versus 44.6%. On the other end of the education continuum, in 1999, 36.5% of all parents had a high school degree or less, while this was the case for only 18.9% of homeschooling parents. By 2003, there was a significant narrowing in this category, however: 31.8% for all parents versus 24.5% for homeschooling parents (i.e., a narrowing from 17.6% to 7.3% from 1999 to 2003).

Two other national studies buttress conclusions presented above. According to Rudner (1999), nationally 15.6% of males and 14.8% of females had earned bachelor's degrees, while fully 37.6% of homeschooling fathers and 47.2% of homeschooling mothers had done so. Ray (1997b), in turn, found that while only 24% of adults had college degrees or higher, fully 53% of homeschooling parents had this level of education.

Two caveats merit introduction here. First, information on post–high school work tells us little about what course of study parents are pursuing (for exceptions, see Parker, 1992; Sutton & Galloway, 2000). Second, and more important, data about the education of homeschooling versus non-homeschooling parents, while informative, do not provide the best comparison set. As Lange and Liu (1999) remind us, because we are examining homeschooling parents as instructors, the most appropriate comparison would be of education between homeschooling parents and teachers in public and private schools.

❖ FAMILY INCOME

Middle Class

Analyses of family income over the last quarter century present home-school families as solidly middle class and financially stable, with medium to medium-high amounts of income (K. Bauman, 2002; Belfield, 2005; Kleist-Tesch, 1998; Mayberry et al., 1995). In none of the empirical studies do we find a significant percentage of low-income homeschooling parents. On the opposite end of the income spectrum, homeschool parents are not heavily represented in the upper end of income bands, either (Belfield, 2004a; Nemer, 2002). This, Belfield (2004a, 2005) suggests, may be attributable to the fact that higher-income families may find it wiser to garner a robust second income and use the money to pay for private education than to forgo income for one parent to stay at home. The takeaway conclusion from the research is that homeschooling families are likely to be neither rich nor poor but of middle-income status.

Better Off

Reports of family income in dollars confirm this summative conclusion. Gustavsen (1981) reported an average homeschool income in the $15,000–$20,000 range. John Wesley Taylor (1986a) added that the income for homeschool families was higher than for families in the United States in general. In a study from the same era, Gladin (1987) reported an average yearly income of $30,972 for homeschooling families (with only 14.3% making more than $40,000) and $25,757 for the average American family. Mayberry (1989b) also concluded that homeschooling families enjoyed greater economic security than average families. In 1990, Wartes reported a median family income for homeschooling families in the $30,000–$35,000 range. For comparison purposes, in 1989 the U.S. Census Bureau pegged average family earnings at $27,326 (Kelley, 1991).

Throughout the 1990s, the income advantage of homeschooling families continued to be visible. Mayberry and colleagues (1995) found that 57% of Washington, Nevada, and Utah homeschooled families earned in the $25,000–$50,000 range, while only 37% of other adults in the three states earned this much income. Median family income for homeschoolers was $43,000 in 1996 (Ray, 1997b) and $52,000 in 1999 (Rudner, 1999), and $35,000 for all families with children in 1999 (Rudner, 1999).

More recent studies suggest that while the income of homeschooling families is concentrated in the middle-income brackets, it is moving closer to the median American family income (Ray, 2005). That is, the income gap of earlier decades may be closing. For example, Sutton and Galloway (2000) noted a mean family income of $27,160 for homeschoolers attending college, nearly $9,000 less than for college-attending public school students ($36,026). In a more generalizable analysis, Ray (1997b) found that the median family income for homeschool families was $43,000, compared to $47,067 for all married-couple families.

In terms of summary on the income storyline, here is what we can say. Homeschool families are squarely in the middle class. They are underrepresented in both the low- and high-end income streams, a consequence largely due to the fact that almost all of these families forgo one income so that the mother can stay home with her children. While in the earlier years of the homeschooling movement these families enjoyed a slight to significant edge in income, that advantage appears to have been eliminated as the movement has matured. That is, income for homeschooling parents is close to the median income of all families (Basham et al., 2007; Ray, 2004a), $74,049 nationwide versus $75,000–$80,000 for homeschooling families (Ray, 2010). But as we noted above and discuss in more detail in the following section, homeschool families are much more likely than most families to garner income through the work of a single adult. Thus, if rather than comparing the income of homeschooling families to all families, we compare their income to the income of married-couple families with the wife not employed, an advantage to homeschooling families reappears: $43,000 versus $32,375 (Ray, 1997b).

❖ OCCUPATIONAL STATUS

The cardinal conclusion of the homeschooling demographic is that mothers in these families overwhelmingly do not participate in the labor market. They are stay-at-home moms who devote themselves full time to taking care of their families and assume prime responsibility for educating their children. Or, as Mitchell Stevens (2001, p. 85) points out, "home schooling is largely a movement of women." Various studies shed light on the prevalence of this occupational pattern. In a study in Washington State in the late 1980s, Wartes (1987, 1988) reported that 94.4% of homeschooling families relied on one income. In a study of homeschooling in Texas, Parker (1992) found that 89% of mothers were homemakers who worked outside the home fewer than 10 hours per week. In the 1997 report from NHERI, Ray (1997b) reported that 84% of homeschooling mothers did not work outside the home. Those who did so worked an average of 14 hours per week. Rudner (1999) documented homeschooling mothers not in the workforce at 80%.

The most recent data from NHERI (Ray, 2010) show that 81% of home-school mothers continue not to participate in the labor force. Of the 19% that do so, fully 85% are part-time employees. Kurt Bauman (2002) reported that 60% of homeschool youngsters have a nonworking parent in the home. The data from the 1989 National Household Education Survey (NHES) provide a similar storyline. Fully 52% of homeschooled children were in two-parent families in which only one parent was in the labor force, compared to 19% for non-homeschool school-age youngsters (Bielick et al., 2001; Princiotta & Bielick, 2006).

The alternative formulation of the occupational theme just described is that fathers are the main wage earners in homeschooling families. Research shows that these fathers occupy a wide range of positions in the labor market, a narrative that in some ways parallels the national storyline and in some ways is distinct. In particular, researchers have documented that homeschooling fathers are overrepresented in professional jobs, self-employed work, and the religious sector (Gladin, 1987; Mayberry et al., 1995; Parker, 1992; Ray, 1997b). We also learn that homeschooling does not impact labor force participation for these fathers or the number of hours that they work (Isenberg, 2002).

❖ RACE AND ETHNICITY

All analyses conclude that whites are disproportionately represented in the ranks of homeschoolers. The underrepresentation of families of color is most pronounced in studies that rely on surveying from lists of known homeschooled families provided by support organizations and/or inves-tigations anchored in lists of families using popular homeschooling cur-ricular packages. (See the discussion on counting homeschoolers in Chapter 1.) Disproportionality is less dramatic in national census data. This suggests that methods developed prior to national household sur-veys, and still employed, probably underestimate minority enrollment in homeschooling (Mayberry et al., 1995). Let us turn to the data.

Early studies (1980–1995) revealed that whites were greatly overrepre-sented on the rolls of homeschooling families (Chatham-Carpenter, 1994; Rakestraw, 1988), although, as Lines (1991) thoughtfully reports, many of these early studies did not document patterns of race and ethnicity. A 1986 study in Washington State discovered that 96% of homeschool children were white (Wartes, 1987). Parker (1992) established white participation at 93% and Mayberry and colleagues (1995) at 98%.

Studies from 1996 through 2010 divide largely, but not exclusively, along the "methods for counting" fault line. In one of his legendary comprehensive analyses from this era, Ray (1997b) found that 95% of homeschooled students were non-Hispanic white, about 17 percentage points higher than the average school-age child in the nation at the time. Ninety-six percent of mothers and 96% of fathers were classified as white in the same study. In another national study from the early part of this era, Rudner (1999) pegged the white homeschool population at 94.0%, compared to 67.2% white K–12 students nationwide. Another, although state-based, study reported white homeschool enrollment at 93% (Lange & Liu, 1999). (See also Belfield, 2004b; Cogan, 2010.) Ray (2004a) found that 93.2% of homeschooled children were white, compared to 75.1% of all U.S. students. Other studies have pegged white non-Hispanic enrollments at 84.8% (Muntes, 2006), 85% (Ray, 2005), and 91.3% (Ray, 2010), compared to about 57% of school-age children in general.

Census data reveal parallel but less extreme findings in the area of race/ethnicity. For example, in U.S. government surveys white homeschool enrollment was calculated at 86.8% in 1996, 75.3% in 1999, and 77.0% in 2003, compared to 64.7% and 62.3% nationally in 1999 and 2003, respectively (Princiotta & Bielick, 2006).

Regardless of the source of data used to arrive at estimates of homeschool enrollment, there is a recurring claim in the literature that homeschooling is becoming more diverse in terms of race/ethnicity, that increasing numbers of minority children are being homeschooled (Gaither, 2008; McKeon, 2007; Ray, 2005, 2009b; V. Taylor, 2005). Or as Kurt Bauman (2002) nicely phrases it, there is evidence of diminishing racial differences in homeschool enrollment over time. This seems to be a reasonable hypothesis, although it needs to be subjected to much more rigorous testing than it has been to date. We also need to remember that it is comparative data that need attention. Specifically, the percentage of minority students in the nation is increasing and minority enrollment in public schools is increasing even faster. An important question is how the changing racial/ethnic enrollments in America's homeschools line up with these shifting patterns.

❖ MARITAL STATUS

So far we have documented that homeschool families are solidly middle class and likely to be a bit better off financially than non-homeschool families, and considerably better off if the comparison is confined to one-wage-earner families. We have also seen that homeschoolers are overwhelmingly one-income families in which one parent (almost always the mother) stays at home to school the children. We also reported that homeschooled youngsters are more likely to be white than the school-age population in general. We add to the demographic chronicle by marking another hallmark characteristic of these families: strong marital cohesiveness. Specifically, homeschooled children are routinely located in married, intact, two-parent families (Basham et al., 2007; Cai, Reeve, & Robinson, 2002; Lips & Feinberg, 2008). Early studies by Gustavsen (1981), John Wesley Taylor (1986a), Wartes (1990), and Mayberry and colleagues (1995) provided estimates of married, two-parent families as follows: 91%, 94%, 98%, and 97%, respectively. Later studies by Rudner (1999), Ray (2004a), Muntes (2006), and Ray (2010) confirm the marital cohesiveness conclusion, reporting estimates of married, two-parent, intact families as follows: 97%, 95%, 87%, and 98%, respectively.

Here again, we see that national surveys conducted by the U.S. government provide confirming but less dramatic findings. For example, the U.S. Census Bureau and the NHES pegged two-parent homeschooling families at 79.2% in 1996, 80.4% in 1999, and 80.8% in 2003 (K. Bauman, 2002; Princiotta & Bielick, 2006), roughly 15% higher than American families with children in general. We conclude that while marital cohesiveness is not a requirement for home-based education (Sheffer, 1995), it greatly increases the odds of homeschooling (Isenberg, 2002), especially given the prevalence of the one-wage-earner, stay-at-home mom patterns we documented above.

❖ PARENTAL AGE AND RELIGIOUS AFFILIATION

Surprisingly little information has been compiled on parental age. The data that are available suggest that homeschooling parents are likely to be somewhat younger than parents in general (Gladin, 1987; Mayberry et al., 1995).

On the other hand (as we will see in Chapters 3 and 4), because of the central place that religion occupies in the homeschool parental motivational equation and for the support associations that buttress the movement, considerable attention has been devoted to the religious affiliations of homeschooling families. Both nominal affiliations and depth of activity have been investigated. As with education, occupation, race, and marital status, religious affiliation varies by homeschool status. Drilling downward from the general to the specific, here is what we know from the empirical literature. First, homeschooling is overwhelmingly a Christian phenomenon (Ray, 1997b). Second, it is predominantly a Protestant activity (Lines, 1991; Ray, 2004b). Third, fundamentally based religious denominations are overrepresented (Kunzman, 2005). It will come as no surprise, then, to learn that many homeschool families have conservative religious beliefs, ones that tightly align with Christian religious orthodoxy and conservative biblical doctrine (Mayberry et al., 1995; McKeon, 2007; Ray, 2005).

It is worth noting that these patterns do not imply a monolithic phenomenon (Apple, 2007; Mayberry et al., 1995; M. L. Stevens, 2001). It is also sometimes suggested that homeschoolers may be becoming more religiously diverse, an assertion that cries out for more empirical evidence (Gaither, 2008). For example, McKeon (2007) reports that those from the Muslim faith comprise one of the fastest-growing groups of homeschoolers in the United States (see also Gaither, 2008), a finding that is not inconsistent with the centrality of conservative religious doctrine in the movement.

Documentation of these three dynamics nest in a series of studies conducted over the last 30 years. Gladin (1987), for example, found that nearly all (92.4%) of the homeschooling families in his study characterized themselves as evangelical (37.3%), fundamentalist (35.0%), or charismatic (20.1%). Wartes (1990) concluded that 98.7% of his sample of Washington State families were Christian. Well over three-quarters of these were classified as "non-denominational Christian" or "conservative evangelical denomination," religious groups that are also the most active in encouraging homeschooling for their parishioners (Parker, 1992). In their study, Mayberry and colleagues (1995) counted over one-third of homeschooling parents as evangelical Pentecostal and other nondenominational religious groups, with another quarter belonging to mainstream Christian denominations.

In his comprehensive studies for NHERI, Ray has also described the prevalence of a conservative Christian tilt in the homeschooling community. In his 1997 study, he pegged that percentage at roughly 57, most likely an underestimation given that nearly 17% of the sample classified themselves as "other Christian" (5.5%) or "other" (11.5%). He found that 90% of the homeschooling parents classified themselves as Christian, and most of them as born again or basic biblical Christians (Ray, 1997b; see also Gaither, 2008; Luebke, 1999; M. L. Stevens, 2001). In a later study, Ray (2010) provides a similar but a bit reduced number, roughly 49%, for biblically doctrinaire homeschoolers. In his highly cited report, Rudner (1999) estimated that about 63% of homeschooled families were biblically anchored Christians. Cai and colleagues (2002) found that about 75% of homeschooling families can be characterized as conservative, born-again Christians (see also Kunzman, 2005). The lowest figure in the empirical literature to date sets the number of conservative Christian homeschoolers at 57.3% (McKeon, 2007).

Homeschool parents are also highly committed to their faith (Chatham-Carpenter, 1994; Mayberry et al., 1995). Over 90% confirm that their religious commitment is very important to their lives (M. L. Stevens, 2001), compared to 45% of a national sample that report that religion is not very important to them (Mayberry et al., 1995). Seventy-five percent of homeschooling parents attend church frequently (Ray, 2005). Mayberry and colleagues (1995) found that 78% claim to attend church weekly, compared to 30% of the nation as a whole. Gladin (1987) reported even higher percentages: 93% attending church weekly, with fully 72% attending at least twice a week.

❖ POLITICAL VIEWPOINTS

Given the narrative provided on the dominance of conservative religious doctrine in the homeschooling movement, it should come as no surprise that researchers report that as a group homeschoolers are politically and socially conservative as well (Collom & Mitchell, 2005; Mayberry et al., 1995). Turning first to party affiliation, we learn that homeschoolers are overwhelmingly Republicans, 93% in the Parker (1992) investigation and 76% in the study by Mayberry and colleagues (1995). Nationally, affiliation with the Republican Party is around 50%. Looking next at labels of political perspectives, we discover that homeschoolers fall overwhelmingly into the conservative and extremely conservative categories (Houston, 1999), far more so than the general population in the United States (Cai et al., 2002; Mayberry et al., 1995). Based on their research, Mayberry's team concluded that 77% of the homeschool population fell into these categories, with the balance falling into the liberal and highly liberal categories.

Scholars have also discovered that social and political conservatism, coupled with a suspicion of social institutions (see Chapter 3), does not translate into withdrawal by homeschool parents from the larger social order. That is, homeschooling does not equate with social disengagement (Isenberg, 2002; Ray, 2004a; M. L. Stevens, 2003). To the contrary, findings from 1981 through 2010 suggest that homeschooling families fall somewhere between moderately and highly active in community endeavors (Parker, 1992; Ray, 2004a; J. Taylor, 1986a). Homeschool parents tend to vote more frequently than the general public and are often involved in political activities in their communities (Parker, 1992).

As is the case with many of the demographic domains reviewed in this chapter (e.g., race), there are assertions in the literature that political dynamics are changing in the homeschooling world. In particular, some analysts suggest movement away from the far right and toward the center of the political spectrum (Reich, 2005; Somerville, 2005). To date, these claims do not enjoy much empirical support.

❖ GEOGRAPHICAL LOCATION

Two issues around geography have interested homeschool analysts over the years: geographical emphasis of homeschooling in the various regions of the nation and degree of *urbanicity* of the movement. At first blush, it seems that homeschooling is not spread evenly across the United States. However, when patterns are lined up against the general population in the regions of the country, these differences become muted. For example, John Wesley Taylor (1986a) found that only 19.6% of homeschool students were located in the Northwest. However, only 21.1% of the population is in this geographical region. Looking at student enrollment numbers by region also damps down suspected differences, leading the analysts who conducted the NHES to conclude that homeschooled students are distributed roughly similarly across the nation as are public school students. The one meaningful regional difference is that homeschooling students have been, and continue to be, slightly underrepresented in the Northeast (Belfield, 2004a; Princiotta & Bielick, 2006).

Turning to type of community (i.e., degree of urbanicity), researchers across the last 30 years have consistently reported that homeschooling is more of a rural and small-town phenomenon than an urban one (Luebke, 1999; J. Taylor, 1986a; Wenders & Clements, 2007). Consistent with this conclusion, analysts have found that homeschooling families generally populate the nation's most affluent counties and most frequently live in single-family homes (Gustavsen, 1981; Belfield, 2004a).

❖ FAMILY SIZE

Researchers have also long been interested in the issue of family size, especially the number of children in the home. There is consensus that, compared to national norms, large size is a defining characteristic of homeschooling families (Rudner, 1999); that is, they have more children than the average U.S. family, about 50% above the mean (Ray, 2005). Investigators provide averages in two forms: medians and modes. The median homeschool family size in terms of number of children has been recorded as follows: 2.54 (Kelley, 1991), 2.69 (J. Taylor, 1986a), 2.73 (Parker, 1992), 2.78 (Gladin, 1987), 2.80 (Gustavsen, 1981), 3.26 (Muntes, 2006), and 3.33 (Ray, 1997b). The U.S. average is 1.9 children per family. The mode is always recorded as either 2 or 3 children for homeschool families.

Thus, homeschooling families typically have two to three children. Compared to national norms, they are much less likely to have only one child in the family and much more likely to have three or more children (Princiotta & Bielick, 2006). In his most recent comprehensive analysis, Ray (2010) provided the following data on the number of children in homeschooling families: one (6.6%), two (25.3%), three (26.0%), four (20.2%), and more than four (22.0%). These are in line with the findings from his early systematic reviews of the topic. Rudner's (1999) findings on number of children are roughly parallel: one (8.3%), two (29.6%), three (28.6%), four (18.6%), and more than four (14.9%). He reveals that while nationwide 79.6% of families have one or two children, only 37.9% of homeschooling families do so. On the other hand, national survey data reveal less discrepancy. While nationwide 44% of families have three or more children, fully 62.1% of homeschool families do so (Bielick et al., 2001; Princiotta & Bielick, 2006).

❖ SCHOOLING-RELATED DEMOGRAPHICS FOR STUDENTS

In Chapter 6, we peer deeply into the activities in homeschools. We explore what the research tells us about teaching practices, the structure of the school day and year, curriculum employed, and so forth. We set the stage for that analysis here with a few demographic notes about homeschool youngsters and their schooling situations. So far we have seen how home-school youngsters and their parents are a unique demographic subset of the national family portrait. We report here that this is not always the case. In many ways, for example, homeschooled children are a good deal like their non-homeschooled peers. We know, for instance, that the two groups are equivalent in terms of gender (Princiotta, Bielick, & Chapman, 2004). For example, in John Wesley Taylor's (1986a) study, 50.4% of the home-schoolers were male and 49.6% were female. Nearly isomorphic figures were provided by Rudner (1999) a decade later and Ray (2010) one more decade hence.

Not surprisingly, in the early years of the modern homeschool move-ment, about 93% of the children were found in the elementary and middle grades (i.e., they were young; Gladin, 1987; J. Taylor, 1986a). By 2010, this was no longer the case. Today there is rough equivalence in the ages, as defined by grade levels, between homeschool and public school youngsters (Ray, 2010). Ray (1997b) recorded average age for homeschoolers at 10.5.

A number of other questions about homeschoolers have engaged the research community to a lesser extent. Answers to these inquiries are less robust and most likely have shifted since the beginning of the modern homeschooling movement around 1975. For example, early on most home-schooled youngsters were pulled from another school to start the home-schooling process: 82.6% according to John Wesley Taylor (1986a) and 65.0% in the Gladin (1987) study. We lack reliable current data on this issue, although we do know that more families are starting homeschooling in kindergarten, and more and more parents (76%) tell researchers that they intend to educate their children through the high school years (Ray, 1997b). Somewhat surprisingly, given the centrality of disappointment with public education as a motivation for homeschooling, withdrawals from private schooling are not uncommon (Cibulka, 1991). That is, while the typical homeschool student was formerly in a public school (Wartes, 1987), previously private-schooled students in general and Christian-schooled students specifically are overrepresented in the homeschool com-munity (Gladin, 1987; Wartes, 1988).

Length of time that youngsters are homeschooled is also not as well documented as are issues such as race, income, and related demo-graphic dimensions of homeschooling families. Earlier studies suggest shorter stays, while more recent work uncovers more extended periods of homeschooling (Luebke, 1999). The length question has become difficult to address because of the growth of the hybrid models of homeschooling over the last decade (see Chapter 3).

In 1986, John Wesley Taylor (1986a) informs us that as many as three-quarters of first-generation homeschooling students were returning to public or private schools (see also Williams, Arnoldson, & Reynolds, 1984). Other researchers (Gaither, 2008; Isenberg, 2002, 2007) maintain that high rates of attrition define later generations of homeschoolers as well. The most recent data reveal that this pattern may be slowing, with increasing numbers of families staying with homeschooling (Ray, 2010). Belfield (2004b) contends that the duration of homeschooling is probably bimodal, with many students returning to regular schools after a year or two and many others being educated at home across their school careers. This, of course, makes measures of central tendency less valuable. There is also some evidence that regardless of how long they educate their children at home, parents make the decision to continue homeschooling on a year-to-year basis (Mayberry, 1992).

While there is less certainty here than one would desire, the evidence suggests that a decision to homeschool one child does not necessarily mean homeschooling for all the children in the family (Isenberg, 2002). Indeed, in the majority of the cases it does not. We also discover that religion plays a role here. Parents who homeschool based on religious motivations are considerably more likely to homeschool all of their children (Isenberg, 2007).

❖ CONCLUSION

In this chapter, we compiled data on the demographics of homeschooling families. We noted at the outset that conclusions often rest on where one looks on these data portraits. Whereas many scholars attend primarily to the similarities, others focus on differences in the patterns. We found that homeschool parents tend to be better educated than non-homeschooled parents. Homeschool families are solidly middle class, and they achieve that status while relying on one wage earner. The mother is almost always a stay-at-home educator. While there is some reason to believe that homeschool families are becoming somewhat more ethnically and racially diverse, whites continue to be dramatically overrepresented in their ranks. Homeschool families are also defined by an unusually high amount of marital cohesiveness. That is, more so than their peers, homeschool children are located in married, intact, two-parent families. We know that homeschoolers are overwhelmingly Christian, usually Protestant, and often fundamentalist. They tend to be socially and politically conservative, but not withdrawn from issues of the larger community in which they live. Homeschool families also tend to be larger than the average U.S. family and to reside with greater frequency than the norm in small towns and rural areas.

3

Riding History

The Origins and Development of Homeschooling

The history of modern homeschooling has its roots in the counterculture Liberal Left, but within twenty years, the movement was fully adopted by the equally counterculture Conservative Right. (Taylor-Hough, 2010, p. 2)

⤳◌⃝⤳

What was once countercultural has become a generally acceptable educational choice. (M. L. Stevens, 2003, p. 96)

⤳◌⃝⤳

There is certainly a bright future for home-based education in the United States. (Gaither, 2008, p. 226)

⤳◌⃝⤳

In this chapter, we explain how homeschooling came to life in America, describing the forces that pushed it from the margins of acceptability to the center of the national political and social stage and to near normalization within the educational industry. In reality, however, we cannot contain this line of analysis to a single chapter. The narrative on the development of homeschooling is ribboned throughout the book. For example, in Chapter 1 we described development in terms of growth of homeschooling families. In Chapter 2 we discussed how demographic patterns have shifted from 1970 through 2010. In later chapters on homeschooling curriculum and impacts, developmental themes will also be evident.

Our focus here is more constrained. We explore the origins of homeschooling by exposing its intellectual and cultural roots. We outline the dynamics propelling the movement forward—often, as we saw in Chapter 2, at a quite rapid pace. That is, we explain how homeschooling has become mainstream in America in such a short period of time. We then review in some detail two of these dynamics: the legalization of homeschooling throughout all 50 states and the development and actions of support organizations and associations. We close with a description of the evolution of models of homeschooling over the last 40 years, from pure homeschooling that is 100% detached from public education to the development of a plethora of hybrid or mixed public-home designs.

❖ FOUNDATIONS OF HOMESCHOOLING

We would be wise to examine how the contemporary movement toward home schooling evolved. (Rakestraw & Rakestraw, 1990, p. 68)

~◠✦◠~

Home-school advocates claim a long heritage. (Knowles, Marlow, & Muchmore, 1992, p. 200)

~◠✦◠~

The existing scholarship suggests that the home school movement emerged as an embodiment of both radical reform from the left and conservative Christianity. (Cochran, 1995, p. 1)

~◠✦◠~

Stages

Scholars of the homeschooling movement have devoted considerable attention to exploring its foundations. There is a deeply held belief among these analysts that the use of historical lenses provides important insights into the shape, texture, and animating spirit of this unique historical phenomenon (Gaither, 2008; Rakestraw & Rakestraw, 1990; M. L. Stevens, 2001). These reviewers help us understand that homeschooling has a long heritage and deep roots (Lyman, 2000; Nemer, 20002; Whitehead & Bird, 1984). It is, according to most analysts, not a new phenomenon but one that traces back to the foundation of the nation (Carper, 2000; Hill, 2000; Wilhelm & Firman, 2009). The narrative these scholars craft unfolds in three stages: the period before compulsory public schooling; the stage when required, institutionalized schooling moved to the high ground; and the modern homeschooling era.

In the first chapter of the homeschooling history book, academics and advocates alike document that prior to the formation of a system of compulsory public education, homeschooling was at a minimum widely practiced and most likely the primary, if de facto, form of education in the United States (Carper, 2000; Cogan, 2010; J. D. Marshall & Valle, 1996). They are quick to portray all the great figures of our nation who were educated at home. These analysts describe homeschooling as a long-chained phenomenon, one that has witnessed many twists and turns (Nemer, 2002).

In the second chapter of the historical chronicle of homeschooling, reviewers explore the growth of compulsory education in the United States and its impact on home-based education. For a variety of cultural, social, economic, and political reasons, between 1850 and 1918 a system of formal education on a state-by-state basis was forged throughout America. Among the many consequences of this development, the most important for our analysis here is that family and parental influence and choice gave way to government control (Murphy, 1991, 2006). Accolades about the abilities of governments and professional experts were increasingly accompanied by lamentations about the appropriateness and effectiveness of parents as educators. In many ways, the school began to be seen as a substitute for the family, and families began to be judged as incapable of educating their children (Blok, 2004; Carper, 2000). In the process, home-based education was transformed from a normal state of affairs into an oddity, something distinctly old-fashioned, an aberration clung to by misguided parents who could not accept the new order. Later it came to be viewed as an actual attack on the new educational order. All of this activity, as we documented in Chapter 1, nearly drove homeschoolers to extinction (Cai, Reeve, & Robinson, 2002; Houston & Toma, 2003).

In the third and final chapter of the homeschooling history book, reviewers provide rich narratives about the birth and growth of the modern era of homeschooling. Two different interpretations are found therein. The first viewpoint holds that modern home-based education is part of the larger historical mosaic of homeschooling (Gladin, 1987; Lyman, 1998; Whitehead & Bird, 1984). Here we see the contention that homeschooling is not a new educational form but rather a continuation of (or return to) models that have been on the educational landscape for hundreds of years. A second group of scholars suggests that the purported linkages between contemporary homeschooling and homeschooling in the 1700s and 1800s is somewhat artificial. These analysts contend that it only makes sense to understand homeschooling as a response to the compulsory education movement that dominated the educational terrain during the 20th century (Erickson, 2005; Glenn, 2005; Hadeed, 1991). They maintain that homeschooling today is indeed something distinct and different from its pre–compulsory education ancestor. They see the contemporary home-schooling phenomenon as something relatively new and unique, not a resurgence of an old idea.

It does seem that the second group of scholars provides considerable wisdom and many useful insights about the dynamics of homeschooling development. While homeschooling today does share genes with its pre-industrial ancestors, there really is something different and unique about the contemporary homeschooling movement. However one sees the contours of the third stage of the homeschooling story, however, there is considerable agreement about when it began to take root and develop. Lines (2000a) provides the oldest start date, around the mid-20th century. Advocates from the conservative Christian wing of the homeschooling family, who are likely to slight the early liberal roots of the movement (Gaither, 2008), provide the newest start date, around 1980 (Farris & Woodruff, 2000). Most analysts, however, place the start of the modern homeschooling movement in the 1960s (Knowles, 1991; McKeon, 2007; Wilhelm & Firman, 2009), the 1970s (Guterson, 1992; Isenberg, 2007), or some blend of the two decades (Collom & Mitchell, 2005; Green & Hoover-Dempsey, 2007).

The Contemporary Taproots

In the early stages of this contemporary movement, most were pursuing a philosophy of child-led learning. Later, many families with strong religious convictions also turned to home schooling. (Lines, 1995, p. 1)

⌇∽⌇

The movement straddles two cultural landscapes.
(M. L. Stevens, 2001, p. 175)

⌇∽⌇

Homeschooling, as we know it today, may not have existed if not for a pair of Paul Reveres who alerted parents to the pitfalls of dispatching their children off to schools. The seeds of what has grown into the modern-day American homeschooling movement were planted by them 30 years ago.
(Lyman, 2000, p. 23)

⌇∽⌇

Nearly all the archeologists of the contemporary homeschooling move-ment identify two core foundational pillars and two founding figures, one for each of the cultural traditions. The first seeds were planted by pioneers from the liberal left, with John Holt as their chief spokesperson and strate-gist. Later seeds were planted and nurtured by advocates from the Christian right, with Raymond Moore occupying the role of founding father. At one level, as Mitchell Stevens (2001, 2003) eloquently details, these two platforms share some common ground. Most important, the core rationale of the group is the same: the legitimization of the demand for parental control of the education of their children. In addition, both sub-movements see themselves as occupying space outside the mainstream—trailblazers, if you will, but with quite different viewpoints (Apple, 2007; Collom, 2005). Both the liberal and conservative arms of the movement also see homeschooling not as an isolated activity but as part and parcel of a more comprehensive worldview. For the liberal left, it is a commitment to a new world order. For the conservative right, homeschooling is an aspect of a commitment to life as religious persons, overwhelmingly Christian religious persons. While these two submovements share this geographical space, they also have major differences. They rest on distinctly different cultural traditions, espouse different values, have different understandings of the problems in American schools, contain distinct educational philosophies, and pose alternative ways of thinking about themselves as communities (or as social movements; Cochran, 1995; Gaither, 2008; Lyman, 2000; M. L. Stevens, 2001). We crack open that door here and explore similarities and differences in greater detail in Chapter 5.

We begin our examination of the two roots of homeschooling with two caveats. The first one is required in almost all historical analysis. That is, while we examine homeschooling through the work of its two founding fathers, it is essential to remember Tolstoy's great lesson: that leaders are as much products of as they are directors of historical movements. Gaither (2008), in particular, warns us against this danger, reminding us that homeschooling is at heart a grassroots movement. The second codicil is that our focus here is on the early stages of the movement. The names and ideas of other key leaders will surface below when we analyze the role of support organizations and associations.

Holt and the Liberal Left

John Holt, a leading and quite popular school reform advocate from the 1960s and 1970s, is consistently acknowledged as one of the two founding fathers of the contemporary homeschooling movement (Divoky, 1983; Moore & Moore, 1994), evolving from a reformer of public schooling to the *de facto* head and chief tactician of the branch of homeschoolers known as the *unschoolers* (Farenga, 1998; Luke, 2003; Lyman, 2000). The unschoolers were (and are) defined by their liberal and humanistic orientations. They were the countercultural or humanistic left and the libertarian political left (Collom, 2005; Reich, 2002; Wilhelm & Firman, 2009). The intellectual framework for unschooling was forged with materials mined from the progressive quarry (Knowles et al., 1992). In particular, wisdom from the Romantic tradition and ideas from both historical (e.g., Dewey, Pestalozzi, Rousseau) and modern (e.g., Neill, Illich, Kohl) progressive educators were crafted into an ideological platform to support the unschooling version of homeschooling. All of the elements of this platform are visible in the works of Holt (see especially 1964, 1967, 1972) and in historical reviews of his contributions to homeschooling (see especially Gaither, 2008; M. L. Stevens, 2001).

As with all homeschoolers, the liberal left, which represents almost 10% of the movement (Kunzman, 2009b), leveled some ferocious attacks on the public school system, most centrally that it harms children (Holt, 1964, 1967). These beliefs form a major part of their platform. On the constructive side of the ledger, the following four beliefs are the load-bearing walls in the unschoolers' home. Two are general in nature and two are education specific. On the general front, unschoolers contend that persons are basically good and that they can safely pursue their own best interests. They also hold that children have the same rights as other persons in society, rights that need to be acknowledged (Cochran, 1995; Guterson, 1992; M. L. Stevens, 2001). On the education front, the cardinal dimension of unschooling is child-centered learning. Included here is the passionate belief that children have an innate propensity for learning. Concomitantly, unschoolers believe that a child's needs and interests should direct his or her education (Holt, 1964, 1967, 1972). The second key, and well-aligned, educational idea is that the learning environment should be flexible. The environment bends to the learner, not the other way around as is common in schools.

Moore and the Christian Right

The second founding father of the contemporary homeschooling movement is Raymond Moore, the figure whose early research was the major catalyst in the development of homeschooling as a national social and educational movement (Gaither, 2008). Like Holt, Moore began as a school reformer. He was particularly troubled over the burgeoning early childhood movement that was sending children to institutionalized schooling at earlier and earlier ages. Moore found no empirical support for this development. On the contrary, he discovered evidence of harm (Moore & Moore, 1981, 1994). Also, as was the case with Holt, frustration in his reform efforts led Moore to endorse homeschooling as a preferred alternative to the public schools (Gaither, 2008). Known also as the grandfather of home-based education (Kleist-Tesch, 1998), Moore became the most visible and most celebrated homeschool leader in the nation (Gaither, 2008), one who would play a foundational role in the development of this new social and educational movement.

If Holt and the unschoolers steered to the left and were in the gravitational pull of Romanticism and progressive education, Moore and his followers were animated by religion (Basham, Merrifield, & Hepburn, 2007; Knowles et al., 1992; Mayberry, Knowles, Ray, & Marlow, 1995). Their north star was a conservative, far-right version of Christianity (Apple, 2000b; Arai, 2000), a pattern we documented in Chapter 2. In short order, riding the crest of the wave against secularism and its ill effects on children and their families, by the mid-1980s the Christian fundamental wing had moved into a very dominant position in the world of homeschooling in the United States (Arai, 2000; Knowles et al., 1992; Marlow, 1994). According to Mitchell Sevens (2001), by the mid-1980s their numbers began to dwarf those of the unschoolers, they had taken definitional control of the movement, and they exercised control over the organizational architecture of the homeschoolers. Again, as was the case with Holt and the unschoolers, power for the fundamentalist conservatives grew partially from their scathing critiques of the system of compulsory public education in the United States at the time. As we will explore in more detail in Chapters 4 and 5, the critical aspect of their lament rested on two ideas. First, it was argued that the public schools had birthed a belief system that was at odds with the one expressed by conservative Christian parents (Carper, 2000). Second, the academic program and social climate that flourished in these schools were inimical to children and undermined the values of the home (Cochran, 1995; M. L. Stevens, 2001). In sum, homeschooling was to be a counterweight to the ungodly influences and secularism that washed over America's children in its public schools.

Other ideas were also welded into the intellectual platform being used to support the conservative branch of homeschooling promulgated by Moore. As we reported above, unschoolers featured the child in his or her inherent goodness. Autonomy and self-direction were privileged under the banner of children's rights. Child-centered education placed the youngster squarely on center stage. Homeschoolers following the ideas of Moore saw things differently (M. L. Stevens, 2001). Based on their religious faith, this wing of homeschoolers held that all persons, including children, were both good and sinful. In short, each group possessed quite discordant views about the nature of the person. They also, as Mitchell Stevens (2001) goes on to document, maintained incompatible views about authority. With the conservatives, parental authority, not child freedom, occupied the high ground. The family, not the child, held center stage. Traditional family values and role conceptions were underscored.

❖ TOWARD THE MAINSTREAM

Home education emerged as a deviant practice in the USA in the late 1970s and became an acceptable alternative to conventional schooling in a remarkably short period of time. (M. L. Stevens, 2003, p. 90)

~✿~

Homeschooling is now a widespread, diverse, and important segment of education in America. (Nemer, 2002, p. 5)

~✿~

The home education movement is a growing one. Its numbers are growing, its acceptance is growing, and its power to affect the political environment is growing. (McDowell & Ray, 2000, p. 2)

~⌒⭒⌒~

A Rise in Legitimacy

As one of its founders argued it might (Holt Associates, 1999), on the broad landscape of culture and politics, homeschooling has become a national phenomenon (K. Bauman, 2002) and an important social movement (Hadeed, 1991; Mayberry et al., 1995; Reich, 2002; M. L. Stevens, 2001), one that has been integrated into the larger society quite successfully (M. L. Stevens, 2003). Looking more narrowly on the educational part of the terrain, it has, as its other founder suggested, become a formidable educational movement (Moore, 1982), one that is beginning to act as a catalyst for change in the larger education sector (Wilhelm & Firman, 2009). Indeed, it remains the fastest-growing form of education in the United States (Hardenbaugh, 2005; Ray, 2009b).

This is a major accomplishment, considering that less than three decades ago homeschooling was viewed as little more than a fringe phenomenon (Collom, 2005; Hardenbaugh, 2005; Reich, 2005), "an uprising perceived by many as a sort of insult" according to Guterson (1992, p. 6)—an attack on the fabric of society (Knowles, 1989). It was illegal to homeschool in most states, and legal action against homeschoolers was not uncommon (Gladin, 1987; Welner, 2002). The educational establishment and many mainstream educators viewed the movement with skepticism, if not outright hostility (Knowles, Muchmore, & Spaulding, 1994; M. L. Stevens, 2003). The general public and governmental figures were by and large not supportive (Gladin, 1987; Hertzel, 1997; M. L. Stevens, 2003), although many were simply uninformed (Wilhelm & Firman, 2009). In short, disapproval, if not outright rejection, was the norm (Dahlquist, York-Barr, & Hendel, 2006; Gorder, 1990; Rakestraw & Rakestraw, 1990). Homeschooling at the time was considered to be a "social and educational aberration" (Aurini & Davies, 2005, p. 462), a product of extremism operating under an evil cloud of suspicion (Klugewicz & Carraccio, 1999; Knowles et al., 1994; Wilhelm & Firman, 2009).

Over the last quarter century, home-based education has gone from the closet or the outhouse to the mainstream (Ray, 2009b; Reich, 2005). Although still the subject of controversy, misunderstanding, debate, critique, and the concerns of dyspeptic scribblers, the dark clouds surrounding homeschooling have broken and homeschooling has come to enjoy considerable legitimacy and support (Gaither, 2008; Romanowski, 2001). It is now legal in all 50 states, and most states and districts have stopped hectoring homeschool families. Many politicians have become advocates.

The professional geography in this area has changed as educators, especially practitioners, have tempered some of their distrust, becoming less enamored with hauling around old habits of oppositionality. Deeply etched and negative contours of policy in this domain have been more favorably reshaped in many states and districts. And the general public has warmed up to the idea. We explore the dynamics behind this metamorphosis in Chapters 4 and 5. Here we simply report the conclusion: Homeschooling has become a socially acceptable and educationally appropriate means of schooling for increasing numbers of America's families (M. L. Stevens, 2003).

Overall, then, as Farris and Woodruff (2000) and Romanowski (2001) maintain, homeschooling is well integrated into the American social fabric, an option unlikely to disappear from the educational portfolio any time soon (Dalaimo, 1996). And as Mitchell Stevens (2001, 2003) concludes, this normalization of homeschooling in the United States represents a significant accomplishment for supporters who only 30 years ago confronted the thick crust of negative culture outlined above, one that foreshadowed the promise of failure (Gaither, 2008; M. L. Stevens, 2001).

Analysts affirm the expanding acceptance of homeschooling in a variety of ways. To be sure, they document the increasing enrollment reported in Chapter 1. They point to the fact that questions about homeschooling have found a home on federal surveys, such as those from the U.S. Census Bureau (Basham et al., 2007). They document the changing legal environment, from illegality in 30 states in 1980 to legality in all 50 states today (McCulloch, Slocum, Kolegue, & Montaudo, 2006; Reich, 2005). They tabulate the data on the massive increase in the availability and sale of resources to homeschool families (Arai, 1999; Basham et al., 2007). They chronicle the dramatic growth in the number of support groups for homeschooling families and students, the equally impressive growth of participation in these associations, and the significant influence of these groups in the legal and political decision-making realms and the court of public opinion (Gaither, 2008). They narrate the development of a more hospitable public school environment for homeschooling youngsters (Kunzman, 2005). And they tabulate changing public attitudes toward homeschooling. For example, numerous analysts spotlight the growth of public acceptance of home-based education in the regularly administered *Phi Delta Kappan* poll, from 16% in 1985 to 28% in 1988 to 36% in 1997 to 41% in 2001 (Belfield, 2004a; Cooper & Sureau, 2007; Kunzman, 2009b).

Explanations

The questions at hand, of course, are: Why and how has this normalization occurred? How did homeschooling go from being on the fringe, and often a hostile venue on the fringe, to the mainstream? As noted above, the answers are threaded throughout the remainder of this volume and highlighted here. As an advance organizer to that line of analysis, we offer the following insights. We note at the start of this quest for answers that it is difficult to untangle causes and effects. We also remind the reader that the search takes us to those factors listed above in our discussion of the ways analysts have documented the development of homeschooling (e.g., the changing political context).

As we discuss in detail in Chapter 4, larger political, cultural, and social forces underway in America (e.g., privatization, localism, deinstitutionalization) have combined to create a culture that is hospitable to the growth of homeschooling (Cooper, 2005; Mayberry, 1989b). The shift from conditions conducive to the rise of the liberal democratic welfare state to those supporting market and client approaches to education have unquestionably fueled the growth of homeschooling (Murphy, 2000; Murphy, Gilmer, Weise, & Page, 1998). At the same time, there is a new willingness to rethink the once almost unassailable position of compulsory education (Guterson, 1992; Mayberry & Knowles, 1989). Coupled with these forces are often ferocious attacks on government provision in general and of public schooling in particular, assaults that can encourage parents to examine alternatives for the education of their children—often, it turns out, homeschooling.

In social movements in general (Holt Associates, 1999) and in the homeschooling movement in particular, awareness and familiarity help people get beyond their biases. In the 1970s and 1980s, the public was almost completely unaware of homeschooling (Ray, 1997a), and almost no one knew of a family that engaged in this odd-to-deviant practice (Luebke, 1999). Today, homeschooled children are commonplace in many neighborhoods (Luebke, 1999). Such familiarity has often promoted support or at least ameliorated concerns about homeschooling (Klugewicz & Carraccio, 1999). Relatedly, the growing regard in which homeschooled youngsters are held by universities has helped make the process both more normal and more special at the same time (Jones & Gloeckner, 2004; Scheps, 1998; Wilhelm & Firman, 2009).

Triumphs in the courthouse have powered growth as well (Fager & Brewster, 2000; Isenberg, 2007; Knowles et al., 1992). It is much safer to homeschool today than it was in the 1980s and 1990s (McCulloch et al., 2006). Reviewers routinely single out the creation of legal rights for homeschoolers as an explanatory variable in the growth algorithm (Lips & Feinberg, 2008; Wenger & Hodari, 2004). So too is growing support on the political front, from both legislators and members of the executive branch (Basham et al., 2007; Luebke, 1999; McDowell & Ray, 2000).

As we have seen, at the outset homeschooling was the purview of the far left and later of the far right. As the movement has matured, it has become more diverse, generating a larger gravitational force that is pulling increasing numbers of parents from the center into its field of influence. And, as Whitehead and Bird (1984) predicted, proliferation has produced more proliferation. Certainly the growing sense of community within the homeschooling world has helped families make, and be successful with, the traditionally unorthodox decision to educate at home (Lips & Feinberg, 2008). So too the at least partial dismantling of the Berlin Wall between public schools and homeschooling has made home-based education more feasible for some families (Gaither, 2008; Fager & Brewster, 2000). Growth is attributable to the expansion of new technologies as well (Apple, 2000b; Basham et al., 2007; Dahlquist et al., 2006; Wilhelm & Firman, 2009).

It is also important to note that the popular press has done much to influence the positive growth of homeschooling in the last 15 years (Gaither, 2008). While news reports in the 1970s and 1980s often portrayed homeschooling as an extreme and problematic if not harmful endeavor (Cooper & Sureau, 2007), the pendulum and the received wisdom have swung 180 degrees (Apple, 2005). As far as homeschooling is concerned, the media's ancestral tapestry has been cleansed. Positive features are often reported on the nation's airwaves and in its publications (Basham et al., 2007; Lyman, 1998; Wilhelm & Firman, 2009). Homeschooling is often presented in the garb of "savior," a powerful alternative to the corroding public school system (Apple, 2000a, 2000b).

Finally, there is a sense that homeschooling is growing because it is being successful (Cibulka, 1991; Taylor-Hough, 2010). That is, it is doing what parents want (e.g., keeping their children at arm's length from negative peer environments, forging healthier families). At the same time, homeschoolers are more than holding their own on measures often used to judge student success (e.g., academic achievement). The counsel of despair in the area of student socialization in particular is poorly supported in the research literature available to date.

❖ THE DNA OF NORMALIZATION

Home educators do not tend to act in isolation. They work together through networks and organizations. (Collom & Mitchell, 2005, p. 279)

～◯˙◯～

Today, homeschooling is legal in every state. (Dahlquist et al., 2006, p. 355)

～◯˙◯～

As we discussed above, many factors and conditions assisted in the formation and normalization of the modern homeschooling movement in the United States. Two of these forces merit special attention: the creation of a network of support groups and the legalization of a practice that was on the margins of legality only 30 years ago.

Creating Support Groups

Networking is now widespread, particularly among religiously motivated home school families, and is probably the single most important factor in the continued consolidation of the home education movement.
(Mayberry et al., 1995, p. 19)

~⌒ॐ⌒~

The support group has given homeschooling its power.
(Moore & Moore, 1994, p. 251)

~⌒ॐ⌒~

Focusing on the size of the phenomenon, Moore and Moore (1994) inform us that by the early 1990s there were thousands of local, regional, and state support groups throughout the United States. The prevalence of these support groups has increased over the last two decades. Gaither (2008) reports that these associations held more than 500 homeschooling conventions in 2001, 75 of which garnered enrollments of more than 3,000 people.

Turning to the use of support groups, we learn that they form a key pattern in the homeschooling mosaic, have been visible since the start of the movement, and are becoming increasingly important (Hadeed, 1991; Gaither, 2008). In the first major study of homeschooling, Gustavsen (1981) discovered that 45% of parents were members of at least one home school organization. A few years later, Wartes (1987) reported that 62% of homeschooling parents participated in a support group meeting at least once every 2 months. Parker (1992) found that all of the families in his study belonged to at least one homeschool support group; over one-third were members of two or more groups. A few years later, Mayberry and colleagues (1995) uncovered a participation rate of 86%. At the turn of the 21st century, Lyman (2000) documented a similar pattern, 85%.

Support groups operate at the local, state, and national levels (Hadeed, 1991; Mirochnik & McIntire, 1991). As we will see, the boundaries between groups at all three levels are often formed from religious or other ideological values and beliefs. To begin, we know that national organizations provide an important source of support (M. Martin, 1997). National support groups include over two dozen suppliers of homeschool curriculum packages (Houston, 1999). They encompass associations such as the Home School Legal Defense Association (HSLDA), the National Association for the Legal Defense of Alternative Schools, and the Rutherford Institute that provide legal information and support (Cibulka, 1991; Whitehead & Bird, 1984). National homeschooling organizations have also been created to deliver periodicals across the country (Knowles et al., 1992) and to serve as clearinghouses for resources (Schemmer, 1985). Finally, at least one well-regarded and influential national association, the National Home Education Research Institute (NHERI), was crafted in 1992 with a mission to produce and disseminate research findings about homeschooling (Cooper & Sureau, 2007; Klicka, 2004).

Statewide organizations are also an essential part of the homeschooling movement (Cooper & Sureau, 2007; Knowles et al., 1992). There is at least one such association in every state (Lines, 1995). Regional associations also populate the networking landscape, with some states having a dozen or more (Lines, 1995). Finally, thousands of local homeschooling groups are found in communities throughout the country, pursuing the wide assortment of goals we outline below. These local groups range from highly informal (e.g., a small cluster of parents who coplan a field trip for a few families) to highly formal (e.g., groups with well-defined organizational structures; Knowles et al., 1992; Luebke, 1999). The focus of local support groups can also vary. Some are created to support homeschooling children directly. Others are designed to help the parent as teacher (Perry & Perry, 2000). In summary, we learn that support groups can be differentiated along the following criteria: cultural orientation (i.e., religious versus secular); level (i.e., local, state, national); target (i.e., children, parents, some combination of the two); educational philosophy (i.e., traditional versus alternative); and organizational structure, including leadership arrangements (Gaither, 2008; Knowles et al., 1992; Luebke, 1999).

Support Grid and Goals: The Macro View

Joining a homeschooling organization is akin to choosing sides in a battle.
(Guterson, 1992, p. 244)

～⌒⟨⚜⟩⌒～

Scholars are consistent in highlighting the cardinal role of associations in cementing the modern homeschooling movement into place. (See especially the excellent historical analyses provided by Gaither, 2008; M. L. Stevens, 2001.) They reveal that contrary to common stereotypes, homeschoolers are not generally isolated families educating their children in unconnected enclaves (Apple, 2007; Collom & Mitchell, 2005; M. L. Stevens, 2001). Rather, these analysts confirm that from the earliest phase of the modern era, parents were moved to create support groups, especially local networks of similarly situated parents (Holt, 1983; Lines, 1991; Mayberry et al., 1995)—what Knowles and team (1992) describe as support systems to aid independent homeschool endeavors. By the mid-1990s, these numerous and varied associations were wired into an expanding homeschooling support grid. By the end of the 20th century, this grid had become denser and more intertwined (Lyman, 2000) as parents increasingly realized the value of these communal connections—and associations were active in helping parents discern such value (Cooper & Sureau, 2007; Mayberry et al., 1995).

Homeschool analysts also explain that as the support grid matured it fractured into distinct sectors. That is, different clusters of linkages began to occupy specific vectors on the grid, and connections between vectors began to atrophy. Analysts return us to the past to see how and when this fracturing process unfolded, as well as to view the resulting homeschool geography. (See especially Gaither, 2008; M. L. Stevens, 2001.) The major berm was constructed between the early homeschoolers from the liberal left and the next generation of homeschoolers from the conservative Christian right. These reviewers also document that it was the home-schoolers on the right who built almost all of the dividing walls; they sealed themselves off from those who did not value what they believed in. Or more accurately, they created conditions that prevented nonbelievers from joining them. They also constructed a distinct organizational archi-tecture for their support groups, one that reinforced their separation from nonevangelical homeschool associations. As Mitchell Stevens (2001) explains,

> home schoolers have built two quite distinct movement infrastruc-tures. Committed to ideas of individual freedom and ideological diversity, the inclusives have created an organizational system that is built around individual decision making and that amply accom-modates difference. Committed to an idea of godliness, the believ-ers have created a system that is built around leaders and that discourages dissent. (p. 115)

So we see in the first phase of separation that the conservative right pushed nonreligious homeschoolers onto a small and isolated sector of the support grid. A second break then split the religious right sector of the support group grid (Gaither, 2008; Mayberry et al., 1995; M. L. Stevens, 2001). The associations and leaders who were instrumental in pushing the formation of religious-based support groups (i.e., Moore and his follow-ers) became increasingly marginalized and isolated by the evangelical Christians who assumed the dominant position in the modern homeschool movement and its affiliated network of support groups. By the dawn of the 21st century, then, when the support group fracturing process had been completed, both of the founders of the homeschool movement and their accompanying associations had been pushed off center stage and replaced there by more evangelical and more dogmatic figures. What once had been a loose if somewhat uncomfortable coalition with tethers across the full homeschooling support grid had become a divided and quite polarized network with many linkages within but few connections across sectors. Or as Mayberry and team (1995; Knowles et al., 1992) explain it, the homeschool support associations have become quite homogeneous.

Each sector of the grid has different members, rules of working, and cultural orientations (Cibulka, 1991; M. L. Stevens, 2001).

Turning to the dominant Christian conservative sector of the homeschooling support grid, we see that associations and related organizations at the broadest level are about three goals: the Christianization, collectivization, and politicization of homeschooling. First and most important, these groups have an explicit goal to nurture and support Christian beliefs in families and Christian ideology in the nation as a whole (Gaither, 2008; Klicka, 2004). Second, they are about weaving individual families together into a collective form of action. While, perforce, relying on the actions of hundreds of thousands of individual households, the goal is to de-atomize homeschooling by building communication networks, ones in the service of the Christian agenda (Collom, 2005; Hadeed, 1991; M. L. Stevens, 2001). The third goal, also placed in the service of the larger Christian agenda, is the politicization of the homeschooling movement via support organizations. According to scholars such as Cibulka (1991) and Cooper and Sureau (2007), the homeschooling movement, or at least the dominant evangelical sector thereof, has through its support groups morphed from an educational to a political movement.

Purposes of Support Groups: The Micro View

At a more micro level, homeschool support groups and organizations exist to meet an assortment of academic, emotional, social, and spiritual needs of children and their parents (Bates, 1991). Employing the student lens, we find that these associations and networks sometimes are designed to engage in collective instructional activities such as arranging a science fair or teaching a foreign language (Lips & Feinberg, 2008; Luebke, 1999). They also often provide socializing experiences such as teen socials (Luebke, 1999; M. L. Stevens, 2001). And, of course, they undertake activities that cut across both areas, such as sponsoring field trips and arranging for service learning activities.

Using the parent (teacher) lens, we discover that support groups sometimes provide curricular resources and assessment materials that can be used in the home, as well as information on teaching methods (M. Martin, 1997; Mayberry et al., 1995). Network associations often provide legal information and services (Erickson, 2005; Whitehead & Bird, 1984). They organize to achieve political goals (Cibulka, 1991; Isenberg, 2007). They monitor actions related to homeschooling and push that knowledge downward to their members (Apple, 2007; Schemmer, 1985).

Especially at the state level, support groups are active in organizing conferences for parents (Gaither, 2008; Lyman, 2000), conferences that attend to many of the other purposes we describe in this section. These support groups provide a support structure, a community, for homeschooling parents, especially moms, to learn from one another (Schemmer,

1985; M. L. Stevens, 2001) and to discover what is afoot in the larger world that may be of interest to homeschoolers (Bates, 1991; Perry & Perry, 2000). They often provide moral support (M. Martin, 1997) and the emotional buttressing to stay the course with homeschooling (Mayberry et al., 1992). Religious-anchored support groups also provide frameworks to reinforce religious values (Bates, 1991) and build linkages to churches (Cooper & Sureau, 2007).

Support associations often offer assistance in getting started in home-schooling (Lines, 1991; Luebke, 1999) and navigating relationships with the public schools. They distribute publications (newspapers, magazines, and books) with a wealth of information on potential homeschool resources as well as stories on the triumphs of homeschooling families (Gaither, 2008; Knowles et al., 1992). These support groups sometimes are active in distributing and providing speakers to educate the general public about homeschooling (Lyman, 2000), what Whitehead and Bird (1984) refer to as building public awareness. They often take it upon themselves to educate policymakers at all levels of the government. National organi-zations sometimes provide guidance and assistance to state associations, and state associations often perform the same functions for local support groups (Scheps, 1998).

The Fight for Legalization

The home schooler often has the perspective of a minority, of a reformer,
of one who stands to lose the most precious things in his or her life at the
stroke of a legislative pen. (Farris & Woodruff, 2000, p. 252)

~⌒⚬⌒~

The courts have proved critical to the politics of homeschooling,
for without the right to argue and defend, homeschooling would
have disappeared or been forced underground as an illegal activity.
(Cooper & Sureau, 2007, p. 122)

~⌒⚬⌒~

As we have just illustrated, much of the normalization of homeschool-ing over the last 30 years can be traced to the work of support groups and associations. Normalization is also the product of some hard-fought legal wars. And it is important to note at the outset that most of the major bat-talions in the legalization wars were some of the very support groups examined above. Or as Cibulka (1991) reminds us, the legal and regulatory frameworks in place at the start of the modern era of homeschooling pro-vided a good deal of the impetus for the collective work of the homeschool community. In the balance of this section, we analyze the central themes in the struggle for legitimacy and freedom in the legal arena. It is not our intention to provide a deep historical treatment that examines court decisions across time. That work has been completed by others (see, in order, Whitehead & Bird, 1984; Richardson & Zirkel, 1991; Somerville, 2005; Gaither, 2008). Neither is it our goal to provide a review of laws and regulations across the 50 states. HSLDA makes this information available on an ongoing basis. Rather, we review the essential elements and outcomes in the struggle to create an environment of freedom for homeschooling families.

Legal analyses in this area confirm that while constitutional cases decided by the Supreme Court provide a platform for the right of parents to control the education of their children (Guterson, 1992; Richardson & Zirkel, 1991; Whitehead & Bird, 1984), federal courts generally have not been receptive to arguments that state mandates in the area of homeschooling infringe on the First or Fourteenth Amendment rights of families (Knowles et al., 1992; Richardson & Zirkel, 1991). While that battle has not been completely abandoned, reviews show that the major fights have unfolded in the various state legislatures throughout the country (Gaither, 2008) and in the state courts, where state mandates impacting home-based education are adjudicated (Somerville, 2005). Here the track record for opening up homeschooling has been nothing short of remarkable (Houston, 1999), and the speed with which this deregulation occurred has been exceptional (Cibulka, 1991). At the start of the 1980s, it was illegal to homeschool in most states (Aurini & Davies, 2005; Cooper & Sureau, 2007), or more accurately, it was only clearly legal to homeschool in a few states (Klicka, 2004). That is, for the average family, homeschools operated under the veil of excessive if not crippling regulations. According to Mayberry and team (1995), during the 1980s alone 27 states passed laws permitting homeschooling. By the mid-1990s, homeschooling had been legalized in all 50 states (Gaither, 2008; Klicka, 2004; Somerville, 2005).

> After a flurry of activity in the 1980s, home-schooling is now legal throughout the nation, and more than thirty states have enacted explicit statutes. The remaining jurisdictions make home-schooling legal under laws dealing with alternative, comparable, equivalent, or other instruction (including tutors) and/or private, church, or parochial school exceptions. (Russo, 2006, pp. 33–34)

Since the mid-1990s, when the struggle to legalize home-based education was achieved, the fight has moved to the regulatory battleground. The focus has shifted to the extent to which homeschooling should be controlled by the state. As Somerville (2005) captures the change, forces have been redirected from the battle for making homeschooling legal to keeping it free. Because states are the prime mover in the area of education, each one has a regulatory framework in which home-based schooling is nested (Dahlquist et al., 2006; Russo, 2006). Historically, there has been considerable variability in these frameworks, in what they control and the restrictiveness of these mandates (Klicka, 2004; Lines, 2000a; McKeon, 2007). Indeed, state laws form what Basham and colleagues (2007) and Reich (2005) refer to as a patchwork of rules.

Regulatory action in the area of homeschooling derives from the fact that a triad of interests is in play here, those of parents, children, and society at large (Kunzman, 2009a). As with all political engagements, the debate is about how to value the various interests (Cibulka, 1991), with homeschoolers often viewing government regulation as simply an intrusion into their sphere of influence (Kunzman, 2009a) while homeschool critics tend to place more emphasis on the interests of the children and the larger society (Apple, 2000b; Berliner, 1997; Lubienski, 2000; Reich, 2002). According to Ray and Eagleson (2008), rationales for and against homeschooling regulations rest on four pillars—philosophical, academic, human development, and sociopolitical—and the empirical evidence that informs the four avenues of learning.

Regulation of homeschooling is found in a variety of domains such as attendance, curriculum, student assessment or academic testing, time requirements, qualifications of home-based instructors (i.e., parents), and compliance reporting (Dahlquist et al., 2006; Reinhaller & Thomas, 1996). It is the differences in each of these domains that create the regulatory patchwork we referenced above (Houston, 1999). To provide one example, Kunzman (2009a, p. 320) informs us that in the area of curriculum, current regulations imposed by states range from Indiana's remarkably vague mandate for "instruction equivalent to that given in public schools" (with no further details and no authority to review homeschool curricula) to Pennsylvania's requirements of a portfolio of student work, standardized testing, and a written report from an outside evaluator. Many states fall somewhere between: 35 mandate the study of particular subjects, 14 require parents to maintain curriculum records, and 7 require student work portfolios to be kept.

Based on the number and robustness of the rules in these various domains, scholars and advocates alike often place states into one of four categories—no regulation, low regulation, moderate regulation, or high regulation (Basham et al., 2007; Kunzman, 2005)—with homeschoolers assessing states in the first two categories most favorably (Klicka, 2004). Ray (2010, p. 17) supplies the following definitions:

1. Low regulation—no state requirement on the part of the homeschool parents to initiate any contact with the state

2. Medium regulation—state requirement that homeschool parents send to the state notification of homeschooling or achievement test scores and/or evaluation of the student's learning by a professional

3. High regulation—state requirement that homeschool parents send to the state notification of homeschooling or achievement test scores and/or evaluation by a professional as well as other requirements (e.g., curriculum approval by the state, teacher qualifications of parents, home visits by state officials)

According to HSDLA (see Belfield, 2004a; Kunzman, 2005; Lips & Feinberg, 2008) and NHERI (Ray 2009a, 2010), most states fall under the medium regulation label, with fewer located in the high regulation (7) and low regulation (11) categories.

The current regulatory environment is quite different than it was only 20 years ago. There has been a considerable loosening of regulations across the nation (Hardenbaugh, 2005; McKeon, 2007). In many states, homeschooling has been significantly deregulated (Basham et al., 2007). Most homeschooling families have few deep disagreements with the extant regulatory environment (Lyman, 2000), and there is a sense that the current equilibrium is about where it needs to be (Gaither, 2008), with the possible exception of student participation in state association–sponsored athletic programs (Cooper & Sureau, 2007; Webb, 1997).

What should be clear at this point is that support groups and efforts to legalize and deregulate homeschooling are heavily intertwined. Indeed, it is fair to claim that the success of homeschooling in the postfoundational era is largely due to the efforts of homeschool associations, especially the Rutherford Institute and, to an even larger extent, HSLDA (Gaither, 2008). HSLDA was formed in 1983 by Michael Farris and Michael Smith, and directed in its early years by Christopher Klicka (Kunzman, 2009b). Over the last two decades, it has developed into the most influential of the national homeschool associations (Gaither, 2008). In 1983, 200 families belonged, and by 1985, 1,200. Fifteen years later, at the turn of the 21st century, the organization was supported by 53,000 dues-paying members and 45 employees. By 2010, membership had increased to around 85,000 families, assisted by more than 60 staff members (Gaither, 2008; Klicka, 2004; Kunzman, 2009b; Lyman, 1998). The HSLDA mission is to provide legal information and to defend the rights of its members across the nation. As the contest for dominance over regulation has become settled, HSLDA has branched out to take on new assignments anchored in its core values of parents' rights (freedom and primacy of the family) and Christian doctrine (Cooper & Sureau, 2007; Klicka, 2004).

❖ EVOLVING HOMESCHOOLING MODELS

Although some consider homeschooling as a "world apart," the relationship between public school districts and home schools is dynamic and evolving.
(Muntes, 2006, p. 12)

~∿◌∿~

Recent political and legal developments have made it much more difficult to draw sharp distinctions between homeschools and plain old schools. Homeschoolers are increasingly creating hybrids that blend elements of formal schooling into the usual pattern of a mother teaching her own biological children at home. (Gaither, 2008, p. 211)

~◦᠃◦~

It appears that the "home" in homeschooling is rapidly becoming a misnomer. (Kunzman, 2005, p. 4)

~◦᠃◦~

For much of the modern history of homeschooling, the struggle for parents was to pull free of government schools, to create an alternative to public school education. When the battle was first enjoined, the lines between homeschool and public school were clearly demarcated and populated by vigilant sentries who helped ensure that the two choices were indeed distinctly separate options. Sociologists help us understand that this is the normal flow of development for the creation of new roles and organizations from old ones; meaningful separation is sought. In the case of homeschooling, as we report in detail below, the pulling away was reinforced by a good deal of ideological buttressing (Frost & Morris, 1988). In recent years, however, it is clear that this state of affairs is evolving. Divisions are softening (Cooper & Sureau, 2007; Dahlquist et al., 2006). Ideological flourishes have become tempered. As a consequence, a variety of mixed or hybrid models are finding their way into the homeschool narrative.

This evolution is in many ways quite logical. Endowed with the clarity of time and association, a good deal of the antagonism that marked the perceptions of public school educators toward homeschooling has cooled (Cibulka, 1991; Gaither, 2008). More and more parents who were not part of the fight to make home-based education a meaningful option for their children are joining the ranks of the homeschool population. Many of these see advantages in mixing the two forms of schooling—whereas those who preceded them saw (often correctly) only problems (Luebke, 1999). Districts for their part have often by necessity become more client sensitive, more market oriented, and more entrepreneurial. Some were always open to new ways of doing business. Others have been forced by law and public pressure to become so. Cooperation that provides half a loaf (i.e., some tuition from partially enrolled homeschoolers) seems more desirable than the empty coffers of righteous indignation (Fager & Brewster, 2000; Knowles, 1989). In short, districts have begun to see the incentives of engaging with homeschoolers (Dahlquist et al., 2006; Lines, 2000b). Others see the advantages of co-opting homeschoolers. Also, as one would expect, as cooperation has materialized homeschooling educators and public school educators have begun to see the benefits of collaboration that were only dimly visible in the recent past (Fager & Brewster, 2000; Holt, 1983; Jackson, 2007). All of this has been reinforced by an expanding definition of what counts as schooling in America, as well as a proliferation of acceptable ways to bring that understanding to life. It has been supported as well by a shift from a nearly universal focus on issues of control to greater attention to issues of quality.

We need to be clear, however, that the deep-seated skepticism and disagreements that define relationships between homeschoolers and public educators have not disappeared. More important, neither have the reasons why parents have been drawn to homeschooling from the outset. There remains considerable angst, if not outright distrust, by many about mixed models of schooling (Gaither, 2008; Kunzman, 2009b; Lines, 2004). This is especially the case for those who fought so assiduously to make homeschooling a possibility (see, for example, Erickson, 2005; Klicka, 2004) and for the diehard opponents of homeschooling (Apple, 2000b; Berliner, 1997).

Table 3.1 provides a snapshot of the variety of options available. As we reported in our discussion of the definition of homeschooling, four criteria can be applied to place educational alternatives: funding (who pays), control (who regulates), provision (who teaches), and venue (where schooling occurs). If the answers to the "who" questions are "parents" and the venue is the "home," then we have a pure version of homeschooling, or a homeschooling-only situation (Belfield, 2005; Bielick, Chandler, & Broughman, 2001). Here we see the parent educating one or more of their children completely in the home environment. "Mom schools" also appear in the pure homeschooling category. A mom school occurs when an individual mom invites children to join her family for some lessons (Gaither, 2008). We also find here the use of homeschool cooperatives, the clumping together of homeschool families to provide some of the homeschool activity (Dahlquist et al., 2006; Hill, 2000), often selected subjects (e.g., foreign language), programs (e.g., soccer), and extended learning opportunities (e.g., a science camp). At times, these cooperatives are so extensive that they resemble schools (Gaither, 2008; Hill, 2000; Kunzman, 2009a). Also in the pure homeschool category we find limited public school support of homeschool families, support that stops short of having home-educated youngsters participate in public school classes and extracurricular activities (Lines, 2000a, 2000b). For example, schools sometimes make available, and homeschool families sometimes partake of, services and resources such as testing, access to school facilities, resource centers, websites for parents and/or children, and books and other institutional materials (Bielick et al., 2001; Dahlquist et al., 2006; Fager & Brewster, 2000; Mayberry et al., 1995, Muntes, 2006; Reich, 2002). Currently, 80%–85% of all homeschooled children fit into the pure homeschool model (Bielick, 2008).

Table 3.1 Models of Homeschooling

	Types					
	Pure Homeschooling			*Mixed Model*		
Criteria	*Single Home*	*Mom Schools and Collaboratives*	*Public School Support*	*Dual Enrollment*	*Independent Home-Based Education*	*Pure Public Schooling*
Funding	Parents	Parents	Parents	Both	Government	Government
Control	Parents	Parents	Parents	Both	Government	Government
Provision	Parents	Parents	Parents	Both	Parents (or both)	Government
Venue	Home	Home/ collaborative space	Home/ collaborative space	Both	Home	School

To the far right of Table 3.1, we see the traditional public school where resources to fuel the enterprise are garnered from taxpayers, government is in charge of regulation, students are taught by government employees, and the school building is the center of activity.

The middle columns are where the blending of the two types of schooling occurs (Blok, 2004; Isenberg, 2002). While there are a variety of models in play and scholars employ varied terms to capture these hybrids, it is reasonable to divide them into two largely separate categories: dual enrollment and independent home-based (public) education. The former is closer to the pure homeschooling end of the continuum, while the latter is much more in line with traditional public school education.

Dual enrollment (also known as shared services, shared schooling, and part-time enrollment) is a straightforward concept. It means simply that for part of the day (or week) a student is educated at home and for the remainder is at school (either public or private; Fager & Brewster, 2000; Holt, 1983; Lines, 1995; Pearson, 1996). Children in dual enrollment status often take targeted classes and co-curricular activities at the public school (K. Bauman, 2002; Dahlquist et al., 2006; Kunzman, 2005; Lips & Feinberg, 2008). Data from NHES reveal that about one in five home-schooled students is also enrolled in public or private school on a part-time basis, most for fewer than 10 hours per week (Bielick, 2008; Princiotta & Bielick, 2006).

Independent home-based education (also known as enrolled-home study and off-campus home study) means that students are enrolled full time in the public school but educated by parents at home—under the control of the public school (Lines, 2004). Since these students are enrolled in the public school, the district receives full public support for each independent homeschooled child. Independent home-based education has been fueled by the emergence and rise of the charter school movement (Collom & Mitchell, 2005; Dahlquist et al., 2006; Isenberg, 2002). (Remember that all charter schools are public schools.) Indeed, a fair number of charter schools are virtual institutions or cyber schools that cater specifically to parents who want to teach their children at home (Gaither, 2008; Luebke, 1999). Note that these parents forgo many of the core values of homeschooling when they engage in independent homeschooling. Funding and regulation reside with the government. This, not surprisingly, has caused considerable pushback by some in the vanguard of the homeschooling movement (Gaither, 2008; Klicka, 2004).

❖ CONCLUSION

In this chapter, we examined the origins and development of homeschooling in America. We were particularly attentive to the foundations of the modern home-based education movement, as seen through the efforts of its founding fathers. We explored the forces that pushed and pulled homeschooling from the educational and societal margins to the mainstream. We also reported on the hybridization of homeschooling that has accompanied its legitimization.

4

Seismic Shifts

Exploring Environmental Conditions That Foster Homeschooling

The increasing number of home schools nationwide is occurring in a specific historical period. (Mayberry, Knowles, Ray, & Marlow, 1995, p. 100)

⋘⋗

Contemporary home education emerged and flourished in the USA at a particular point in time, and that temporal specificity says something important about the cultural context surrounding its emergence. (M. L. Stevens, 2003, p. 96)

⋘⋗

❖ THE ESSENTIAL HYPOTHESIS

Societal forces have enabled, even prompted, the present upsurge in homeschooling. (Nemer, 2002, p. 20)

⋘⋗

> *Large scale cultural, social, and economic forces played a significant role in the development of homeschooling. (Luebke, 1999, p. 10)*

⸺◠⸰◠⸻

> *Interest in home education bears a relationship to larger social trends. (Mayberry et al., 1995, p. 100)*

⸺◠⸰◠⸻

One of the major goals of this volume is to explain why homeschooling has taken root and flourished over the last 30–40 years. In the last chapter, we provided a partial answer to that question by examining factors that nurtured home-based education once it began to germinate. In the next chapter, we add to our storyline by exploring the reasons parents offer for selecting homeschooling. In this chapter, we deepen the explanatory narrative by considering the larger contextual forces that allowed the movement to take root in the first place.

The conundrum we confront is this: Some analysts contend that there is an abundance of homeschooling today because there is a biblical command for parents to take personal control of the education of their children. Others maintain that the phenomenon can be yoked to the visible shortcomings of schools. Both of these points are accurate. However, the biblical rationale is hardly new. And schools have been systematically lambasted for their failures for a century. Indeed, since the 1950s critical analysis of education has become a cottage industry. Yet before 1970 there were almost no homeschoolers and today there are over 2 million. The pertinent question is, Why now? Why not in the 1930s or the 1960s, for example?

The answer to this fundamental question can be found in an analysis of the changing sociopolitical and economic calculus of the nation writ large. That is, homeschooling is thriving because the essential pillars of society that made it anathema for over a century are being torn down and replaced with scaffolding that supports homeschooling. The argument we develop in the following pages progresses as follows: As the nation birthed and developed (1800–1890), important cultural, economic, political, and social ideas were forged into a foundation for government action, or lack thereof. As the nation evolved from an agricultural to an industrial society (1890–1980), much of this initial foundational framework disintegrated. Different economic and sociopolitical ideas were cobbled into a new platform for government action. The liberal democratic welfare state was formed over this industrial ideological scaffolding. The anchors in this new platform—government control and professionalism (i.e., the reliance on experts to solve societal problems)—made homeschooling nearly impossible. Beginning in the last quarter of the twentieth century (1970 on), this second national social and political infrastructure also began to crumble, severely undercutting the growth and health of activist government.

A third infrastructure began to take shape, forged from very different cultural, economic, social, and political ideas. It is this new scaffolding that makes social movements such as homeschooling possible.

❖ SOCIAL CONTEXT: BEFORE HOMESCHOOL (1800–1890)

Shifting Environmental Context

External currents in the larger sociopolitical and economic environment helped form the first period of American education. The *economic* dimensions of this phenomenon can be traced to a new economic order taking root in the mid to late 1800s (Reese, 1995). One aspect of the new economy was the decay of the older system, including the twin pillars of the barter economy and economic self-sufficiency. The other aspect was the emergence of a market economy. With the advent of this new order, the connections between schooling and the economy became more robust. Education now provided a competitive edge in the world outside the pulpit and the university classroom. School was seen increasingly as an avenue to opportunities in the free market. Demand for schooling was on the rise (Anderson & Gruhn, 1962; Sizer, 1964).

Concomitantly—and often in response to changes underway in the economy—powerful *social and political* forces also began to influence the transformation of schooling. Specifically, Reese (1995) avers that bedrock shifts in the economy eroded "familiar social patterns and relationships" (p. 167), widened class divisions, and "generated new questions about social relationships and the place of schools in society" (p. 2). He suggests that schooling increasingly came to be seen as a solution for these profound social changes. In particular, Reese holds that the following key ideas about the role of schooling in relation to society's needs flowered in the mid to late 1800s—all of which promoted the development of new forms of public education: (a) the well-being of the nation depended on the knowledge of its citizens, (b) an extensive middle class was essential to the prosperity of the country, (c) education provided the key for the creation of productive workers for the new economy, and (d) education was directly linked to social harmony. In other words, schools could help socialize workers into accepting the emerging changes associated with industrialization (Vinovskis, 1985).

Changing Architecture of Schooling

Reese (1995) and Tyack (1974) have uncovered the roots of important governance issues in this era, roots that have occupied a central place in the development of public education. According to these scholars, the key governance issues were forged on the anvil of control. Their work exposes two major points.

First, throughout this era, a rather robust struggle was taking place between divergent ideologies. One side was populated by reformers who believed that centralized control was imperative for fostering the widespread implementation of the public school and for strengthening the quality of the educational system. These progressive reformers were guided by the values of centralization of power, specialization, and professional expertise. They supported a larger role for the state, especially in the area of financial support for education. Decentralized or local control infuriated these reformers. For them, a system of local governance was "archaic, unprofessional, and too decentralized" (Reese, 1995, p. 26). They regularly "highlighted the foibles of local school politics . . . before professional educators set things straight" (p. 26). The local control advocates were, according to the reform crowd, "drags on social progress" (p. 70).

On the other side of the debate were citizens who were leery of the ideas and the initiatives of the reformers. Many simply did not accept the values of the reformers, especially notions of professional control and expert knowledge. They believed in citizen control and self-governance. They emphasized personal liberty and family responsibility (Reese, 1995). Not surprisingly, and unlike the reformers, they "chafed at state intrusiveness in education" (p. 75), believing that central control undermined democracy. For them, decentralized school control was viewed as an asset, not a liability.

Second, by the close of the formative era of the development of public schools, the local-control camp was ascendant. The efforts of the progressives had largely "foundered on the shoals of localism" (Reese, 1995, p. 215). A pattern of decentralization was visible across the nation, and local control became the dominant form of governance.

❖ SOCIAL CONTEXT: BEFORE HOMESCHOOL (1890–1970)

Shifting Environmental Context

According to Tushman and Romanelli (1985), environmental shifts provide an important axis on which major institutional changes are scaffolded, especially significant alterations in the ambient political, social, and economic contexts. On the *political* front the change with the most impact on education was the rise of progressivism and the development of the liberal democratic state (Murphy, 1996). Rooted in discontent with political corruption and an expanded recognition of government as too limited for the new industrial era, the political landscape was noticeably recontoured in the late 19th and early 20th centuries. Direct citizen control and machine politics gave way to bureaucratized institutions led by a cadre of educational experts.

The *social* tapestry was also being rewoven during this period. The central dynamic was "the transformation of American society from one characterized by relatively isolated self-contained communities into an urban, industrial nation" (Kliebard, 1995, p. 2). Most important from our perspective here is the fact that these significant shifts in social conditions resulted in important changes in schools (Willing, 1942). As Cremin (1961), Kliebard (1995), Tyack (1974), and Wraga (1994) have all demonstrated, with the recognition of social change came a significantly revised vision of the role of schooling.

Turning to the *economy*, we see the emergence of "new economic realities brought on by the industrial revolution" (Wraga, 1994, p. 2). At the core of the matter was the transformation from an agricultural to an industrial economy—or, perhaps more accurately, given the social changes outlined above, to an industrial society (Cremin, 1955). The nation was witnessing the "advent of machine production and its accompanying specialization of occupation" (Koos, 1927, p. 310). Stated in language that eerily would be reintroduced nearly a century later in reshaping the school to the realities of a postindustrial world, it could be said that by 1890 national worries about international economic competition (Spring, 1990) and the demands of advancing technology (Krug, 1964) began to influence the design of the blueprints being used to shape the foundations of the newly emerging model of public education. In ways that were not previously evident (Sizer, 1964), schools became yoked to the needs of the economic system (Spring, 1990): "In effect, some saw the school as a critical means of transforming the preindustrial culture—values and attitudes, work habits, time orientation, even recreations—of citizens in a modernizing society" (Tyack, 1974, p. 29).

Changing Architecture of Schooling

Given this shifting sociopolitical and economic environment, the methods used to govern education and the designs employed to structure schools underwent significant alterations. The defining element of the organizational revolution was the shift from lay control, which dominated the governance landscape before 1890, to a corporate bureaucratic model of governance (Tyack, 1974) to a managerial state (Apple, 2000b). The new scientific models of organization and governance provided some of the defining components of public schooling during the 20th century (Erickson, 2005).

The organizational transformation that marked the evolution of the school within the new industrial world was laced with two central ideologies, a "corporate form of external school governance and internal control by experts" (Tyack, 1974, p. 146). Both elements drew freely from models supporting the development of the postagricultural business sector (Callahan, 1962; Newlon, 1934). The external dimension focused on the transfer of power and control from lay citizens to elite decision makers in government (Erickson, 2005; Kirschner, 1991; Tyack, 1974). "Working under the banner of the depoliticalization of schooling and eliminating political corruption, reformers sought to remove the control of schools as far as possible from the people" (Tyack, 1974, p. 167), to eliminate community control. The struggle to separate education from politics was powered in part by both antidemocratic ideology and class prejudice. In terms of influence, we know that this movement accomplished much of its goal, "for it destroyed the decentralized power which had sustained a grass roots lay influence in the schools" (Tyack, 1974, p. 3). During most of the 20th century, throughout the nation, a closed system of governance had replaced much of the more open system that had prevailed at the end of the 19th century. Control had been passed from parents to state agents and professional educators (Murphy, 2006); localism had been eviscerated (Erickson, 2005; Kirschner, 1991).

Shifts in the basic governance equation were accompanied by a reconfiguration in the way schools were managed and structured (Callahan, 1962). One distinctive development was the appearance of a class of administrative experts to whom governance elites delegated control for the management of schools (Gaither, 2008; M. L. Stevens, 2001; Tyack, 1974). Borrowing from the new models of organization and management being forged in the corporate sector, reformers began to draw a "strict parallel" (Tyack, 1974, p. 143) between the leadership of business enterprises and the management of schools (Callahan, 1962; Tyack, 1974). They argued that "to change schools, . . . one first needed to concentrate power at the top so experts could take over" (Tyack, 1974, p. 3).

In order to facilitate the use of this centralized power and to maximize its potential to effect change, reformers drew up blueprints for a new structure for schools (bureaucracy) and cobbled together a new philosophy of leadership (scientific management) borrowing freely from material originally crafted in the corporate sector (Callahan, 1962; Newlon, 1934). In so doing, they brought forth the array of operating principles that would form the organizational backbone for public education for most of the 20th century, principles that collectively represent a distinct break with the model of organization in play before 1890.

❖ SOCIAL CONTEXT: HOMESCHOOLING (1970 ON)

The presence and growth of home schools is also a reflection of economic, political, and cultural developments and conflicts that have occurred over the last two decades. (Mayberry & Knowles, 1989, p. 209)

~◠⸙◠~

The growth of home-schooling can also be related to social and structural phenomena. (Belfield, 2004b, p. 6)

Normalization of home education is best understood as a reflexive phenomenon: peculiar cultural and institutional conditions provided a hospitable context for the early development of a home education movement. (M. L. Stevens, 2003, p. 90)

Dismantling the 20th Century Environmental Architecture

Some of the fuss over homeschooling may be due to the fact that it has been on the cutting edge of a larger renegotiation of the accepted boundaries between public and private, personal and institutional. (Gaither, 2008, p. 4)

One of the dynamics we are seeing is social disintegration, that is the loss of legitimacy of a dominant institution that supposedly bound us together—the common school. (Apple, 2007, p. 127)

The DNA of the Storyline

At one of the most fundamental levels, the issue is whether the parents or the state should have primary authority and responsibility for the education of a child. (Ray & Eagleson, 2008, p. 8)

Home education in the United States is a vivid example of an increasing number of families attempting to reverse the history of their diminished control over the education of their children. (Mayberry, 1989b, p. 172)

As we have attempted to make explicit throughout these pages, the hallmark issue in the homeschooling movement is control. As power and influence were passed from parents and communities to government agents and professional experts throughout the 20th century, real costs were experienced by parents, costs calculated in terms of loss of control over the schooling of their children (Kirschner, 1991). That is, while the liberal democratic state brought activist government that assumed ever-expanding responsibility for social life (Apple, 2005), it also diminished the influence of parents (Erickson, 2005).

Homeschooling, then, can be examined as part of an ongoing debate about who should control the education of America's children, government or parents (Moore & Moore, 1981; Ray, 2000a; Riegel, 2001). It is also an essential dynamic in a larger movement to reverse the status quo in the area of control (Bates, 1991; Reich, 2002). Its success rests on a foundation quite different than the architecture supporting the liberal democratic state (Gaither, 2008), one that replaces the corporate bureaucratic model of governance that displaced parents as controlling agents in the 20th century. The fight for the high ground has been and continues to be waged on two highly overlapping fronts: against government domination of schooling and against the dominant role played by professional educators in the production known as schooling.

The Attack on Government Domination

It is not possible to understand the growth of home schooling unless we connect it to the history of the attack on the public sphere in general and on the government (the state) in particular. (Apple, 2005, p. 82)

⁓ⓞ⚡ⓞ⁓

Home schooling is part of the trend away from the reliance on American institutions. (Gorder, 1990, p. 10)

⁓ⓞ⚡ⓞ⁓

The Sociopolitical Critique. One critical strand of the current sociopolitical mosaic is plummeting support for government. Not surprisingly, indicators of dissatisfaction and discontent provide ample support for the claim that something is happening to traditional approaches to public governance in general and school governance in particular (Gaither, 2008).

Critics maintain that government in the United States is troubled and is becoming more so—"that conventional ways of doing business in the public sector [have] failed to deliver acceptable results" (Hassel, 1999, pp. 35–36). They discern a sense of hopelessness about civic government (Katz, 1992) and a crisis of confidence in public institutions and representative government (Putnam, 1995). They point to surveys and opinion polls showing that citizens are distrustful of government agencies and regularly opposed to government-sector programs and policies. Other chroniclers of this unrest speak of a mounting sense of skepticism about the public sector in general (Fitzgerald, 1988) and skepticism about the government's capacity to meet social goals in particular (Hula, 1990a; Lyman, 2000).

Still other reviewers discern among citizens a more fundamental (Savas, 1982) cynicism toward (Hula, 1990b), animus against (Gaither, 2008), distaste for (Donahue, 1989), or distrust of government and government officials and institutions (Apple, 2000b; Kirschner, 1991; Kunzman, 2009b). They describe a "culture of resistance, bitterness, and adversariness" (P. C. Bauman, 1996, p. 626). They paint a picture of "political bankruptcy, a vaguely defined state of popular alienation and disaffection from government which stops short of revolution" (Hood, 1994, p. 91). These analysts portray a growing discontent with activist government (Hirsch, 1991) and the rise and spread of an antigovernment philosophy (Apple, 2007). They describe a "fundamental concern that government simply 'doesn't work.' Planning is seen as inadequate, bureaucracy as inefficient and outcomes highly problematic" (Hula, 1990a, p. xiii). They go on to argue that the consent of the governed is being withdrawn to a significant degree. In its softest incarnation, this cynicism leads citizens to argue that government is no longer a reasonable solution to all problems and to question the usefulness of much government-initiated activity (Florestano, 1991; Luebke, 1999). At worst, it has nurtured the belief that government is fated to fail at whatever it undertakes (Starr, 1991). In many cases, it has nurtured the development of a variety of antigovernment political and social movements. There is little question that this widespread "disillusionment with government has extended to all sectors, including schooling" (Gaither, 2008, p. 93).

The Economic Critique. It is almost a fundamental law that the economy is undergoing a significant metamorphosis. There is widespread agreement that we have been and continue to be moving from an industrial to a postindustrial economy. What is becoming clearer to many analysts is that with the arrival of the postindustrial society, "we are seeing the dissolution of the social structure associated with traditional industrialism" (Hood, 1994, p. 12) and an environment that is less hospitable to government intervention. With the ascent of the global economy, there is an emphasis on new markets (Dahrendorf, 1995; Lewis, 1993), and a "break[ing] of the state monopoly on the delivery of human services so that private enterprise can expand" (Lewis, 1993, p. 84)—conditions that provide many of the seeds for the debate about appropriate governance structures for society and its institutions. At the same time that the economic policy habitat is evolving, the current foundations of the economy— especially the public sector—appear to be crumbling. In particular, the economic principles that have provided the grounding for government actions for most of the 20th century have been called into question.

The important question here is: What accounts for this discontent and skepticism about the public sector of the economy that is helping fuel privatization initiatives such as homeschooling? Given the cyclical nature of policy development and other value expressions in American society, it should surprise no one to learn that some of this rising tide of dissatisfaction with public sector initiatives can be characterized as a response to the nearly unbroken growth of government over the last three-quarters of the

20th century—a counterreaction to the progressive philosophy that has dominated the policy agenda for so long (Apple, 2007; Murphy, 2000). According to Hood (1994), for example, the growth of the public sector contained the seeds of its own destruction:

> The public sector is, in many ways, simply aging and wearing out. Once a major economic model gains ascendancy, dissatisfaction builds up over time. Unwanted side effects of the policy [become] more clearly perceived. . . . At the same time, shortcomings of the alternative orientation are forgotten, because they have not been recently experienced. Pressure then starts to build for the policy orientation to go over on the other track. (Hood, 1994, p. 15)

Another piece of the discontent puzzle focuses on the widespread perception that the state is overinvolved in the life of the citizenry. Critics note that more and more citizens are chafing under the weight and scope of government activity (Collom & Mitchell, 2005). They characterize a government that has gone too far (Hirsch, 1991). They argue that the state has become involved in the production of goods and services that do not meet the market failure test (Pack, 1991) and that government agencies have pushed "themselves into areas well beyond governance. They [have] become involved in the business of business" (President's Commission on Privatization, 1988, p. 3). The results are predictable: The state, it is claimed, occupies an increasingly large space on the economic landscape, welfare loss due to collective consumption increases, and citizens experience an increasing need for more nongovernmental space (Florestano, 1991). Calls for a recalibration of the economic equation are increasingly heard.

Expanding numbers of citizens begin to experience "some public sector institutions as controlling rather than enabling, as limiting options rather than expanding them, as wasting rather than making the best use of resources" (B. Martin, 1993, p. 8). Of particular concern here is the issue of values. An increasing number of individuals and groups have come to believe that state intrusiveness includes efforts to establish value preferences (Cibulka, 1996)—values that they believe often undermine their ways of life (Collom, 2005; Cooper & Sureau, 2007; Klicka, 2004). Others argue that, at least in some cases, through interest group and bureaucratic capture, some public sector institutions have actually destroyed the values that they were established to develop and promote (Hood, 1994).

The wearing out of the economic foundations of the liberal democratic state can also be traced to recent critical analyses of the model of public sector activity developed to support expanded state control. The critique here is of three types. First, when examined as they are put into practice, the assumptions anchoring public sector activity over the last century look much less appealing than they do when viewed in the abstract (i.e., conceptually).

Indeed, "many of the assumptions and predictions on which the earlier growth of government was based have proved either to be false or at least to be subject to much greater doubt" (President's Commission on Privatization, 1988, pp. 249–250). Thus, the attack on extensive state control rests on the way in which its limitations have become visible. At the same time, much of the critique of the market economy upon which public sector growth has been justified, especially market failure, has been weakened with the advent of sociotechnical changes associated with a shift from an industrial to a postindustrial society (Hood, 1994).

Second, "structural weaknesses inherent in the nature of public-sector supply itself . . . which undermine the whole basis on which it is established" (Pirie, 1988, p. 20) have become more visible—visible to the point that some analysts claim that state ownership and management are inherently flawed. Concomitantly, both the efficiency and effectiveness of governmental activities have begun to be questioned seriously.

Third, it is suggested that the reforms that created the large public sector are themselves much in need of change. Reform is increasingly seen in terms of an alternative to, rather than the repair of, the existing public sector.

The recasting of public sector economic policy can also be attributed to stories of gross government incompetence or scandal and a mounting body of evidence that government enterprises are often inefficient, that it costs more to accomplish tasks in the government than in the primary sector (Gottfried, 1993; Murphy, 1996). Or, stated alternatively, government is consuming more of the nation's resource than it should (Richards, Shore, & Sawicky, 1996): "The government provision and production of many goods and services, including the regulation of market activities, generates substantial deadweight losses" (De Alessi, 1987, p. 24).

While widespread concern over the growing costs of government is an important variable in the algorithm of the discontent—especially perceived waste and inefficiency, an even more significant factor is the expanding disillusionment about the overall effectiveness of government action (Donahue, 1989; Hula, 1990b; Lyman, 2000), particularly the perceived inability of government to meet its goals. Perhaps nowhere is this perception more vivid than in the arena of the large-scale egalitarian programs initiated in the 1960s and 1970s (Hula, 1990b). A number of critics of government control argue that the conditions that led to the development of these policies have not been ameliorated and that they will "not disappear as a result of having responsibility for them transferred from the private to the public sector" (Savas, 1987, p. 290). In fact, they maintain that such transfers often worsen the situation and create even more problems. They go so far as to suggest that many of our social problems are in reality cratogenic—that is, created by the state.

This widespread dissatisfaction with public sector economic activity has led some to question "whether public production . . . is so inherently inefficient that it results in even greater resource misallocation than do the market failures it aims to correct; whether regulation [government control] is even more costly to society than the initial resource misallocations" (Pack, 1991, p. 282). In tangible terms, it has helped foster a taxpayer revolt and has given birth to an array of citizen initiatives designed to seize control away from existing government structures, including, most prominently in the education arena, homeschooling. At the core of these reactions is the "feeling that there must be a better way of doing all those things that governments do not do too well" (Savas, 1985, p. 17): "If government is failing in its efforts to provide essential services, should we not reconsider the role we have given government in these areas?" (Carroll, Conant, & Easton, 1987, p. x).

The Attack on Bureaucracy (Government Agencies and Professional Experts)

These parents are home schooling because they actively question the professionalization and bureaucratization of modern society, and particularly of modern education. (Van Galen, 1991, pp. 72–73)

~◠◡◠~

It would appear, therefore, that the success of the home schooling movement is but another instance of a wider trend toward more public influence over educational policies, in contrast to the wide autonomy professionals once enjoyed. (Cibulka, 1991, p. 117)

~◠◡◠~

Focusing specifically on education, we discover that the attack on government-controlled schooling can be traced to two broad areas: discontent with the processes and outcomes of schooling and critical reviews of the core system of schooling. We defer our treatment of the former to the following chapter, where we allow parents' motivations for homeschooling to animate the analysis. Here we stay focused on the issue of the core system of schooling—governance and control—turning to the theoretical framework developed by public choice theorists and then applying that general framework specifically to the bureaucratic framework of schooling.

The Larger Narrative. At the heart of the critique of existing governance arrangements is a reassessment of the interests of public employees. Central to this reinterpretation is a dismantling of the basic faith in the benevolence of governmental bureaucracy (Apple, 2007; Buchanan, 1987). According to Niskanen (1971), "The beginning of wisdom is the recognition that bureaucrats are people who are, at least, not entirely motivated by the general welfare or the interests of the state" (p. 36). Rather than accepting the assumption that managers of public agencies are "passive agents [who] merely administer and carry out programs" (Bennett & DiLorenzo, 1987, p. 16) with the sole intent of maximizing public interest, some analysts advance the belief that these agents often make decisions in their own interests (Lyman, 2000; Tullock, 1994b). Bureaucrats are much like other people, "people who are less interested in the ostensible objectives of the organization than in their own personal well-being" (Tullock, 1965, p. 21).

In economic terms, this means "that government employees, like other economic agents, respond to the opportunities for gain provided by the structure of property rights embedded in the institutions used to control their choices" (De Alessi, 1987, p. 24) and that bureaus act as a type of special interest group (Hilke, 1992). At the most basic level, this results in the notion of the bureaucrat as a public service maximizer, giving way to the conception of experts who attempt to maximize their own utility functions—utility functions that contain a diverse set of variables: "salary, perquisites of the office, public reputation, power, patronage, [and] output of the bureau" (Niskanen, 1971, p. 38).

Such an analysis continues to argue that because improving one's utility function is directly dependent on the resources available to the bureau, budget maximization becomes the operant goal of bureau managers (Niskanen, 1971, 1994). Consequently, managers have a strong incentive to engage in bureaucratic imperialism (Tullock, 1965) or empire building (Dudek & Company, 1989). Budget maximization and empire building impose real costs on citizens in terms of public control and overall efficiency of the economy (Bennett & Johnson, 1980). The switch from maximizing the public interest to maximizing the discretionary budget means that bureaus have the potential to become producer driven (Pirie, 1988), to capture the agency and to direct its energies toward meeting the needs of government employees (Hardin, 1989; Vickers & Yarrow, 1988). The result is goal displacement (Bates, 1991; Downs, 1967; Tullock, 1965). Some public sector work ends up serving the interest of the workforce more than the interest of the constituents (Apple, 2005; Pirie, 1988).

One avenue of this discourse suggests that because public employees are, next to transfer payment recipients, the most direct beneficiaries of government spending (Savas, 1987), they are likely to use the power of the ballot box to promote the objective of government growth (Tullock, 1994a). A second part of this view holds that public sector unions in particular are key instruments in the growth of bureaus and the concomitant subordination of consumer interests to the objectives of the employees themselves. Ramsey (1987) concludes that when the economic influence of unions is combined with political muscle, public sector unions have considerable ability to tax the rest of society.

A final point of this critical analysis asserts that employee self-interest is nurtured in what might, presented in the best light, be thought of as a symbiotic relationship with the bureau's sponsor—the intersection where the self-interest of the politician and well-organized workers converge to maximize the utility of both groups:

The political power of public employees and their unions is not restricted to their voting strength. Political campaign coordinators and campaign workers are a potent influence on office seekers. The situation lends itself to collusion whereby officeholders can award substantial pay raises to employees with the unspoken understanding that some of the bread cast upon those particular waters will return as contributions. (Savas, 1987, p. 26)

As described above, the well-being of government agents and professional experts, what Hill (2000) refers to as civil service cartels, often comes at the expense of the general citizenry, especially in inefficiencies in delivery and lack of responsiveness to constituents (Hanke, 1985; Hilke, 1992; Hirsch, 1991; Niskanen, 1971, 1994).

The Application to Education

These political and economic concerns were easily transferred to public schooling, since for many people the school was and is the public institution closest to them. (Apple, 2005, p. 84)

⌐◠⌐

The reputation of education's mass institutional form has become tarnished. (Richardson & Zirkel, 1991, p. 159)

⌐◠⌐

Faith in the intellectual elite managing the public school system has failed. (Klicka, 1995, p. 85)

⌐◠⌐

Over the past quarter century, the belief has taken root that many of the difficulties dominating education originate in the way public schools are organized and governed (Loveless & Jasin, 1998; Nemer, 2002), that "some of public education's troubles come not from the problems students bring to school with them but from the educational system that unions, school boards, administrators, and legislators have created" (Nathan, 1996, p. 76). Or even more directly, "the current governance of public education makes effective action at the school level almost impossible" (Hill, Pierce, & Guthrie, 1997, p. 13). Specifically, too much self-interest and too much bureaucracy are at the core of educational mediocrity (Snauwaert, 1993): "In recent years, critics have argued that the reforms of the Progressive era produced bureaucratic arteriosclerosis, insulation from parents and patrons, and the low productivity of a declining industry protected as a quasi monopoly" (Tyack, 1993, p. 3). Consistent with the analysis outlined above, there is a sense that producers have "come to dominate most education decisions and government has become their chosen mechanism for retaining control" (Finn, Manno, & Vanourek, 2000, p. 223)—a feeling that in bureaucracy students can be taken for granted because it is adult concerns that matter (Kolderie, 1994). There is growing sentiment that the existing educational governance and management systems are unsustainable (Little Hoover Commission, 1996; Rungeling & Glover, 1991).

Much of the attack on the bureaucracy is directed at educational professionals (elites), who as we saw above were handed (and took) control of schooling during the early decades of the 20th century, replacing in the process the fairly robust system of local control operating in the nation's formative years. With the growing distrust of government control in general, this outcome in the domain of educational governance is hardly surprising. Authors from nearly every realm of the homeschooling world (e.g., parents, advocacy leaders, developers, researchers) report that the authority claims of experts (Gaither, 2008; Gatto, 1992; M. L. Stevens, 2001) and the accompanying respect (Sheffer, 1995), autonomy (Apple, 2000a) and control (Hill, 2000) are being withdrawn (Kunzman, 2009b; E. Stevens, 1997a; Thom, 1997): "Historic deference to expertise has been eroded dramatically in recent years" (Gaither, 2008, p. 4). This, in turn, has produced two outcomes: a significant crisis in educational legitimacy (M. L. Stevens, 2001) and social resistance (Hadeed, 1991), with the accompanying belief that parents, not professional elites, know what is best for their children (Colfax, 1990; Gaither, 2008; Mayberry, 1989b).

Critics maintain that school bureaucracies, as currently operated, are incapable of providing high-quality education (Elmore, 1993) and, even worse, that bureaucratic governance and management cause serious disruptions in the educational process (Shanker, 1998a, 1998b, 1998c; Wise, 1989), that they are "paralyzing American education . . . [and] getting in the way of children's learning" (Sizer, 1984, p. 206). These scholars view bureaucracy as a governance management system that deflects attention from the core tasks of learning and teaching (Elmore, 1993; Lyman, 2000). Still other reviewers suggest that bureaucratic management is inconsistent with the sacred values and purposes of education. Other reform proponents hold that the existing organizational governance structure of schools is neither sufficiently flexible nor sufficiently robust to meet the needs of students in a postindustrial society (Shanker, 1998a, 1998b, 1998c). Finally, some analysts suggest that the existing structure has produced an insulated political culture (Finn et al., 2000). They contend that the rigidities of bureaucracy, by making schools nearly impenetrable by citizens, impede the ability of parents and citizens to govern and reform schooling (Collom & Mitchell, 2005; Sarason, 1995; Tyack, 1992).

Not unexpectedly, given this tremendous attack on the basic organizational governance infrastructure of schooling, stakeholders at all levels are arguing that significant reforms are needed to rectify this situation (Elmore, 1993), that "the excessively centralized, bureaucratic control of . . . schools must end" (Carnegie Forum, cited in Hanson, 1991, pp. 2–3). Some analysts look to replace government control with market mechanisms. Others appeal to more robust models of democratic governance. It is this context that has propelled homeschooling to such heights in such a short period of time.

The Evolution of a New Social Context Supporting Homeschooling

Homeschooling is a symbol of larger social trends.
(Aurini & Davies, 2005, p. 465)

༁

Homeschooling represents the future of education: deregulated, market-driven, privatized, malleable, liquid. (Gaither, 2008, p. 225)

༁

New Social, Cultural, and Political Foundations

Homeschooling represents a move among some in postindustrial America to rethink patterns of living that have been with us since the Civil War. (Gaither, 2008, p. 224)

༁

In many ways, the movement toward home schooling mirrors the growth of privatized consciousness in other areas of society. (Apple, 2000a, p. 66)

༁

New ideas are emerging to fill the sociopolitical spaces left after the unraveling of the liberal democratic welfare state that has dominated education for the past century. One of the key elements involves a recalibration of the locus of control based on what Ross (1988) describes as "a review and reconsideration of the division of existing responsibilities and functions" (p. 2) among levels of government. Originally called democratic localism by Katz (1971), it has more recently come to be known simply as localization or, more commonly, decentralization (McGree, 1995; Wells, Lopez, Scott, & Holme, 1999). However it is labeled, it represents a backlash against and a reversal of nearly exclusive reliance on control by government and professional elites (Rofes, 1998).

A second ideological foundation can best be thought of as a recasting of democracy, a replacement of representative governance with more populist conceptions (Rofes, 1998), especially what Cronin (1989) describes as direct democracy. While we use the term more broadly than does Cronin, our conception shares with his a grounding in (a) the falling fortunes of representative democracy, (b) a "growing distrust of legislative bodies . . . [and] a growing suspicion that privileged interests exert far greater influence on the typical politician than does the common voter" (p. 4), and (c) recognition of the claims of its advocates that greater direct voice will produce important benefits for society—that it "could enrich citizenship and replace distrust of government with respect and healthy participation" (p. 48).

A third foundation encompasses a rebalancing of the control equation in favor of lay citizens while diminishing the power of the state and educational professionals (Tyack, 1992). This line of ideas emphasizes parental empowerment by recognizing the historic interests of parents in the schooling of their children (Gaither 2008; Gottfried, 1993). It is, at times, buttressed by a strong strand of "profound dissatisfaction with and disappointment in many members of the so-called 'educational establishment'" (Wells, Grutzik, Carnochan, Slayton, & Vasudeva, 1999, p. 525) or antiprofessionalism that subordinates "both efficiency and organizational rationality to an emphasis on responsiveness, close public [citizen] control, and local involvement" (Katz, 1971, p. 306).

The ideology of choice is a fourth pillar supporting homeschooling (Aurini & Davies, 2005; Belfield, 2004a; Whitehead & Bird, 1984). Sharing a good deal of space with the concepts of localism, direct democracy, and lay control, choice is designed to deregulate the demand side of the education market (Beers & Ellig, 1994) and to enable parents to become more effectively involved in the way education unfolds (P. C. Bauman, 1996; Lange & Liu, 1999). It means that "schools would be forced to attend to student needs and parent preferences rather than to the requirements of a centralized bureaucracy" (Hill, 1994, p. 76; see also Hill & Bonan, 1991).

Fifth, it seems likely that something that might best be thought of as democratic professionalism forms a central part of the political infrastructure of schooling in the postindustrial or postmodern world. What this means is the gradual decline of control by elite professionals—by professional managers and more recently by teacher unions—that marked the politics of schooling in the industrial era.

Two highly integrated shifts that we address extensively in Chapter 5 also occupy critical space in the emerging sociopolitical architecture that supports parental control in general and home-based schooling in particular. One is the rise in importance of evangelicalism or conservative Christian ideology as a reaction to the dominant worldview of civil secular humanism that helped form the foundation of society for over a century (Carper, 2000; Gaither, 2008; M. L. Stevens, 2003) and of schooling for the last 50 years or so (Apple, 2005; Nemer, 2002; Van Galen, 1991). The result has been a "morally conservative counter revolution" (Bates, 1991, p. 10). More specifically, what has occurred is the "unboxing" or uncaging of evangelicalism, the spread of conservative Christian ideology to historically nonreligious domains of society, especially in this case to the government sector. God as the source of authority has been infused into all sectors of life; or perhaps more appropriately, there are no nonreligious domains in life. The second overlapping and reinforcing dynamic has been the shift from a middle-of-the-road, slightly liberal ideological foundation to the acceptance of a much more conservative ideological platform in the nation

(K. Bauman, 2002; Murphy, 1996), what Apple (2005) describes as a rightward turn in the country.

One thing becomes clearer as one steps back and reviews the analyses of the unraveling and reweaving of the social and, especially, the political aspects of the educational environment. The dismantling of the dominant foundations of the democratic welfare state has undercut the currency of traditional notions of schooling in general and governance in particular (Fuller, Elmore, & Orfield, 1996; Hassel, 1999). A good deal of space in the quest for school improvement has been opened. The reform game need no longer be played on the margins. Or stated alternatively, construction does not need to proceed by welding additions onto the foundations prevalent in the era of the liberal democratic state.

New Economic Foundations

Homeschooling dovetails easily with the market logic that is becoming pervasive in the US education circles and with a larger, global trend toward neoliberal understandings of states as service-providers and citizens as client/consumers. (M. L. Stevens, 2003, p. 97)

Home schooling is part of a general trend of elevating private goods over public goods. (Lubienski, 2000, p. 207)

Homeschooling is perhaps the ultimate in educational privatization. (Kunzman, 2009a, p. 316)

New ideas are also emerging to define the economic domain of society in a postmodern world, many of which share space with the new social and political ideas we just reviewed. Most of these are contained in what can be described as a recalibration of the equation of market-government provision, with considerably more weight being devoted to the market aspects of the algorithm. Stated more directly, the core idea for the reformulation of economic activity is the introduction of significant market forces into the public sector or, for our industry, the privatization of schooling (Murphy, 1996, 1999). And as we discuss more fully below, homeschooling is the most robust or expressive or radical form of privatization (Aurini & Davies, 2005; Belfield, 2004a; Reich, 2002).

Privatization covers a good deal of ground and has several different meanings (Murphy, 1996). Indeed, analysts have been quick to note that privatization is a multilayered construct (Butler, 1991). A particularly helpful definition has been provided by De Alessi (1987):

The term *privatization* is typically used to describe the transfer of activities from the public sector to the private sector and includes contracting out as well as reducing or discontinuing the provision of some goods and services by government. More accurately, privatization entails a move toward private property and away from not only government and common ownership but also from government regulations that limit individual rights to the use of resources. (p. 24)

At the most basic level, two elements are common to these, and nearly all other, definitions of privatization—a movement away from reliance on government agencies to provide goods and services and a movement toward the private sector and market forces (Murphy, 1996).

An especially helpful way to see how a reweaving of the economic sector supports homeschooling is to examine the objectives of the privatization movement. Some authors perceive privatization to be a vehicle to help "restore government to its fundamental purpose to steer, not to man the oars" (Savas, 1987, p. 290). Others who view privatization as an element of a more extensive neoliberal policy package (B. Martin, 1993) maintain that a key objective, for better or worse, is to reconstruct the liberal democratic state (Starr, 1991), to redefine the operational "set of assumptions about the capacities of democratic government and the appropriate sphere of common obligation" (Starr, 1991, p. 25). Privatization here is viewed, in particular, as a vehicle to overcome the dependency culture (B. Martin, 1993) associated with a social order dominated by government activity. Another aim is to depoliticize service operations (Hanke & Dowdle, 1987). As Pirie (1988) argues, "the actual transfer to the private sector . . . can take the service into the purely economic world and out of the political world . . . freeing it from the political forces which acted upon it in the state sector" (pp. 52–53) and overcoming "structural weaknesses inherent in the nature of public sector supply" (p. 20; see also Lyman, 2000).

Perhaps the central purpose and most highly touted objective of privatization is reduction in the size of the public sector (Pack, 1991). The goal is to downsize or "rightsize" government (Worsnop, 1992). Based on the belief that government is too large and too intrusive and that government's decisions are political and thus inherently less reliable than market decisions (Savas, 1982), the focus is on "rolling back either the rate of growth or the absolute amount of state activity in the social service delivery system" (Ismael, 1988, p. 1).

A further objective is to enhance the overall health of the economy: "If reducing the size of the public sector is the dominant theme in the work of privatization advocates, enhancing the efficiency of the economy as a whole and the public sector in particular is their *leitmotif*" (Pack, 1991, p. 287). The secondary aims are to enhance efficiency and responsiveness (Bell & Cloke, 1990), to promote productivity and growth (Starr, 1987), to enhance the use of scarce resources (Miller & Tufts, 1991), to ensure that customers are served more effectively (Hanke & Dowdle, 1987), and to promote cost-effectiveness by getting prices right (Starr, 1991). Related to the issue of cost-effectiveness is still another objective of privatization: to diminish the power of public sector unions (Hardin, 1989).

Finally, privatization is often portrayed as a tactic for promoting choice and accountability in public services (Marlow, 1994; Savas, 1987). "The key word is *choice*. Advocates claim that privatization will enlarge the range of choice for individuals while serving the same essential functions as do traditional programs" (Starr, 1987, p. 131). According to Gormley (1991) and other analysts, "privatization enable[s] individual consumers to pursue their private choices more freely" (p. 309). These same analysts further posit that more choice will generally produce a more equitable distribution of benefits (Starr, 1987).

A review of the literature in this area shows that privatization represents a particular public philosophy (Van Horn, 1991) and that advocates of privatization fall into a distinctive ideological camp. In particular, as we discussed in the section on the rebuilding of the sociopolitical foundations, privatization draws strength from political movement toward the right (Apple, 2007; Brazer, 1981) and the fact that "Americans have turned to conservatives for the answers to the most important problems facing the U.S." (Pines, 1985, p. v). The fusion of a political agenda increasingly dominated by conservative politics (B. Martin, 1993) and an economic theology signaling a return to fundamentalism (Thayer, 1987) has given birth to the doctrine of neoliberalism (Apple, 2000a, 2000b; Aurini & Davies, 2005; Seldon, 1987) and to "the ideological and profit-oriented agenda of the New Right" (B. Martin, 1993, p. 182), the conservative understanding of government as an economic black hole (Starr, 1987). In the process, "an ideology which has long lurked in the darkest shadows of right-wing thinking [has been] transfer[red] into an apparatus at the very center of the policy process" (Bell & Cloke, 1990, p. 4).

Given the central role of the individual consumer in the market narrative and the reality that privatization represents a shift from government to private provision (and funding and regulation), it will come as a surprise to no one that individual freedom and choice (at least for parents, if not children) is at the heart of the newly forming economic foundation on which homeschooling rises. While there is considerable debate about the benefits and costs of privileging "the force of individualism" (Smith & Sikkink, 1999, p. 16; e.g., where some see the virtues in the right to be left alone [Klicka, 2004], others discern atomization, fragmentation, isolation, and an accompanying loss of community [Apple, 2000a; Lubienski, 2000]), analysts on all sides of the homeschooling debate confirm its critical placement in the newly emerging economic architecture of the nation in general (Gaither, 2008) and in the homeschooling movement in particular (Lubienski, 2000). Indeed, as Mayberry and team (1995, p. 102) remind us, "the home school movement perhaps to a greater extent than other movements . . . exemplifies the principles of individualism."

When viewed through a pragmatic lens, privatization is about the more efficient delivery of higher-quality goods and services. However, "as an ideological principle, privatization equals smaller government, lower taxes, and less government intervention in public affairs" (Van Horn, 1991, p. 261). Fueled, as we have seen, by citizen discontent with activist government, newly formed conservative winds are pushing society away from the agenda of the progressive era and toward a reconstruction of (some would argue, undermining of) the liberal democratic welfare state (Apple, 2005; Riegel, 2001; Starr, 1991).

Finally, consistent with an increasingly popular libertarian philosophy, there is an ongoing reassessment of the appropriate size of government in general and certain units of government in particular (Tullock, 1988), an emerging "belief that small is beautiful when applied to domestic government" (Fitzgerald, 1988, p. 21), and a rekindling of belief in the appropriateness of self-help and local initiative, especially of traditional local institutions (Savas, 1987). As noted earlier, these winds are blowing us in the direction of decentralization (Murphy, 2000), a "rebuilding [of] America from the bottom up—and the trend away from reliance on political institutions in favor of individual self-help initiatives" (Fitzgerald, 1988, p. 16). New attention is being devoted to "the potential of 'mediating structures'" (Savas, 1987, p. 239)—and the deleterious effects of large government on these structures—that are situated between the individual and the apparatus of government (Fitzgerald, 1988), such as families, churches, neighborhood groups, and voluntary associations. According to proponents of privatization, based on the belief that "creative local initiatives, informal person-to-person efforts, local role models, and intra-community pressures are more likely to be effective than bureaucrats" (Savas, 1987, p. 239), "we are witnessing the revival of self-help strategies and voluntarism as expressions of independence from government" (Fitzgerald, 1988, p. 26).

Central to this reweaving narrative is a set of key ideas, some more explicit than others, but nearly all of which support the formation of homeschooling as a social and educational movement. Some of these overlap and reinforce the bundles of ideas we saw emerging in our analysis of the shifting sociopolitical environment, ideas such as decentralization, choice, conservatism, and the privileging of citizen control over government action. Others, such as the power of voluntary association, competition, an emphasis on enhancing supply, and the empowerment of the consumer, are additions to the reform engine powering homeschooling.

❖ CONCLUSION

In this chapter, we examined the context that has allowed homeschooling to grow. Our central argument is that prevailing economic, political, social, and cultural forces during most of the 20th century precluded homeschooling from taking root. As those forces have been transformed, an environment conducive to homeschooling has materialized. We examined both oppositional and supportive forces in detail.

5

The Calculus of Departure

Parent Motivations for Homeschooling

Common to these parents is the belief that the traditional schools available to them are not meeting the needs of the total child. (S. Gray, 1993, p. 9)

～✧～

Home schoolers proceed from the insight that the institution of public education cannot adequately serve their children in the ways they want them served. (Lubienski, 2000, p. 211)

～✧～

*The home school parents believed that the public schools were academically and, more importantly, spiritually bankrupt, and that placing their children there was to put them at great risk—spiritually, intellectually, socially, and all too often physically.
(Cochran, 1995, p. 278)*

～✧～

In the previous chapter, we employed a wide-angle lens to explore the larger social, cultural, political, and economic forces that have formed a robust context for the growth of homeschooling in the United States. Here we examine the causal universe with a narrower lens, the views of parents who have selected homeschooling for their children. In the first part of the chapter, we provide a few general clarifying notes on parental motivations. We then investigate how context influences motivations. In the second part of the chapter, we forge and then employ a motivational scaffold to examine the homeschooling tapestry. We begin by reviewing major frameworks provided by scholars from 1980 to 2010. We then deepen our analysis by exploring the four major motivations for homeschooling in detail, those based on religion, academics, school environment, and family.

❖ MOTIVATIONAL DYNAMICS

Home education represents an exit from the formal educational system, an exit based on a complex set of needs, motivations, and expectations that are often idiosyncratic when examined individually but are united collectively into an organized and sophisticated sociopolitical movement.
(Marlow, 1994, p. 440)

～◦✦◦～

Prime Motive

The different rationales that parents have for home instruction are obvious. The underlying commonality between them, however, is less apparent. In each instance, homeschooling provides parents the opportunity to expand personal and family rights, regardless of their secular or religious orientations. Looked at in this way, the growth of the home school movement represents the attempt of a widely diverse group of parents to decide how their children will be educated, what values they will learn, and which socialization experiences they will encounter.
(Mayberry, Knowles, Ray, & Marlow, 1995, p. 39)

～◦✦◦～

The right of parents to raise and educate their children—and the complete lack of government authority in that regard—is perhaps the foundational conviction in homeschooling. (Kunzman, 2009b, p. 181)

～◦✦◦～

Before we travel too far in our trip, we need to be explicit about the universal, prime motive for homeschooling, one that is somewhat under-emphasized (or assumed and skipped over) in much of the empirical literature on home-based education. Specifically, parents homeschool for one overarching reason: They want control of their children and their education (Lines, 1991; Mayberry et al., 1995). They do not want to give that authority away to the school (Caruana, 1999; Colfax, 1990). This is the foundation that informs all other motives. It is the vehicle to meet other goals—for example, to impart cherished values or to protect children from social harm.

Three Sources of Motives

Parents' recollections of school and of learning environments thus figured prominently in their thinking about home education.
(Knowles, 1991, p. 219)

~◯◌◯~

Their rejection of the public school is often shaped by the experiences they have had while their children have been enrolled in public schools.
(Mayberry, 1989b, p. 177)

~◯◌◯~

Researchers help us discern the wellsprings from which homeschooling motives flow. To begin with, as Knowles (1988, 1991; Knowles, Muchmore, & Spaulding, 1994) was the first to systematically document, motives for homeschooling are nurtured by the schooling and family experiences, especially unpleasant ones, that parents had when they were children (Arai, 2000). These, Knowles maintains, are as important as present conditions in convincing parents to educate their children at home. Knowles and team (1994), for example, document a need for some parents to protect their children from the type of unhealthy learning environments that were in play when they were students. Other scholars report on parents hoping to shield their children from the less-than-stellar academic regimen they experienced in school (Williams, Arnoldson, & Reynolds, 1984). Second, motives grow from the challenges and problems freighted on children by today's schools (Groover & Endsley, 1988). Third, reasons emanate from a ferocious critique of America's schools in general, independent of one's own experiences and the experiences of one's children (Van Galen & Pittman, 1991).

Push and Pull Dynamics

Combined frequencies suggest that choices for homeschooling are made for both reactive and proactive reasons. (Dahlquist, York-Barr, & Hendel, 2006, p. 366)

~◯◌◯~

We also learn from a rich trove of studies that there are both positive and negative reasons for homeschooling, with the former featuring the perceived benefits of educating at home (e.g., building a stronger family) and the latter underscoring the personal costs of public schooling (e.g., becoming peer-dependent)—what Hertzel (1997) calls push and pull factors. We have much to report on findings in each of these two domains in the sections that follow. Our only objective here is to confirm the dual nature of motives. We also note that positive motives are under-emphasized in the general literature vis-à-vis their importance in the empirical studies.

Figure 5.1   Parent Motivations for Homeschooling

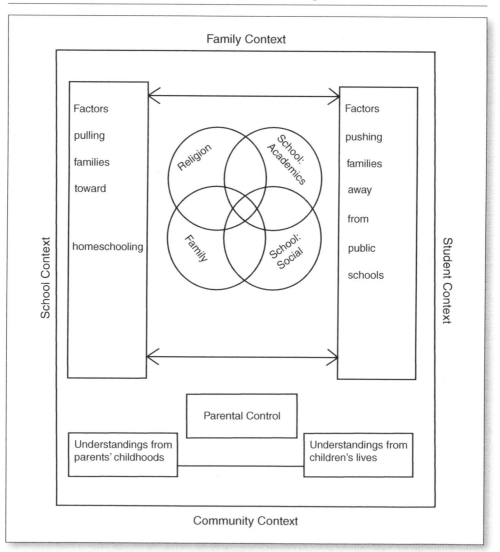

Complexity and Overlapping Rationales

The reasons to homeschool are as diverse as the methods employed.
(Lyman, 2000, p. 14)

～⌒⁖⌒～

The decision to educate at home involves a complex set of motivations.
(Marlow, 1994, pp. 441–442)

～⌒⁖⌒～

Reasons which compel home education families to teach their children at
home may not be mutually exclusive. (J. D. Marshall & Valle, 1996, p. 4)

～⌒⁖⌒～

Research consistently reveals that the attribution of uniformity in homeschooling motives often seen in the literature is inaccurate. Studies generally confirm that the motives of homeschooling families are multi-dimensional (Ray, 2009b; Sutton & Bogan, 2005). They also document that there is considerable variety in the reasons parents supply for homeschooling their children (Apostoleris, 1999; Nemer, 2002), what Mayberry and colleagues (1995) refer to as a myriad of perspectives and beliefs shaping homeschooling decisions. Motives also tend to be complex (Wartes, 1987), making understanding more arduous than often assumed (Knowles, 1988). Finally, there seems to be considerable overlap in motives (Dahlquist et al., 1996). Fixed boundaries between motives that defined the early modern era of homeschooling seem to be disintegrating (McKeon, 2007; Muntes, 2006), and motivational bundles seem to be more varied today (Isenberg, 2007).

Shifts in Motivations

There is some important empirical work that reveals that the motivational geography of homeschooling is changing. For example, one conclusion is that ideological rationales in general and religious-based motivations in particular, although still quite significant, are becoming less important (Bielick, 2008; Green & Hoover-Dempsey, 2007). Another finding is that as a new generation of middle-grounders has moved onto the homeschooling stage, motivations are less polarized (Collom & Mitchell, 2005; Gaither, 2008).

Investigators are also documenting that even in the same family, motivations for homeschooling are not fixed (Collom, 2005). Analysts have discovered that families sometimes begin homeschooling for one set of reasons but reference a different bundle of motivations for continuing the practice (S. Gray, 1993; Nemer, 2002). Dobson (2001) and Ray (2004a), for example, suggest that there may be movement from reactive to proactive rationales as parents settle into homeschooling. More specifically, the case has been made that involvement in the work of homeschooling can transform motives (Collom, 2005). Relatedly, investigators document that parental motives vary by the age of the child (Isenberg, 2002). For example, Muntes (2006) finds that parents place more weight on the importance of developing character and values for younger than for older children.

Three other insights merit note in any review of homeschooling motives. First, there is at least a hint in the literature that motivations follow from the decision to homeschool rather than drive the original choice (McKeon, 2007), a finding not inconsistent with the larger stream of research on human motivation. Second, for many families motives for homeschooling are a piece of a larger perspective on life (Kunzman, 2009b); they are nested in a web of motivations that power particular lifestyles (Nemer, 2002). Finally, almost no one has addressed the motivational quandary first surfaced by Mayberry and team (1995); that is, why do some roughly equivalent families in terms of demographics, values, and lifestyles vary in their selection of homeschooling as an educational option?

Context Considerations

A parent's decision to homeschool is motivated not only by the parent's psychological beliefs but also by the parent's perception of contextual variables that influence the feasibility of homeschooling.
(Green & Hoover-Dempsey, 2007, p. 272)

⋽⌒⋎⌒⋞

The propensity to home school is not only responsive to observed characteristics of schools, but also to household characteristics.
(Isenberg, 2002, p. 23)

⋽⌒⋎⌒⋞

One of the essential laws of social science is that context almost always matters. Nowhere is this conclusion more obvious than in the realm of homeschooling. Employing nomenclature such as *environmental variables, economic determinants,* and *structural conditions,* scholars identify four bundles of contextual conditions that can differentially shape motivations to homeschool: the school, the household, the student, and the community.

Schooling Characteristics

These results indicate that public school quality issues are important when a family considers the choice between public and home education.
(Houston, 1999, p. 101)

⋽⌒⋎⌒⋞

The leading economically grounded scholar in the area of home-schooling divides schooling conditions in two categories, those that relate directly to the quality of the public schools and those that measure environmental conditions in the school district in which a given school is located (Houston, 1999). We also learn from other researchers that the state context plays a role in influencing decisions to homeschool (Isenberg, 2007).

Turning first to *measures of school quality,* Houston (1999) in his path-breaking research concluded that when the quality of schools goes down, homeschooling increases. Or, stated inversely, the availability of quality schools decreases homeschooling (Isenberg, 2007). While acknowledging that identifying the best measure of public school quality is not an easy assignment, Houston identifies some proxies that are linked to home-based education. Examining one indicator, expenditure level per student, he affirms that lower investments of resources in a public school increase motivation to homeschool and, subsequently, home-based enrollment. Alternatively, higher levels of expenditures are associated with an increased likelihood of selecting public schooling (Houston & Toma, 2003; Isenberg, 2002). These scholars also demonstrate that school quality as measured in terms of low levels of student achievement has a small effect in pushing up homeschool enrollment. A parallel finding is reached when dropping out is the measure of school quality. When schools have difficulty holding youngsters in school, more families turn to homeschooling (Houston, 1999). Finally, Isenberg (2007) has shown that when relationships among students are used as an indicator of quality, homeschooling increases as negative peer socialization in schools increases.

As noted above, Houston (1999) has investigated a second cluster of school characteristics that shape parental motivation to engage in homeschooling, what might best be described as school *environmental conditions.* Collectively, the storyline runs as follows: "If schools are unable to deliver a product that is valued by the household because of the prevalence of negative environmental factors then the household will seek out alternative forms of education, including home education" (p. 86).

One school environmental factor is level of income. The higher the poverty level in the district, the more push and pull there is toward home-based education. More specifically, researchers affirm a positive correlation between the percentage of children in the free and reduced lunch program and the extent of homeschooling in a district (Thompson, 1994), suggesting that this socioeconomic condition in a district "does influence parents to homeschool their children" (p. 16). Houston (1999) arrives at a parallel conclusion, employing the percentage of people living below the poverty line in the district as the measure of low income. An even stronger association has been drawn between heterogeneity of income in a school district and homeschooling (Houston, 1999), with greater heterogeneity associated with expanded homeschool enrollment (Houston & Toma, 2003). An empirical relationship has also been documented between race and homeschooling, at least for African Americans. Houston and Toma (2003) find, for example, that a higher percentage of African Americans in a district increases the probability of homeschooling.

Investigators have also established a connection between the robustness of state regulations and the motivation to homeschool. Analysts affirm that greater amounts of regulations in general will push homeschool enrollment downward (Houston & Toma, 2003). More specifically, they find that states that mandate testing dampen enthusiasm for homeschooling (Houston, 1999). Finally, there is evidence that a context rich in options for schooling, both public and private, will act as a brake on homeschooling (Houston, 1999; Houston & Toma, 2003).

Household Characteristics

The actual decision to homeschool is often triggered by unique circumstances that vary from family to family. (Collom, 2005, p. 309)

~✧~

Certain characteristics of the household may predispose a family to home education. (Houston, 1999, p. 105)

~✧~

Analysts bundle a second group of context conditions into a category labeled *household characteristics.* Generally included here are family income, education level of the parents, race/ethnicity, religious affiliation, and marital status, conditions on which considerable data were provided in Chapter 2 on homeschooling families. In regard to income, scholars document an interesting pattern. Up to a point on the income continuum, greater wealth is positively associated with additional homeschooling, most likely because higher income provides the opportunity for one parent to stay at home. But past some point on the continuum, homeschooling turns downward as costs of forgone income by keeping one parent out of the labor force rise to unacceptable levels. At this point, paying private school tuition costs can become a more attractive option than homeschooling (Houston, 1999; Isenberg, 2002). Not surprisingly, the findings on education are similar to those on income. As Houston (1999) has documented, more highly educated women (those with a bachelor's degree or more) are less likely to homeschool because of reluctance to forgo returns from the labor market.

Race also appears as a variable in the household characteristics equation. McDowell, Sanchez, and Jones (2000) maintain that African American families that mirror white families in income and education often are motivated to homeschool for different reasons. Involvement in the labor force is another relevant household characteristic, with job holding by the mother pushing down homeschooling (Belfield, 2004b). So too is marital status. Indeed, it is the strongest household determinant of homeschooling (Houston, 1999). Finally, there is evidence that another contextual condition, religious affiliation, influences the homeschooling decision of families. Membership in the Catholic faith has historically depressed homeschooling (Belfield, 2004b; Houston, 1999). On the other hand, affiliation with an evangelical community of faith enhances the likelihood of homeschooling (Houston, 1999).

Student and Community Characteristics

Households are more likely to choose public schools over home schools in more densely populated areas. (Houston & Toma, 2003, p. 930)

~✲~

Surprisingly, little empirical work has been completed that examines how student characteristics beyond special needs status influence families to homeschool. There is a discernible line of argumentation in the literature that families with special education students, both gifted and learning disabled, may be attracted to homeschooling. But there is almost no systematic research on the issue (Kunzman, 2009b).

Conditions in communities, which overlap considerably with environmental conditions in districts, are also known to influence homeschooling (Houston & Toma, 2003). Ruralness pulls families toward homeschooling, while urban environments depress homeschooling (Thompson, 1994). We also know that vis-à-vis rural families, urban parents have somewhat different reasons for homeschooling (Isenberg, 2002). The density of schooling options in a community is also important in the homeschooling narrative. An absence of private school options, for example, will increase homeschooling (Isenberg, 2007). The perceived ability of parents to influence local policy is a relevant contextual variable as well. For example, the greater the percentage of funding for education provided by the state (as opposed to the local community), the higher the level of homeschooling (Isenberg, 2002).

❖ MOTIVATIONAL FRAMEWORKS

While reasons for homeschooling are wonderfully diverse . . . they tend to fall into roughly defined categories. (Dobson, 2001, p. 5)

~✲~

Introduction

> *The idea of two distinctly motivated types of homeschoolers—the Ideologues (religiously motivated) and the Pedagogues (academic and methodology motivated)—is a recurring theme throughout the available literature. (Taylor-Hough, 2010, p. 4)*

⁓◠◡◠⁓

> *There is a general consensus among researchers that the decision to home school is motivated by four broad categories of concern: (a) religious values, (b) dissatisfaction with the public schools, (c) academic and pedagogical concerns, and (d) family life. (Collom & Mitchell, 2005, p. 277)*

⁓◠◡◠⁓

Prevalent Typologies

Analysts over the last three decades have devoted considerable energy exploring the reasons why parents choose to educate their children at home. At one end of the workbench are investigators who present answers in unbundled form—that is, in lists of motives. At the other end of the workbench are researchers who aggregate rationales to create more comprehensive motivational categories. Collectively, these motivational detectives provide an especially rich understanding of the calculus of departure—that is, why families are turning to this historically unorthodox educational option. In this introductory section, we review in historical sequence some of the most important frameworks that these scholars have provided. In the next section, we collapse all the findings on motivations into a four-dimensional framework.

One of the earliest motivational frameworks was provided by Holt (1981, p. 23), who answered the question of why parents choose homeschooling as follows:

> mostly for three reasons: they think that raising their children is their business not the government's; they enjoy being with their children and watching and helping them learn, and don't want to give that up to others; they want to keep them from being hurt, mentally, physically, and spiritually.

In the first major study on homeschooling, Gustavsen (1981, p. 3) listed four major motivational categories:

> concern about the moral health and character development of their children; detrimental effect of rivalry and ridicule in conventional schools; parent-perceived poor quality of public school education; and the desire to extend parent-child contact.

In 1984, homeschool parents provided the rationales that allowed John Wesley Taylor (1986a, p. 29) to craft this motivational typology:

(1) academic—children can learn better, (2) religious—it is a better way to foster religious beliefs and values, (3) social/moral—avoid negative influences and reinforce family values, (4) intuitive—the family offers a more natural and nurturing environment, and (5) philosophical—avoid undesired philosophies such as humanism and socialism.

Williams and colleagues (1984, p. 1) collapsed their case study findings on reasons for homeschooling as follows:

unsuitability of children for school, desire of parents for control, socialization, conceptualization of the learning process, ideas about content, and personal interest.

In the late 1980s and throughout the 1990s, Knowles and Mayberry added entire new chapters to the book on homeschooling motivations and deepened existing sections of the book as well. In an early investigation, they uncovered

four groups of rationales for home school operations: family environments of the home school parents; parents' schooling and other learning experiences; contemporary problems children experienced in schools; and parents who believed they could provide a superior learning climate. (Knowles, 1988, pp. 73–74)

Based on their studies in Oregon and Utah, Mayberry and Knowles (1989) discussed two overarching bundles of motivations, in priority order: (1) religious, sociorelational, academic, or New Age reasons and (2) protection, control, self-actualization, and closeness.

Van Galen (1991) has provided the most cited and most well-regarded framework in the homeschooling literature, collapsing motivations into four categories in an overarching, two-dimensional design: ideologues (strengthen relations with one's children and opposition to what is taught [or not taught] in schools) and pedagogues (problems with academics, problems with school climate).

In his dissertation, Parker (1992, pp. 167–168) bundled rationales into four categories: religious convictions, parental concerns, the goal of academic excellence, and the goal of providing children with a healthy socialization experience. In his review, Jeub (1994) distilled motivations into four areas: social, academic, family, and religious. Hertzel (1997) has provided a seven-part motivational architecture:

1. Instructional and curricular issues

2. Safety issues

3. Social issues

4. Convenience issues

5. Health/handicap issues

6. Values issues

7. Self-esteem issues

Lyman (1998), based on an analysis of 300 magazine and newspaper articles, created four categories to house rationales for homeschooling: dissatisfaction with the public schools, the desire to freely impart religious values, academic excellence, and the building of stronger family bonds. Lange and Liu (1999, pp. 14–15) forged 18 separate boards into five broad motivational beams: educational philosophy, special needs of the child, school climate, family lifestyle and parenting philosophy, and religion and ethics.

In an especially important historical analysis, Mitchell Stevens (2001) designated two motivational groupings, inclusives and believers. In his work for the National Home Education Research Institute, Ray has explored the issue of family motivation for homeschooling numerous times. His framework is representative of his work. It includes four categories: "Teaching specific philosophical or religious values, controlling social interactions, developing close families, and high level academics" (Ray, 2001, p. 1). Boyer (2002, p. 21) provides the following motivational categories: "psychological and emotional well-being, relevant involvement of family, personal safety, and pedagogical needs." Collom (2005) and Collom and Mitchell (2005) have also explored the motivations of homeschooling families. They discuss four categories: "religious values, dissatisfaction with the public schools, academic and pedagogical concerns and family life" (Collom & Mitchell, 2005, p. 277). Using the data from the National Household Education Survey, Isenberg (2007) sorts motivations into three large bins: religion, education, and behavioral or special need. Using a psychologically-grounded lens rather than economic and sociological lenses, Green and Hoover-Dempsey (2007) weave together two bundles of motivations: psychological motivations and perceptions of personal life context variables.

Building from these frameworks and factoring in the balance of empirical work on homeschooling motivations, we employ the following four categories to capture a deep understanding of reasons why parents choose to school at home: (1) religion; (2) schooling: academics; (3) schooling: socialization; and (4) family (see Figure 5.1). We unpack each of these four dimensions in detail below. Before we do so, however, we note a few of the lesser-noted reasons for homeschooling.

Lesser-Noted Motives

Perhaps most surprising, while not completely ignored in the literature (see Kunzman, 2009b; Ray, 1997a), few of the lists of motives include parents moving toward homeschooling because of evidence that it works (i.e., "we homeschool our children because we are impressed with the evidence of its success"). On the other hand, the belief that parents can do a better job than the school is ribboned throughout the literature (Mayberry et al., 1995; Perry & Perry, 2000). Relatedly, there are indications that some parents are pulled toward homeschooling by learning about other families that have been successful in implementing this innovative approach to education (Mayberry et al., 1995). As we saw in earlier chapters, support organizations often play an important role here. There is some evidence that parents can be motivated to homeschool by interest in the concept expressed at the houses of faith they attend (Knowles, 1991).

There are also some references to the fact that homeschooling occurs for some children because it ends up being easier to keep youngsters home than to battle with school authorities. This rationale is often linked to special needs children (Peterson, 2009). Costs appear as a light thread in the motivational fabric as well (Wartes, 1987). Specifically, it is argued that the high costs of private schools may direct parents to the homeschooling option (J. Taylor, 1986a; J. D. Marshall & Valle, 1996). Finally, analysts have uncovered evidence that some parents choose homeschooling to avoid desegregation in general and busing in particular (Reinhaller & Thomas, 1996; J. Taylor, 1986a). Others are less circumspect, suggesting that the data may implicate racism in the motivational algorithm of some homeschooling families (Cochran, 1995; Kunzman, 2009b).

Religious-Based Motivations

Participation in social movements such as the home education movement is often motivated by perceived threats to particular moral understandings and a desire to reinforce and protect the beliefs and values to provide a stable worldview and guide to life. (Marlow, 1994, p. 441)

❧

The extant body of research illustrating the motivations of home educators reveals that the goals are not mysterious or hidden. Repeatedly, consistently, unequivocally, the finding is reported that the primary motivation for most home educators reflects a moral, spiritual, or religious component. (Cizek, 1993, p. 1)

❧

Religiosity has long been associated with homeschooling. (Clements, 2002, p. 3)

❧

In the material that follows, we discuss spiritual motivations in two sections: the significance of religion in the lives of many (most) homeschooling families and the secularization of public schooling.

The Religious Life

Many families are motivated by their religious beliefs to begin home schooling. Their home school activity can only be understood within the context of their religious philosophy. (Mayberry & Knowles, 1989, p. 215)

✺

But even more central in the mindset of conservative Christian homeschoolers is the fundamental conviction that educating their children is a God-given right and responsibility, and one they can delegate only at great moral and spiritual peril. (Kunzman, 2009b, p. 6)

✺

As we reported in Chapter 3, while religious motivations did not fuel the initial phase of the modern homeschooling movement, within a decade religious convictions had become a critical variable in the homeschooling algorithm. For about 20 years beginning in the early 1980s, studies consistently documented that homeschooling families were motivated primarily by religious convictions and spiritual beliefs. On surveys and in interviews throughout this period, parents routinely told researchers that God was behind their decision to homeschool (Dahlquist et al., 2006; Parker, 1992). And because religious ideology is often intertwined with other choice options in these surveys and interviews (e.g., build strong families), religion is probably even a more potent motivational force than it appears.

More recent studies add to the spiritual motivational story in two ways. They confirm that religious convictions remain at or near the top of the list of reasons why families homeschool (Bielick, 2008; Princiotta & Bielick, 2006). At the same time, they reveal that there has been a narrowing of the gap between religious and other rationales for choosing home-based education (Bielick, 2008; Muntes, 2006).

The Moral Imperative. One of the most interesting themes in the religious motivational chronicle is that a large number of homeschoolers believe that they are commanded by God to keep their children at home (Gladin, 1987; Van Galen, 1991; Wilhelm & Firman, 2009). They often make this point with specific references to scripture (Nemer, 2002; Schemmer, 1985). They are apt to discuss homeschooling in terms of divine will (Guterson, 1992; M. L. Stevens, 2001).

In many instances, this scriptural obligation is linked to the belief that public schools morally harm children (Klicka, 1995; Welner, 2002), thus adding significance to the admonition. But this coupling is hardly universal. Some who homeschool from religious convictions do not anchor this work in the moral hazard of public education. It is sufficient to know that God has given parents sole responsibility for the education of their children, especially inculcation of moral values (Kunzman, 2009b; Parker, 1992).

To fulfill the call to integrate Christian doctrine into the lives of their children (Klicka, 2004) and to bring unity to and to maintain the family (Knowles, 1991), many parents believe that they must (a) form a wall between home and state, to take control, and (b) have their children with them for significant parts of the day (Gorder, 1990; Kunzman, 2009b). In total, then, for a large number of parents homeschooling has the potential both to protect children from the unacceptable values in play in public schools and society at large and to foster the Christian perspective that is the lifeblood of their families (Mayberry & Knowles, 1989; Van Galen, 1991).

The Integrative Principle. It should be clear from the analysis above that religiously motivated homeschooling parents do not divide the world into discrete units—home, school, afterschool activities, and so on. They see their faith as an animating force that places God at the center of their lives and pulls all dimensions of their lives into a principled whole (Klicka, 2004; Wilhelm & Firman, 2009), a force that organizes all dimensions of their existence. Homeschooling for many of these believers becomes an essential, if not *the* essential, vehicle for this integrative work (Mayberry et al., 1995; Van Galen, 1991).

The Centrality of Values and Evangelical Beliefs. Margaret Martin (1997) reminds us that as we move into the content at the heart of religiously motivated homeschooling, two issues stand out. First, homeschooling is fundamentally about values (Kunzman, 2009b). As we discuss below, homeschooling happens for these families because first and foremost parents want to inculcate in their children the values they consider important for life and essential for salvation (Gorder, 1990; Klicka, 2004; Welner, 2002). Second, homeschooling happens because parents want to integrate these values and beliefs into all dimensions of the curriculum; each subject is taught from the perspective of scripture (Gaither, 2008).

On the first issue, researchers consistently demonstrate that religiously motivated parents have specific values they want their children to absorb (Aurini & Davies, 2005; Basham, Merrifield, & Hepburn, 2007). It is also clear to them that these values are not being directly taught or indirectly learned in public schools (Nemer, 2002). Worse, they perceive that deviant values are being taught and absorbed by America's youngsters (Williams et al., 1984). Particularly salient here, and consistent with the integrative principle just analyzed, homeschooling permits parents to reproduce their spiritual way of life in their children (Apple, 2000a; Mayberry, 1989a), to mold the life of their youngsters in significant and enduring ways (Kunzman, 2009b), what advocates think of as positive indoctrination and critics define as possible brainwashing (Apple, 2000a; Berliner, 1997).

The general storyline here is about the centrality of moral and ethical character development (Welner, 2002). The particular narrative is about the induction of religious values (Collom, 2005), most often conservative and fundamentalist frames of reference (Cochran, 1995; McKeon, 2007), what Klicka (1995) describes as traditional Christian values and John Wesley Taylor (1986b) labels a Christian conception of God's laws.

On a second front, we also learn from the research that religious-based rationales for homeschooling grow from the desire by some parents to thread these critical spiritual values and beliefs throughout the curriculum and across the school day (Mirochnik & McIntire, 1991; Parker, 1992). According to Klicka (1995), the hallmark point here is that scriptural lessons should stretch across all aspects of life. Therefore, it is essential that all subjects be investigated through the prism of doctrine. Sacred ideology and subject content, according to these homeschoolers, should be inexorably intertwined (Hertzel, 1997; Mayberry et al., 1995). Personal beliefs and values need to be integrated into each curricular domain (Romanowski, 2001). Instruction should unfold from religious perspectives (Whitehead & Bird, 1984). The bible is the architecture on which all learning is to be scaffolded (Kunzman, 2009b). Faith and the divine become the reference point from which all subject area exploration occurs (Klicka, 1995) in the service of guiding children into a comprehensive Christian worldview (Kunzman, 2009b).

The Secularization of Public Schools

Probably a majority of home schoolers are religious fundamentalists, unhappy with the failure of public schools to teach religious and spiritual tenets and with what they sometimes describe as the "secular humanism" that these schools allegedly espouse. (Divoky, 1983, p. 396)

~◠◡◠~

Religiously motivated parents tend to regard secular humanism and apparent student immorality as characteristics of public schools that they wish to counteract by operating home schools for their children. (Knowles et al., 1992, p. 196)

~◠◡◠~

Christian fundamentalists firmly believe that schools are battlegrounds in struggles between Christians and their opponents. (Van Galen, 1991, p. 69)

~◠◡◠~

The Meaning of Secularization. As we just reported, on one hand many families are being pulled to homeschool because of a deep commitment to their faith. At the same time, many of these families also feel pushed away from public schools by what they view as the growth of an educational system at odds with that faith (Apple, 2007; Klicka, 1995).

This divergent moral system was arrived at, according to these parents and many faith-based support groups, by two paths. The first path comprises a series of actions that removed core religious planks that had been part of the foundation of public schools for over a century (Erickson, 2005; Kirschner, 1991), what Houston (1999) describes as a growing away from a Protestant-grounded to a nondenominational, nonreligious system of public education. Central here is the separation of the sacred and secular into two distinct spheres (Holt, 1981), with the former, according to many homeschoolers, being shown the schoolhouse exit door. Essential markers here were a series of Supreme Court decisions in the 1960s that (a) made prayer unconstitutional in schools, (b) prohibited school-sponsored bible reading, and (c) outlawed the display of the Ten Commandments and other symbols of Christianity (Gaither, 2008; Klicka, 2004).

The second path toward the formation of a public school system at odds with faith was what religious-based homeschoolers and support groups see as the active secularization of education (Carper, 2000; Lines, 1991; Reich, 2002). This idea is laced throughout the literature, although it is not especially well defined by homeschooling advocates. It is never discussed in a positive sense. It is seen as an insidious historical pattern, one defined by both the good ideas it precludes as well as the bad ideas it nourishes—"a destructive force that directly opposes their fundamental religious and moral principles" (Marlow, 1994, p. 441). It means in the broadest sense what is left when faith and the divine are displaced, "a philosophy of the absence of a God" (Gorder, 1990, p. 50). Still, at a high level of abstraction, it has been defined by Klicka (1995) and others as the belief that man is the center of all things. Moving a bit closer to the concrete end of the definitional yardstick, analysts define secular humanism in terms of the loss of traditional values and moral absolutes (S. Gray, 1993; Van Galen, 1991). Here some homeschoolers discern a dismantling of foundational moral pillars of society, such as the traditional family, conservatism, and a melting pot culture (Mayberry et al., 1995).

The Impact of Secularization. A major outcome of the secularization movement for many families has been the loss of a well-defined and quite visible Christian culture in the public schools (Gaither, 2008), the removal of the divine commandments and guiding moral worldview (Klicka, 1995). In turn, there has been a palpable sense of disenfranchisement among homeschoolers (Apple, 2000b; Klicka, 2004). At the least harmful end of this disenfranchisement continuum, we find those who believe that Christian values are insufficiently acknowledged in public schools (Jeub, 1994) and that religion is conspicuous by its absence (Basham et al., 2007; Mayberry, 1992). They see a moral vacuum in school (Cai, Reeve, & Robinson, 2002; S. Gray, 1993). In the middle of the continuum are the many homeschooling families who discern not only the absence of attention to religion but also the development of a hazy, antireligious perspective in public schools (Erickson, 2005; Riegel, 2001).

At the far end of the disenfranchisement continuum are homeschool parents who see secular humanists wielding their philosophical tools to actively strangle religion in education (Jeub, 1994; Romanowski, 2001). They discern a school system working assiduously against their convictions and perspectives (Isenberg, 2007; Klicka, 2004). They believe that their values and morals are being intentionally and aggressively undermined (Hadeed, 1991; Parker, 1992). Specifically, these parents point to collections of school programs and interventions that they believe subvert Christian values and honor humanistic worldviews. They observe schools emphasizing what they hold to be immoral ideologies such as political correctness (Lyman, 2000), socialist values (Welner, 2002), moral relativism (Gorder, 1990), consumerism/materialism (Apple, 2005), careerism for women (Welner, 2002), pluralistic values (S. Gray, 1993), social liberalism (McKeon, 2007), humanism (Klicka, 2004), and statism (Glanzer, 2008).

In the instructional program domain, religiously motivated homeschool parents often express an uneasiness about teachers, pedagogy, and curriculum in public schools that they consider to be oppositional to doctrine and their deeply held beliefs (Klicka, 1995; Mayberry, 1989b; Nemer, 2002). In particular, faith-based homeschoolers express considerable angst over subject matter such as evolution, sex education, and life adjustment (Gladin, 1987; Gorder, 1990; J. Taylor, 1986a). They also are troubled by frames such as "values clarification," a perspective that they believe undermines Christian commitment to moral absolutes (Wilhelm & Firman, 2009). The perceived amoral culture of schools is also of concern to many religiously motivated homeschooling parents (Klicka, 1995).

The closing chapter in this story should be fairly transparent by this point in the analysis. First, for many faith-based families, whether by negligence or active design, public schools have become unhealthy places, both morally and spiritually. Through their programs and culture they teach children the wrong lessons. As a consequence, at a minimum, they are likely to confuse youngsters. Worse, they can cause children to reject the values of the home and church (Klicka, 1995; Parker, 1992), thus turning them from God and their families (Apple, 2000b). Second, because of this children are placed at spiritual risk. Their faith and Christian worldviews are threatened (Gaither, 2008; Welner, 2002). The souls of children are thought to be in danger (Apple, 2005; Klicka, 1995). In the worst case, schools are seen as the enemy, one that is consorting with the devil (Knowles, 1989; Kunzman, 2009b). Third, it is the moral obligation of Christian parents to save their children—and their families—from the public school system (Knowles et al., 1992; McCurdy, 1997) and from eternal damnation (Bates, 1991; Welner, 2002). Finally, for many religiously motivated parents this means educating their children at home (Klicka, 1995; Kunzman, 2009b).

School-Based Motivations: Academic Deficiencies

One of the major reasons why people are turning to home schooling is because the state-run public school system has become academically bankrupt. (Klicka, 1995, p. 19)

∽◠ᵛ◠∽

Clearly, home schools are often an expression of intense dissatisfaction with public school outcomes. (Knowles, 1989, p. 393)

∽◠ᵛ◠∽

In the next two sections, we explore school-based motivations for homeschooling, looking first at academic reasons and then at social rationales. Before we begin, however, it is instructive to remind ourselves of two caveats introduced earlier. First, almost all homeschoolers are motivated by multiple factors. Second, the four categories we highlight in this chapter are not mutually exclusive. For example, there is a good deal of faith-based ideology in the family-based motivational category.

Starting with academics, reviewers routinely find that parents are motivated to homeschool because of the poor quality of the public schools available for their children (Lines, 2000a, 2000b; J. Webb, 1989). Alternatively, homeschooling provides an important condemnation of America's public schools (Colfax & Colfax, 1988; Nemer, 2002). The academic critique, reflected in parental disenchantment, discontent, dissatisfaction, and despair (Hadeed, 1991; Moore, 1982; Van Galen, 1991), is constructed on 30 years of reports about the academic shortcomings of public schools (Basham et al., 2007; Isenberg, 2002). Under an avalanche of negative news, some parents have become profoundly dispirited; they have lost faith in the public schools. More join the carousel of despair every day. They have come to believe that schools will harm their children academically (Holt, 1981; Riegel, 2001). As they have, many others have elected to educate their children at home (Mayberry et al., 1995; Whitehead & Bird, 1984). We examine academic motivations below in two sections, a more general critique of public schooling that informs homeschooling decisions and a more localized analysis that relies on the voices of homeschooling parents.

The General Storyline

Two tributaries of critique mix to form the larger river of academic discontent fueling homeschooling: the sense that the current system of public education is failing and the belief that it is incapable of reforming.

A Sense of Failure. On the first matter, many homeschool parents have come to believe that public schools are broken academically. Moore (1982, p. 373) captured this angst at the outset of the homeschool movement when he reported that an increasing number of parents "are rising in anger and despair at the course the schools are taking." What analysts see as parental frustration over the continuing inadequacies of primary and secondary education in the United States is a multifaceted phenomenon. Stated in an alternate form, the perception that the level and quality of education in the United States is less than many desire is buttressed by data on a wide variety of outcomes. Specifically, according to many analysts, data assembled in each of the following performance dimensions provide a not-very-reassuring snapshot of the current academic performance of the American educational system: (a) academic achievement in basic subject areas (compared to student performance in other countries), (b) functional literacy, (c) preparation for employment, (d) the holding power of schools (dropout rates), (e) knowledge of specific subject areas such as geography and economics, and (f) mastery of higher-order skills (Committee for Economic Development, 1994; Murnane & Levy, 1996; Murphy, 2010). Perhaps even more important than the data is the fact that "the experience of most Americans tells them that the nation's school system is in trouble and that the problems are getting worse" (Mathews, 1996, p. 1).

Two issues in particular define analyses of academic outcomes: (1) the inability of the educational enterprise to enhance levels of productivity to meet the needs of the changing workforce and (2) the failure of schools to successfully educate all of the nation's children, especially the poor (Fusarelli, 1999; Murphy, 2010). Analysts fault the education enterprise for its inability to keep pace with the increasing expectations from a changing economy.

One side of the problem these critics discuss is the belief that systems that hold steady in today's world are actually in decline (Murphy & Meyers, 2008). They see "increasing obsolescence of the education provided by most U.S. schools" (Murnane & Levy, 1996, p. 6). The other side of the productivity issue raised by these reviewers is the claim that because of the changing nature of the economy outlined in Chapter 4, the level of outcomes needed by students must be significantly increased. Critics find that the schools are not meeting this new standard for productivity. They argue that many students fail to graduate with the skills they need (R. Marshall & Tucker, 1992), that "American schools are not providing students with the learning that they will need to function effectively in the 21st century" (Consortium on Productivity in the Schools, 1995, p. 3).

An Inability to Reform. Analysts also have a good deal to report about the second tributary feeding the river of discontent over academics in America's schools—that is, the failure of the system to heal itself (V. Taylor, 2005), or growing skepticism about the effectiveness of various educational reforms (Luebke, 1999). What has resulted from nearly 40 years of unbroken efforts at reform, critics argue, has not been an increase in academic quality but rather a proliferation of professional and bureaucratic standards (Hill, Pierce, & Guthrie, 1997), the creation of subsidies for bureaucracy (Beers & Ellig, 1994), a deepening rift between professional educators and the public (R. Marshall & Tucker, 1992), and the strengthening of a centralized educational system (Bulkley, 1998; Tyack, 1992) in which downside risks are passed onto parents and children (Payne, 1995). The effect, analysts assert, is that reform has reinforced the very dynamics that are promoting the imploding of public schooling. The natural consequence, they maintain, is the emergence of new forms of education. And homeschooling may end up as the most prominent of the new models (Collom, 2005).

The Localized Storyline

Home schooling parents are dissatisfied with the quality of education they see. Teachers and academic programs are held suspect in the minds of many of these parents. (S. Gray, 1993, p. 9)

～∩ᵥ∩～

Most of the recent homeschoolers joining the ranks appear to be motivated primarily by academic reasons. (Taylor-Hough, 2010, p. 4)

～∩ᵥ∩～

While the analysis above featured the push and pull dynamics in the general critique of academics in public schools, here we examine academic motivation more specifically through the eyes of homeschooling parents. Case studies of homeschools and surveys of homeschooling parents consistently converge on a concern about academic quality (Dahlquist et al., 2006; Ray, 1997b). When ranked in order of importance, academic motivations usually follow religious rationales and concerns about the social environment in schools (Princiotta & Bielick, 2006; Princiotta, Bielick, & Chapman, 2004). At the same time, researchers are discovering that these academic concerns are rising in importance in the motivational hierarchy of homeschoolers.

Pedagogy. A variety of patterns are visible in the motivational tapestry of academic deficiencies that has been thatched together from insights provided by homeschooling parents. One pattern highlights inadequate teachers (McKeon, 2007; M. L. Stevens, 2001). A second reveals poor-quality instruction (Lange & Liu, 1999; Van Galen, 1991). A third features teaching methods that are troublesome to some parents (Knowles, 1988; Welner, 2002). For example, some homeschooling parents are opposed to whole language instruction (Lyman, 2000). In general, however, it is safe to conclude that the counsel of despair among homeschoolers around pedagogy remains fairly abstract. Reviewers provide only an incomplete analysis of the geology of instructional problems.

Content. Homeschoolers also express concern about the inappropriately low academic standards they believe characterize the schools their children could be attending (Dobson, 2001; Duvall, Ward, Delquadri, & Greenwood, 1997). A general refrain is expressed that their children are not being asked to master ambitious learning targets, that they are insufficiently challenged academically (Muntes, 2006; Ray & Weller, 2003; Winstanley, 2009).

Relatedly, concerns about the curriculum in their local public schools add fuel to the motivational fire for some homeschooling families (Pearson, 1996; Schemmer, 1985; Welner & Welner, 1999). This includes worries both about content that is featured and about content that is not covered. One codicil is that there is considerable entanglement here with religious-based motivations, many of which, as we saw, are rooted in disillusionment with the secular humanistic underpinnings of the public school curriculum. A second codicil is that concerns about content vary a good deal depending on the perspective informing a homeschooling family. That is, curricular deficiencies that trouble homeschoolers from the more liberal wing of the movement are distinctly different than those that motivate more conservative families. For both wings of the movement, however, the heart of the issue is the same: a perceived incongruity between a preferred cultural identity and the one they see in the school curriculum (Glanzer, 2008; Welner, 2002).

Structure. The structure of the academic program also raises alarms among some families, thus pulling them into the orbit of homeschooling (Guterson, 1992; Lange & Liu, 1999). One element of the structural critique centers on schooling's regimentation of children, having all children in lockstep in an instructional dance that requires them to learn the same material at the same time (Arai, 2000; Colfax, 1990). For some parents, this regimentation is inexorably linked to an academic program defined by uninspiring routines and deadening, purposeless activities (Knowles, 1991; Parker, 1992).

The major structural problem for homeschoolers, and one that shares considerable space with the regimentation critique, is the belief that public schooling fails to provide needed individualization for children (Dalaimo, 1996; McKeon, 2007; Nemer, 2002). Almost by necessity, it is held, teachers teach to the children "in the middle" (Kerman, 1990; Holt, 1981). Youngsters who are capable of moving more quickly are, it is argued, held back, while students who are struggling are left behind (Aurini & Davies, 2005; S. Gray, 1993). And even for the children in the middle, the instructional match can be less than ideal. It is argued, therefore, that unique individual academic needs and interests for many go unmet (Colfax, 1990; Delahooke, 1986; Welner, 2002). The cardinal point is that clumping youngsters together by age for 6 or more hours per day makes desired individualization nearly impossible to achieve (Hanna, 2011; Wartes, 1987). Overcrowding or creating larger and larger clusters of children is seen as especially troublesome for homeschooling families (Hertzel, 1997; Schemmer, 1985).

Impact. These pedagogical, curricular, and structural deficiencies in schools lead to a number of problems, according to homeschooling parents. Learned passivity is often noted in this regard (Riegel, 2001), as are its handmaidens, diminished interest in learning and withdrawal (Dobson, 2001; Knowles, 1991; M. L. Stevens, 2001). Also noted are the stifling of independent thinking and the tamping down of creativity (Dalaimo, 1996; Nemer, 2002). Most important, academic failure, or at least what is seen as woefully insufficient academic progress, is found on the list of problems (Knowles, 1989; Mayberry et al., 1995). Or as Holt (1981, p. 25) nicely put it near the inception of the modern era of homeschooling, "One reason people take their children out of school is that they aren't learning anything."

School-Based Motivations: Social/Environmental Problems

Home schooling is partly about saving children from multiple contaminants. (M. L. Stevens, 2001, p. 53)

~◠✣◠~

In spite of the diverse reasons that draw parents to home schooling, they share a profound belief that the public schools are not providing a healthy environment for their children. (Divoky, 1983, p. 397)

~◠✣◠~

A major category of reasons for homeschooling relates to the parents' perception that the public or private school environment is harmful to their child. (Lange & Liu, 1999, p. 5)

~◠✣◠~

Deeply embedded in the studies that investigate parental motivations for homeschooling is the trenchant belief that public (and private) schools at a minimum expose children to harm and at worst actually damage them. According to parents and homeschool support groups, damage can stretch across five domains: spiritual, academic, physical, emotional (psychological), and social. In our earlier analysis, we explored spiritual and academic harm in some detail. Here we turn the spotlight on the last three domains, which aggregate into a bundle we label *school social environment*. The entry point into the analytic narrative is that assessments of school climate often lead parents to conclude that schools are bad places for their children—physically, emotionally, and socially (Fager & Brewster, 2000; Ray & Weller, 2003)—and that they can provide a much healthier environment for learning in the home (Knowles, 1989).

Over the last 30 years, studies have consistently documented that school social/environmental issues rank high on the motivational lists of homeschooling families (Dahlquist et al., 2006; Gladin, 1987; Lyman, 1998). In the 2003 National Center for Educational Statistics study, fully 85% of homeschooling parents identified concerns with the school environment as important in their homeschool calculations, more so than the religious (72%) and academic (68%) rationales discussed previously. Social concerns also edged out religious motivation as the single most important motivation (31.2%–29.8%; Princiotta & Bielick, 2006)—a change from a few years earlier, when religion was chosen as the most important reason for homeschooling (Bielick, Chandler, & Broughman, 2001).

Protection From Physical and Emotional Harm

For an increasingly large number of parents, public schools are now seen as threatening in an even more powerful way. They are dangerous bodily; that is, they are seen as filled with physical dangers to the very life of one's children. (Apple, 2000a, p. 70)

~◌⚬◌~

The second strongest PULL factor was that parents believe it is "safer at home." (Hertzel, 1997, p. 71)

~◌⚬◌~

One reason parents decide to homeschool is that they are worried about the physical well-being of their children when they are at school (Boyer, 2002; D. W. Gray, 1998). While this concern has been on the motivational landscape for some time, it appears to be increasing in significance. Of particular importance here is the uneasiness that gnaws at parents because of perceived violence in schools (Mayberry et al., 1995; Ray, 2004a). Gang problems, drug use, bullying, and weapons are often singled out by homeschooling parents (Lyman, 2000; McKeon, 2007; Nemer, 2002). Feelings run hot on this issue, and there is a sense among some in the homeschooling literature that crime is unfolding unchecked across America's public schools (Klicka, 1995).

Parents are also motivated to homeschool to protect their children from emotional harm (Gorder, 1990; Moore, 1982). They sometimes attempt to shield their children from what they view as an overly competitive environment, one that promotes unhealthy rivalry, ridicule, and meanness (Holt, 1997; J. Taylor, 1986a; Williams et al., 1984).

Protection From Social Harm

Home school parents often claim that the current social environment of formal schools is actually a compelling argument for operating a home school. (Mayberry et al., 1995, p. 3)

⌒⌒

Other studies that have surveyed parents' reasons for home-schooling commonly report that parents see socialization as a negative aspect of school. (Rakestraw & Rakestraw, 1990, p. 74)

⌒⌒

For some parents, this issue of socialization is at the head of their decision to homeschool. (Moore & Moore, 1994, p. 61)

⌒⌒

The hallmark environmentally anchored motivation for homeschooling is the prevention of the dysfunctional socialization that many parents believe defines public schooling (Kitchen, 1991; Winstanley, 2009). Some parents see schools enveloped in a dark cloud of poor health (Collom, 2005; Luke, 2003), one that bodes ill for children (Cochran, 1995; Medlin, 2000). They judge the public school to be "a socially corrosive institution" (Riegel, 2001, p. 91), little more than a chalice of social wretchedness (Klicka, 1995). They maintain that homeschooling provides the only effective antidote to the public school socialization problem (Dalaimo, 1996; Medlin, 2000).

Analysts who study these matters inform us that socialization problems, according to some in the homeschooling community, are spawned in a hideous brew of peer pressure (Boone, 2000; J. D. Marshall & Valle, 1996), in a caldron that in turn is supported by an ill-framed scaffolding of age segregation (Moore, 1982; Smedley, 1992; Tillman, 1995) and the separation of youngsters from ongoing, meaningful interactions with adults (Erickson, 2005; Lines, 2000a, 2000b), a collective condition perhaps best defined as social stagnation (Gorder, 1990; Riegel, 2001). This, in turn, fosters the formation of a negative school climate (Holt, 1981; Kitchen, 1991), one that promotes peer dependency and drives wedges between children and their parents (Gaither, 2008; Groover & Endsley, 1988; Parker, 1992).

The avoidance of this negative socialization is often cited by parents to explain their commitment to home-based education (Ray & Weller, 2003; Saunders, 2010). They see their children avoiding the grim harvest of bad habits and traits associated with peer pressure (Divoky, 1983; Gatto, 1992; Lyman, 2000). And they believe that homeschooling will prevent accompanying and equally negative outcomes such as rejection of parental values, diminished self-worth, and reduced personal accountability (Glanzer, 2008; Kelley, 1991; Parker, 1992).

Family-Based Motivation

Several factors account for the home school movement, including a desire to strengthen the family. (Cai et al., 2002, p. 372)

～ი؎ᴖ～

Parental interest in participating in the education of their children is a primary reason for starting home schools. (Mayberry, 1989b, p. 178)

～ი؎ᴖ～

Many parents report homeschooling to meet the individual needs of their child or children or to meet the needs of their family and their chosen lifestyles. (Lange & Liu, 1999, p. 14)

～ი؎ᴖ～

So far we have examined three of the four essential bundles of motivations for homeschooling: religious-based reasons, academic-grounded reasons, and school social/environmental reasons. While generally highlighted less than these rationales, there is considerable agreement that parents also homeschool to strengthen the family (Hertzel, 1997; Mayberry, 1989a). And there is accompanying evidence that for some parents, family-based rationales are the central theme in the homeschooling motivational portrait. Based on the work of those who have preceded us, we cluster family-based motivations into five categories: parental responsibility for the education function, desire to be with one's children, meeting the requirements of special needs students, special circumstances, and promoting healthy families.

Responsibility for Education

Homeschool parents appear to decide to homeschool because they believe that they are personally responsible for their child's education. (Green & Hoover-Dempsey, 2007, p. 278)

～ი؎ᴖ～

Home schooling was a part of their perceived parental duties. To them, putting their children in any educational environment without them (the parents) in direct control would have been like placing their children in foster homes. (Parker, 1992, p. 166)

～ი؎ᴖ～

In our discussion of religious motivations for homeschooling, we noted that some parents maintain that they do not want the state to hold responsibility for the education of their children. We also reported that they believe that this obligation has been handed down from God. They find scriptural confirmation for this belief. This same sense of obligation is found among parents who homeschool for family reasons as well. For many of these families, the handiwork of the divine is evident. For others it is not. What is shared, however, is the idea that parents are responsible for the development of their children, and this obligation extends into formal education (Kunzman, 2009b; Parker, 1992; Riegel, 2001).

Desire to Be With One's Children

It was as though we had assumed that going to school was simply something children did—no questions asked, and when we finally learned to ask those questions, we felt somewhat cheated by the years our children had been away from us. (Ressler, 1997, p. 51)

⌒✦⌒

Some parents simply like to watch their children learn. They enjoy being parents and enjoy learning with their children. (Williams et al., 1984, p. 10)

⌒✦⌒

A number of parents tell researchers that they are sensitive to the chill of separation. They homeschool because they want to be with their children, to be a part of their growth and learning to a much greater extent than is possible when children are away at school (Gustavsen, 1981; Lyman, 2000). They enjoy being with their children and do not want to turn them over to the care of others no matter how well intended or competent those others may be (Hegener & Hegener, 1997; McCurdy, 1997). To do so, they maintain, would be to deny themselves critical aspects of satisfaction that accompany the parental role (Guterson, 1992).

Special Circumstances

*One group of homeschoolers is the conglomerate of children who engage in one form or another of intensive extracurricular activity.
(Gaither, 2008, p. 223)*

⌒✦⌒

Although not a major theme in the overall motivational narrative, special circumstances do pull some families into home-based education. For example, the desire for a flexible lifestyle and schedule can lead some families toward homeschooling (Dahlquist et al., 2006). Relatedly, irregular work patterns (e.g., intermittent work abroad) are sometimes noted as a motivation to homeschool (Blok, 2004). Finally, intensive activity on the part of some children in careers (e.g., music, acting) or areas of interest (e.g., athletics) can nudge families toward homeschooling as a preferred option (Gaither, 2008; Perry & Perry, 2000).

Meeting the Requirements of Special Needs Children

Although no comprehensive research exists, homeschool advocates contend that the customized, individual attention made possible in a homeschooling context can be of particular benefit to students with special needs.
(Kunzman, 2009b, p. 54)

~⌒◌⌒~

Homeschooling can be a last resort for frustrated families where gifted children are not having their complex needs met through mainstream schooling. (Winstanley, 2009, p. 347)

~⌒◌⌒~

Some parents are motivated to homeschool because they conclude that their children have special needs that schools do not, will not, or cannot address appropriately (Collom, 2005; Mayberry, 1989a). Here we see considerable overlap with other themes in the larger motivational portrait, particularly with the academic deficiency rationale (i.e., schools failing to do their jobs well). Some parents believe that the additional time and attention that can be provided at home may be the only thing that can save their children. Special needs children usually fall into three overlapping categories: children who are simply lost and floundering in formal educational settings (Lines, 1987; J. Taylor, 1986a), youngsters whose parents believe they need to learn in unique ways (Van Galen, 1991), and traditionally defined special needs students such as learning disabled and gifted youngsters. This latter group occupies almost all the space in this sub-area of the homeschooling literature. There is also evidence that homeschooling of gifted and learning disabled students has been increasing in recent years (Ensign, 1998). We highlight each of these two groups below.

According to various studies, some families are turning to the homeschooling of their gifted children out of frustration with the education available in public schools (Knowles, 1991; Nemer, 2002; Winstanley, 2009). These parents find that their children are not being sufficiently challenged by the curriculum or the pedagogy in schools (Arai, 2000; Perry & Perry, 2000). Parents also sense that their gifted children receive insufficient personal attention in school (M. Martin, 1997; Pearson, 1996). They discern less than luminous results. Overall, then, these parents conclude that the special gifts of their children are not being recognized or nurtured sufficiently in public schools (Nemer, 2002). The home, it is argued, is the appropriate remedy for this problem (Ensign, 1997; Knowles et al., 1994).

In a similar vein, frustration with public schooling leads some parents of children with learning disabilities to keep them at home to be educated

(S. Gray, 1993; Hanna, 2011). Parents often fear that their children are being allowed to drop further and further behind age-appropriate standards. They believe that regular classroom teachers are often ill prepared and ill resourced to address the needs of their children, and they question the appropriateness of special education programs (Lange & Liu, 1999; Lyman, 2000). They worry about the social stigmatization that often rides shotgun with the special education driver (Henry, 1997). Concern that their learning disabled children will be poorly prepared for life often looms large on the horizon for these parents. As a result, they often decide that their children need a warmer and more nurturing environment than a regular school can provide (Pearson, 1996). The result is that increasing numbers of parents are choosing homeschooling for their learning disabled children (Nemer, 2002).

Promoting Healthy Families

Most parents express the importance of family relationships and family unity in their decision to teach their children at home. These parents see teaching at home as an essential element in developing close family relationships. (Mayberry & Knowles, 1989, p. 214)

~◌✦◌~

Home school parents want to enhance family relationships between children and parents and among siblings, through more time spent with one another. (Ray, 2004a, p. 4)

~◌✦◌~

The most acknowledged and analyzed family-based motivation for homeschooling centers on the importance of supporting the development of individual families and maintaining the institution of the family (Erickson, 2005; Kunzman, 2009a). The starting point here is that many parents see the family as the most important institution in society, one that is superior to all others, including schools (Jeub, 1994; Parker, 1992; Tillman, 1995). Concomitantly, many parents discern a pervasive weakening of the family unit in American life (Mayberry & Knowles, 1989), especially the decline of the nuclear family (S. Gray, 1993) and the growth of dysfunctional families (Knowles, 1991). They maintain that it is in society's best interest to create policies to strengthen the family (Parker, 1992). One way this can occur, some in the homeschooling community assert, is by consolidating childrearing functions inside the family rather than encouraging them to be spread across a variety of locations. In particular, activities that nurture family relationships as opposed to peer connections are valued (Gatto, 1992; Williams et al., 1984). Fewer substitutes for parents are in order (Gaither, 2008), and more time is to be spent by parents with their children (Mirochnik & McIntire, 1991). The home is to be the core unit of the child's life (J. Taylor, 1986b). And if all this is to be realized, then the education function needs to be housed in the home under the auspices of parents, not in some distant venue under the control of external socialization agents—that is, professional educators (Mayberry, 1989a).

Here, as Mayberry and colleagues (Mayberry, 1989a, 1989b; Mayberry & Knowles, 1989) confirm, homeschooling is essential for more than its effects on individual children. It is a keystone element in the quest to restore and nurture the American family (Marlow, 1994; J. D. Marshall & Valle, 1996). It promotes family cohesion and integrity (S. Gray, 1993; Lange & Liu, 1999). It is the core strategy by which (a) bonds within the family are developed (McKeon, 2007; Romanowski, 1991)—that is, positive relations among family members are knitted (Dahlquist et al., 2006; Ray & Weller, 2003); (b) adult socialization cascades over children (Parker, 1992); (c) parenthood, fatherhood, and motherhood are taught (Erickson, 2005); and (d) family unity is realized (Aurini & Davies, 2005; Mayberry & Knowles, 1989).

All of the healthy family narrative crafted so far rests on the twin pillars of shared time and mutual activity. Better relationships develop because homeschooling parents and children spend more time together (Ray & Weller, 2003; M. L. Stevens, 2001), sharing work that coveys important family values to children (Dobson, 2001; Marlow, 1994; Parker, 1992).

❖ CONCLUSION

In this chapter, we examined the reasons parents cite for homeschooling. We began with a note on control as the keystone in the motivational arch. We outlined the three sources of parental motivations and presented a framework that emphasizes both positive (pull) and negative (push) forces. We discussed at some length how schooling, household, student, and community contexts shape homeschooling decisions. We provided a framework that pulled together all existing research on motivation to homeschool into four categories: religious-based reasons; schooling-based reasons, academic; schooling-based reasons, socialization; and family-based reasons. We unpacked each of these into its component elements.

6

A Ball in Play

Homeschooling in Action

But of course homeschooling is not all of a piece. It is characterized by considerable variety in content and style. (Colfax & Colfax, 1988, p. 37)

❧❦❧

Home schoolers are fractured in a thousand different ways. They are divided on issues like: which textbooks should be used, or whether textbooks should even be used; whether the instruction should be primarily structured and formal, or flexible and child directed, or a combination of both approaches; when to begin teaching reading or mathematics, and what approach to use when it is time. (Parker, 1992, p. 30)

❧❦❧

In this chapter, we accumulate findings from an assortment of studies to illuminate actions inside the homeschool in terms of the instructional program. We begin with some introductory notes, insights that stretch across practices in homeschools. We also introduce the forces that shape instructional and curricular decisions in homeschools. In the second section, we turn the spotlight on pedagogy. The final section addresses what is known about curriculum in homeschools.

❖ INTRODUCTION

There is little research addressing what occurs during home instruction.
(Duvall, Delquadri, & Ward, 2004, p. 140)

The home program varies greatly from family to family. (Lines, 1991, p. 17)

The method of homeschooling is not fixed. (Sheffer, 1995, p. 25)

The first thing one discovers in constructing a composite of the instructional program is that there is not a lot of material from which to build. While attention has been lavished on the motivations for homeschooling and the demographics of these families, considerably less work has been directed to "seeing" inside the homeschool. This is especially the case on the pedagogical side of the instructional program ledger, the methods used in homeschooling—what Green and Hoover-Dempsey (2007) refer to as the parent-child interactions. Research on the quality of these interactions is nearly conspicuous by its absence.

We also know that there is a good deal of variability in the teaching–learning work that unfolds in homeschools, both across homes and within them (Luke, 2003). That variability touches all dimensions of the instructional program—methods, curriculum, and assessment (Clements, 2002; Lyman, 1998; Nemer, 2002).

Researchers document that home-based programs stretch across a continuum from highly unstructured ("freedom reigns") to highly structured ("the school in the home"; Knowles, Muchmore, & Spaulding, 1994; Kunzman, 2009b). As we discuss in later sections, the overall continuum is a composite of continuums in the areas of instruction and curriculum.

Researchers are able to place homeschool families on the structural continuum—that is, establish preference for structure in the instructional program, based on a number of markers. For example, there is considerable evidence that religiously motivated homeschoolers cluster at the more structured end of the continuum (Knowles, Marlow, & Muchmore, 1992; Van Galen, 1991). Formal methods of teaching (e.g., transmission-oriented instruction) and subject-based curriculum materials (e.g., textbooks) tend to be featured in these homes (Parker, 1992; Van Galen, 1991). Other homeschool families, especially those from the unschooling wing of the homeschool community, bunch up at the less structured end of the instructional program continuum, where informal and experiential approaches are more likely to be found (Collom, 2005; Marlow, 1994). Relatedly, researchers have documented that program structure is also a function of the amount of religious content in the curriculum, with more religious content associated with greater structure (McKeon, 2007; Wartes, 1990). There is evidence that the degree of program structure varies depending on whether children attended conventional schools before homeschooling (Parker, 1992). If they did, their homeschool experiences tend to be more formal (Parker, 1992; Williams, Arnoldson, & Reynolds, 1984). There is a hint in the literature of an association between program structure and race, with an emerging hypothesis that African American families operate more structured homeschools (McDowell, Sanchez, & Jones, 2000). There is also an empirically grounded suggestion that parents who are less secure in their subject knowledge gravitate toward the structured end of the program continuum (Knowles, 1988). In addition, investigators have been able to uncover a link between time and structure (Meighan, 1995). Specifically, they find that many homeschools evolve from more structured to less structured instructional programs as they settle into the work (S. Gray, 1993; Ray, 2000b; Williams et al., 1984).

Additional insights on forces shaping the instructional program in homeschools have also been documented in the research. We know from studies over the last quarter century that parents are often apt to employ methods that they experienced as children (Knowles, 1988; Lines, 1991). Religious interest is implicated in the selection of curriculum and the choice of instructional methods (Clements, 2002; McKeon, 2007). So too are instructor characteristics. For example, subject matter knowledge influences the curriculum parents select (Clements, 2002). A parent's personal philosophy of learning shapes decisions about the instructional program as well.

❖ INSTRUCTIONAL METHODS

Teachers and Time

It seems beyond dispute that women do the vast bulk of the homeschooling work. (Kunzman, 2009b, p. 29)

⁓∩⚬∩⁓

A central question is who is doing the teaching in homeschooling families. As we noted in Chapter 2, research from the 1980s (Gustavsen, 1981; Schemmer, 1985), the 1990s (Armon, 1990; Knowles, 1991; Parker, 1992), and the 2000s (Isenberg, 2002; Ray, 2005) consistently finds that mothers carry most of the instructional freight in homeschools. For example, Gladin (1987) reported that mothers did 90% of the teaching, while sharing 9% with their husbands. Ray (1997a) uncovered parallel numbers, finding that 88% of the formal teaching in homeschools was done by mothers. Fathers, according to the literature, are involved in the instructional program in mostly indirect ways. They bankroll the operation through their jobs. They support their wives. And they participate in the informal aspects of the homeschool. On the direct front, they occasionally provide some instruction. In addition, although it is not usually measured in homeschool surveys and observations, there is evidence of some cross-age teaching by children in homeschools, more so than in conventional schools (Parker, 1992; Williams et al., 1984).

Studies confirm that the great majority of homeschool mothers have never been certified by the state to teach (Rakestraw, 1988). Rudner (1999) reported that 23.6% of homeschool students had at least one parent who was certified to teach, although this appears to be an inflated number because of the sample employed (Kaseman & Kaseman, 1999; Welner & Welner, 1999). More recent analysis by Ray (2009a, 2010) finds that only about 10% of homeschool parents are (or ever have been) certified to teach.

Researchers also provide insights into the amount of instructional time in homeschools. We need to introduce a caution here, however. Because many homeschool families do not divide their days into school time and other time (i.e., they have a somewhat seamless conception of instructional time), measures of time in homeschools are sometimes difficult to interpret (Dahlquist, York-Barr, & Hendel, 2006). One strategy analysts employ to address this challenge is to calculate formal instructional time and informal instructional time, as well as planning time for parents. In an early study, Gustavsen (1981) reported a mode of 3 hours of instructional time per day. Parker's (1992) respondents spent an average of 3.7 hours a day and 17.5 hours per week in formal instruction; nearly three-quarters (73%) of them reported that they spent between 3 and 5 hours per day in formal instructional work. Results from Dahlquist and team (2006) mirror these findings. Gladin (1987) documented a mean of 2.58 hours a day of formal instruction in homeschools, with an additional informal allotment of 2.39 hours per day. Rakestraw (1988) calculated 3 to 4.5 hours a day devoted to instruction, with 1 to 1.5 of those hours spent in direct instructional activities. Wartes (1990) reported a mean of 15 hours per week. Collom (2005) noted 4.82 hours a day were devoted to instruction in homeschools. All of this work on time tells us three things. First, because of the caution introduced above, it is indeed difficult to "bunch time" in homeschools. Second, homeschool students spend less time "in school" than do their peers in conventional schools. Third, they spend considerably more time in one-on-one instruction than do their public school counterparts (Lee, 1994).

Very few studies explore the breakdown of how instructional time is allotted across subjects. Even less available are studies that explore usage within subjects. One scholar who has addressed this need is Hertzel (1997), who provides time data in the area of literacy. Results from this work

indicate that the typical range of total minutes homeschool students spend on daily, literacy-related activities ranges from 135 to

225 minutes. Seventy-two to 117 minutes per day are spent reading (parent reads to the child, child reads to parent, child browses through books and reads silently); 22.5 minutes to 37.5 minutes per day are spent on phonics or reading skills instruction; 19.5 minutes to 34.5 minutes per day are spent on writing instruction. The amount of time per day the student actively engages in the writing process is approximately 21.0 to 36.0 minutes per day. (p. 60)

Instructional Activity

Little research has been done specifically on homeschooling teaching strategies. (Ray, 2000b, p. 1)

◦◦◦

The instructional mode of home-schooling appears to be characterized by its heterogeneity. (Belfield, 2004a, p. 3)

◦◦◦

A few scholars have explored the specific teaching methods employed in homeschools, sometimes through direct observations but more often by asking parents about their use of instructional strategies. By and large, however, the research cupboard is fairly bare in this domain (Ray, 2000b). There is a sense in the literature that while sharing ground (Duvall, Ward, Delquadri, & Greenwood, 1997; Duvall et al., 2004), homeschool teaching and public school teaching are somewhat different jobs (Kunzman, 2009b). There is affirmation in the literature that parents develop specific identities as teachers and that these understandings evolve over time as they experience successes and failures (Knowles, 1988). Across the population, there is evidence of considerable variation in methods employed (Schemmer, 1985). There is also a sense that on the pedagogical front, isolation limits opportunities for parents to learn the craft of teaching and to hone their instructional skills (Knowles, 1988).

Most analysts describe instruction as occupying space on a continuum from highly structured methods to highly unstructured strategies, with the scoring metric being the amount of direct instruction occurring in the home (Clements, 2002; McKeon, 2007; M. L. Stevens, 2001). As might be anticipated given that parents frequently lean on their own learning as a model, studies confirm that there is a fair amount of structure to the pedagogy in homeschools (McKeon, 2007). Parker (1992) uncovered six distinct instructional designs in his study of homeschooling, three of which anchor the ends and the middle of the continuum: direct instruction (24.4%) at one end, teacher as guide/facilitator with students working independently (31.7%) in the middle, and teaching in the context of children engaged in real-world activities (17.1%) at the other end.

Consistent with our analyses in earlier sections, studies affirm a linkage between the amount of pedagogical structure and homeschool motivation (Belfield, 2004a). Researchers generally conclude that families that pursue homeschooling for religious reasons engineer more parental control into their instructional designs (Cai, Reeve, & Robinson, 2002; Gaither, 2008). Parent-led learning is the norm here. Families drawn to homeschooling for academic reasons are more likely to supplement or replace parent-led instruction with child-centered learning and self-study (Clements, 2002; Meighan, 1995).

❖ CURRICULAR PROGRAMS

Examining the curricular packages in use in home-schools provides another perspective on the world of home-schooling. These materials reinforce the conclusion that home-schools follow no standard pattern.
(Lines, 1987, p. 512)

∼◠◌◠∼

Some families purchase complete curriculum packages for their children, while others approach homeschooling with only a small degree of preplanned structure. (Ray, 2004b, p. 6)

∼◠◌◠∼

Most families choose an eclectic approach and use a variety of options.
(Hanna, 2011, p. 12)

∼◠◌◠∼

Options

As the homeschool population has grown, so too has the national market for curriculum packages. (M. L. Stevens, 2001, p. 85)

∼◠◌◠∼

Parents may choose materials from a variety of sources. (Hanna, 2011, p. 4)

∼◠◌◠∼

The data on curriculum in homeschools are a little richer than the data on instruction, although gaps in the summative narrative and insufficient depth in areas remain problems. We know that parents have considerable choice in the curricular materials they can use with their children (Kunzman, 2009b; Princiotta & Bielick, 2006; M. L. Stevens, 2001). Much of the curricular landscape is populated with materials developed specifically for homeschool families, especially religiously grounded homeschools. There is a fair amount of general curriculum in homeschools as well (Lyman, 2000). To put the variety in perspective, we need to remember that the homeschool curriculum market is a billion-dollar-a-year industry (Kunzman, 2009a).

Studies across the last quarter century peg average expenditures per homeschool student in the $300–$500 range: Gladin (1987) shows a mean of $175 and a mode of $200–$500, Rakestraw (1988) provides a mean of $280, Parker (1992) offers a mean of $442 and a mode of $200–$299, Ray (1997b) shows a mean of $546 and a median of $400, Rudner (1999) provides a median of $400 and a mode of $200–$400, and Ray (2010) offers a median of $400–$599. None of these numbers are adjusted for inflation. And we would do well to remember that the big costs for homeschooling are in the investment of the time of the parent who stays home to teach (Colfax & Colfax, 1988; Green & Hoover-Dempsey, 2007), which can be measured in terms of income forgone by not participating in the labor force.

The literature also provides some insights into the selection of curricular materials, what draws parents toward certain materials. Match with motivation is important, especially for religiously grounded homeschools (Apple, 2007; M. L. Stevens, 2001). So too are fit with the instructor and fit with the student (Clements, 2002; Perry & Perry, 2000). Ease of use and match with the structural design of the program also come into play in the selection process (Gladin, 1987).

Structure

The degree of structure in the practice of home education varies greatly. It ranges from a very unstructured (unschooling) learning approach, centered upon the child's interests, to the use of a planned, structured, and highly prescribed curriculum. (Ray, 1997b, p. 17)

~᠑᠊~

The only education many of the parents have experienced has been the traditional classroom. Consequently, many adopt the structure of a traditional school when structuring home schools. (Knowles, 1988, p. 77)

~᠑᠊~

Earlier, we documented that instruction in homeschools can be placed along a continuum from highly structured to highly unstructured methods. We find the same theme in play in the curricular domain as well (Moore & Moore, 1994; Savage, 1990; Wallace, 1990), with formal lessons based on textbooks on the highly structured end of the curriculum continuum (the "school at home" model of homeschooling) and real-life materials anchoring the highly unstructured end of the continuum (Parker, 1992; Taylor-Hough, 2010). Studies reveal that homeschool families fall at all points on the continuum, with more bundled up on the structured half of the model (Jaycox, 2001)—that is, using textbooks, sequential learning, formal lessons, subject-centered materials, and tightly scripted schedules. For example, in Wartes's (1987) study, on a 7-point scale with 7 being *very structured*, 28.7% of homeschool parents assigned themselves a score of 4 while another 56.1% gave themselves a score of 5 or higher. The central point of interest here has been nicely penned by Mitchell Stevens (2001, p. 62): "Simply by choosing a curriculum program for their kids, parents enact a tendency toward structure or freedom."

Materials

Parents select a wide variety of curriculum. (McKeon, 2007, p. 8)

❧

Children study a wide range of conventional subjects, with an emphasis on reading, writing, math, science, and integrating faith with living.
(Ray, 2005, p. 2)

❧

Scholars have investigated the subjects taught and source materials employed in homeschools. On the first issue, researchers find, with the one critical exception of bible study, rough parallelism with the subject matter in public schools. In one of the early studies, for example, parents told Gladin (1987) that they viewed the following subjects, in order, to be most important in their homeschools: reading, bible, mathematics, English, and spelling; music, art, and physical education were at the tail end of the importance chart, and practical skills, history, science, and social studies were in the middle. In his investigation, Gustavsen (1981) reported a slightly different list, with mathematics, reading, science, penmanship, English, bible, and history as the most stressed subjects, in that order. Parker (1992, p. 184) found that parents reported spending most time on reading and the bible, with the overwhelming bulk of time devoted "to the 4 Rs—reading, 'riting, 'rithmetic, and religion." Wartes (1990) adds to the curricular narrative when he reminds us that most religiously motivated homeschool parents integrate religion into the other subject areas. Very little subject-based subanalysis is available. About the most we can say based on the extant research base is that in the area of reading, a majority of parents have a commitment to phonics (Gladin, 1987; Hertzel, 1997).

Instructional aids and supplemental resources in homeschools also parallel what a student in a conventional school would encounter, with books occupying the top three positions (dictionaries, library books, and textbooks) in Gladin's (1987) study and the top spot in Gustavsen's (1981) and Parker's (1992) reports. Homeschool families are fairly heavy users of public libraries (Gladin, 1987; Hertzel, 1997; Parker, 1992), with the library showing up as the number-one source of curriculum in the National Household Education Survey (NHES; Princiotta & Bielick, 2006). Ray (1997b) puts this finding in context when he reveals that the average homeschool family visits the library almost once per week (3.8 times per month).

Researchers are also keenly interested in the extent to which homeschool families use curricular materials and other resources from public schools. They document that historically homeschool parents have believed, and acted as if, the most important potential resources reside outside the public school (Mayberry, Knowles, Ray, & Marlow, 1995), thus limiting contact with these institutions (Ray, 2005). The public school resources used most frequently, but still by only a small minority of homeschool families, are testing services (14%), selected classes (14%), textbooks (13%), and school libraries (11%; Mayberry et al., 1995).

Curriculum in most homeschools is seeded in both the relevant disciplines (subjects) and the interests of the child (Gustavsen, 1981; Nemer, 2002; Williams et al., 1984), with the bulk of the weight on subjects (Ray, 2004a, 2004b). That is, the majority of the education homeschool children receive is anchored in academic disciplines and reflected in textbooks. In Parker's (1992) study, for example, only 19% of families focused on individual needs and interests of the child all the time, while 51% focused on disciplines/subjects. Ray (2004a, 2004b) documented that textbooks were the primary source of the instructional program in 24.8% of homeschool families, compared to only 1.6% who made the interests of the child the primary anchor for the curriculum. In short, as Mitchell Stevens (2001) argues, the focus in homeschools is on what youngsters need to be taught rather than their desires and interests.

Forms of Homeschooling

Some families purchase complete curriculum packages for their children, while others approach homeschooling with only a small degree of preplanned structure. (Ray, 2005, p. 2)

~◠⟡◠~

Many programs are available to parents. Sometimes one curriculum can meet a family's needs; other times the "teachers" will need to mix and match to best serve their children. (Lyman, 2000, p. 64)

~◠⟡◠~

Analysts provide another avenue into the topic of curriculum through their analyses of the package of materials used by homeschooling families. While these packages include pedagogy, models of delivery, and organizational arrangements, the anchor is generally the curricular material. A representative sample of one of these packaging systems is the one provided by McKeon (2007, pp. 15–16):

> *Traditional.* This style is also known as the "boxed curriculum" and is the most common type of approach to homeschooling. This style is the traditional, pre-packaged curriculum shipped ready for use.
>
> *Unschooling.* This style can be defined as one that focuses upon the choices made by the individual learner. Those choices can vary according to learning style and personality type of each student.
>
> *Eclectic.* This style is [a] more relaxed or laid back type of homeschool. Parents use a mixed combination of boxed curriculum, homemade curriculum, and/or individualized curriculum. They can operate as borderline unschooling or borderline school-at-home, or anywhere in between and be considered eclectic. Relaxed homeschoolers have many options available to them for homeschooling.
>
> *Classical.* The core of Classical Education is the trivium, a teaching model that seeks to tailor the subject matter to a child's cognitive development. The trivium emphasizes concrete thinking and memorization of the facts of the subjects in grade school; analytical thinking and understanding of the subjects in middle school; and abstract thinking and articulation of the subjects in high school.

Levinson (cited in Taylor-Hough, 2010) provides another portrait of a homeschooling packaging system: unschooling, classical education, unit studies, the Charlotte Mason method, traditional school-at-home, correspondence schools and school-related umbrella organizations, cooperative, and computer-based options. Taylor-Hough (2010, p. 7) describes these forms as follows:

> Unschooling is essentially student-directed learning without a scope-and-sequence plan, focusing on the interests of the child, and allowing the student to pursue their varied interests as far and wide as they personally choose. Classical education has a heavy focus on rote learning and basic facts in the early grades, with an increasing emphasis on critical thinking and oratory in the later years. The Charlotte Mason method is based on the teachings of a British educator from the late 19th and early 20th centuries who focused on children developing a lifetime love of learning. Correspondence and umbrella schools vary greatly depending upon the school they are affiliated with, but usually tend to rely heavily on workbooks, textbooks, and fill-in-the-blank quizzes and tests. Traditional "school-at-home" education attempts to re-create the schoolroom at home, sometimes to the point of school desks

lined up in a row, morning flag salutes, and chalkboards, as well as relying on textbooks, workbooks, teacher-focused lectures, and traditional testing methods. Cooperative schooling is usually done by a group of like-minded homeschooling families with each parent in the group taking on a teaching role in one or more subjects of particular interest or expertise. Computer-based home education can be purchased as a stand-alone curriculum, or as part of a correspondence program with a wide range of methodologies available.

Developing these taxonomies is not the easiest of assignments, and because they mix so many defining program elements (e.g., venue, pedagogy, curriculum), placing families into discrete categories is often difficult. Nonetheless, a number of researchers have undertaken that assignment over the years (e.g., Gustavsen, 1981; Parker, 1992). The best data have been provided by Ray (1997b, 2004a) and the National Home Education Research Institute. Ray's analyses affirm earlier findings that most families use commercial curriculum materials but they often blend them into their own package. Ray (1997b) found that 71% of parents followed this approach. Twenty-five percent purchased a complete curriculum package. By 2010, Ray reported that full-package homeschoolers had declined to about 10% of the population. These recent results are consistent with Rudner's (1999, p. 12) study in which 7.7% of students were enrolled in a full-service curriculum program, one "that serves students and their parents as a 'one-stop' primary source for textbooks, materials, lesson plans, tests, counseling, evaluations, record keeping, and the like for the year's core required subjects such as language, social studies, mathematics, and science."

Treatments of these full-service—and nearly full-service —curriculum providers are ribboned throughout the homeschooling literature. We see examples of providers who offer a full curriculum package and related materials delivered to one's door for use. We also see correspondence programs in which students enroll to receive a specific package of educational experiences. "These programs provide for a structured morning or afternoon of study each day. They also give parents some feedback about their children's progress by evaluating their work, scoring their tests, and reporting back with grades" (Divoky, 1983, p. 397).

Some of the most popular options here include A Beka, the Clonlara School, and the Calvert School (Lyman, 2000). We learn that most of these organizations were formed to serve the needs of religiously motivated homeschool families, and, not surprisingly, the programs they offer often have a unifying bible-based foundation. Some of the better known of these are A Beka, Christian Liberty Academy, Rod and Staff, the Calvert School, Alpha Omega, KONOS, Veritas, Advanced Training Institute International, and Family Centered Learning Alternatives (Hanna, 2011; M. L. Stevens,

2001). The Calvert School is the oldest of these organizations (Lines, 1987); one of the largest is

> Christian Liberty Academy, which provides home schools with an eclectic, individualized package of textbooks and workbooks. The package includes older textbooks, the McGuffey Readers, books from A Beka Publications, and Rod and Staff Publishers (a Mennonite group). Most of their families send tests and other materials to Christian Liberty Academy for evaluation and grading by teachers and other professionals. (Lines, 1991, p. 19)

In an early study, Gladin (1987) listed Bob Jones University Press, A Beka, and Rod and Staff as the three most widely used religiously based, full-service curriculum programs. In his comprehensive analysis a decade later, Ray (1997b) provided these data for families using full curriculum packages: A Beka (31.2%), other complete curriculum (17.4%), Bob Jones University Press (16.4%), and Christian Liberty Academy (11.1%).

The Extended Curriculum

The homeschooler's day is more likely to be seamless. (Sheffer, 1995, p. 30)

~◦❖◦~

Learning to serve and to work frequently finds a meaningful place in the home-school curriculum. (J. Taylor, 1986a, p. 39)

~◦❖◦~

Homeschooling families often participate in community activities and use resources open to the public to enhance the education of the children. (Ray, 2000b, p. 1)

~◦❖◦~

The Integrated Day

> *Learning in the home is unified with other life experiences and is continuous. (Williams et al., 1984, p. 25)*

~◦❖◦~

There is a good deal of information in the homeschool literature about what we call the *extended curriculum,* the use of an assortment of venues to teach. One hallmark issue here is that time for many homeschool families is not set as it is, by necessity, in conventional schools. The other cardinal issue is that schoolwork and life activities often are not divided in homeschools (Schemmer, 1985; Williams et al., 1984), "education is viewed as an interconnected array of subjects related to daily life" (Sheehan, 2002, p. 192). In many homeschools, "the education process is viewed holistically. Home education responsibilities merely become extensions of 'normal' family activities and routines" (Mayberry et al., 1995, p. 49). This perspective greatly extends the definition of schooling in general and the understanding of curriculum in particular. Homeschooling can unfold wherever the family is and at any time of the day—and learning activities occur in the caldron of life experiences (Perry & Perry, 2000; Williams et al., 1984). While the concept and practice of the extended curriculum are often associated with the child-centered wing of the homeschool community, in reality they stretch across homeschool families of various philosophies and those directed by quite varied motivations.

One form of the extended curriculum is teaching through participation in family-based businesses, or what Gladin (1987) refers to as *cottage industries.* Gladin found that fully a quarter of the students in his study were engaged in this type of learning experience. Relatedly, homeschool families often teach by having children participate in the work of managing the household (Divoky, 1983; Pitman & Smith, 1991). Another form of the extended curriculum is linking children with people in the community who possess specific skills that parents want their children to develop (Sheehan, 2002). In this vein, informal apprenticeships and mentors are sometimes part of the curriculum in home-based education (Barker, 1990; Sheehan, 2002). Special events (e.g., local, regional, and national competitions) sometimes make up part of the curriculum (Ray, 2005). Service learning through volunteer community work is a featured dimension of the curriculum in many homeschools (Ray, 2004b). And field trips, including extended travel, are more prevalent in homeschools than conventional schools (Hanna, 2011).

Distance learning is relatively popular in the homeschooling community (Princiotta & Bielick, 2006). We have already reported that this new medium has helped fuel the growth in homeschooling in the United States. We note here that it is a significant source of the curriculum for homeschoolers (Hanna, 2011). For example, in the 2003 NHES, investigators found that fully 41% of homeschools engaged in distance learning.

> Approximately 20 percent of homeschooled students took a course or received instruction provided by television, video or radio. About 19 percent of homeschooled students had taken a course or received instruction provided over the Internet, e-mail, or the World Wide Web. An estimated 15 percent of homeschooled students took a correspondence course by mail designed specifically for homeschools. (Princiotta & Bielick, 2006, p. 18)

The Extended Family

> *Very few home schoolers isolate themselves socially. Rather, other home*
> *schoolers, neighbors, older friends, family, etc., form an important network*
> *which parents and children rely on for ideas and understanding.*
> *(Williams et al., 1984, p. 23)*

~⌒⊙⌒~

The tapestry of the extended curriculum includes a number of loosely connected threads, everything from television viewing to socialization with friends. We pull them together here under the banner of *the extended family*. As in most families today, computers are part of the home life of homeschoolers. Studies suggest that computer use in homeschools lagged behind use by children in conventional schools during the 1980s and early 1990s (Parker, 1992; Rudner, 1999). Over the last 15 years, however, that storyline has been reversed. In his 2010 report, Ray found that 98.3% of homeschool students had a computer in the home, compared to 82% of their traditional school counterparts nationwide whose parents had earned a bachelor's degree. The summative conclusions here are that (a) both formally and informally, curriculum for many homeschoolers is linked to the computer and (b) we know very little about the specific uses of computers in the learning process in homeschools.

There is a fairly lengthy line of survey work that shows that homeschool children watch television less frequently and in smaller doses than other children (Bates, 1991; Burns, 1999). We also discern in that work a tentative hypothesis that television in homeschooling families is used in a more educational manner. In an early study, Gladin (1987) reported that 36.4% of homeschool families watched no television; the average was 1.7 hours per day. Ray (1997a) found that 94% of homeschool students spend less than 3 hours per day watching television and videos. Only 38% of public school children fall beneath this threshold. In his comprehensive study at the turn of the 21st century, Rudner (1999) documented that 65% of homeschool students watched less than 1 hour of television per day, compared to 25% of students nationally. His conclusion on those watching less than 3 hours per day (98.4%) aligns well with Ray's data.

In Chapter 7, we examine the socialization of children educated at home in considerable detail. Our focus there will be on the impact of homeschooling on this critical educational goal, or outcome variable. Here we simply report that socialization activities outside the home are often an essential aspect of the homeschooling curriculum—that is, they impart content knowledge as well as process skills. We begin with the conclusion we reach in Chapter 7: For over a quarter of a century, researchers have consistently documented that homeschool youngsters are not socially isolated. Rather, they engage in ongoing group and community activities (Wartes, 1987; Ray, 2005).

Homeschool families often arrange activities with others in the home-school community, sometimes informally and at other times in a more organized fashion through homeschool support groups (Kunzman, 2009b; Lines, 1995; Ray & Weller, 2003). These networking activities and "satellite" relationships (Gladin, 1987) are widely illustrated in the literature (Hanna, 2011; M. Martin, 1997). Families also deepen the homeschool curriculum by arranging for their children to participate in a variety of community activities, including special studies and events, sporting activities, and art programs (Rakestraw, 1988; Ray, 2005). As noted above, volunteer work is part of the curricular package for a good number of homeschool children. Church activities with peers and adults are an important avenue of socialization and learning for many homeschoolers (M. Martin, 1997; J. Taylor, 1986a). So too are recreational clubs of various sorts (Lines, 1991). In addition, field trips and family travel are heavily used to provide socially anchored learning opportunities for homeschool children (Parker, 1992).

Research also provides some data on the extent of these extended learning opportunities. In his 1987 study, Wartes reported that homeschool parents pegged the extent of involvement of children in organized community activities at 20–29 hours per month. In 1992, Smedley documented that the average homeschool youngster spent 4.2 hours per week in extracurricular group activities, compared to 3.3 hours for public school students. In his 1992 thesis, Parker determined that the modal number of outside social experiences in which homeschool students participated was 6, with a mean of 6.2 per family. Ray (1997a) reported similar findings, pegging the mean of engagements in socialization activities outside the home at 5.2, with 98% of the children involved in 2 or more activities. He found that over one-third of the youngsters were engaged as follows: play with people beyond the family (87%), field trips (84%), Sunday school (77%), group sports (48%), music classes (47%), classes outside the home (42%), bible clubs (35%), ministry work (34%), and volunteer activities (33%). Van Pelt (cited in Basham, Merrifield, & Hepburn, 2007) documented that the average homeschool child is routinely engaged in eight social activities in the community.

Assessment of Learning

There is considerable discussion about the tension between homeschoolers and the state around mandated achievement tests, especially in reports from the early years of the movement. Much of that discussion is freighted with trenchant ideological rigor. There is, however, little research on the topic that carries us beyond the data on state requirements. In one study, Gustavsen (1981) found that 59.7% of homeschool families did not use national standardized tests. Of the 40.3% that did, most used the Iowa (17.3%) and Stanford (17.3%) tests. A decade later, Parker (1992) found that

63% of homeschool children in his sample were taking standardized achievement tests, often more than one. The most popular were the California Achievement Tests, Stanford Achievement Tests, and the Iowa Test of Basic Skills. Access to these tests is often mediated by homeschool organizations. Bob Jones University Press Testing and Evaluation Services is the largest of these agencies (Rudner, 1999). With a few notable exceptions, analyses of assessment methods and strategies inside homeschools are conspicuous by their absence.

❖ CONCLUSION

In this chapter, we traveled to the inside of the homeschool to explore the instructional program. We examined both aspects of these programs, instructional methods and curricular materials. On the pedagogical front, we reviewed what we know about the teachers in homeschools and how much time is devoted to education in the average homeschooling family. We also explored the knowledge base on instructional methods found in home-based education. On the curriculum issue, we reviewed findings around the structure, materials, and forms of homeschooling in the United States. We also discussed curriculum in the context of the extended day and extended family, concepts at the center of homeschooling.

7

The End Game

The Impact of Homeschooling

The lives of the home educated in decades to come and the heritage that they bequeath to their children may inscribe a sweeping, indelible, and immeasurable mark on the history of 21st-century America.
(Ray, 1997b, p. 102)

∽∾∿∾

Any explanation of homeschooling must recognize its multiple and diffuse aims. (Aurini & Davies, 2005, p. 471)

∽∾∿∾

So far, we have explored all the essential dimensions of homeschooling, with one critical exception. We have said almost nothing directly about the impact of homeschooling, what its effects are. As appropriate, we turn to this topic here in the concluding chapters of the book. We commence with a general discussion of the quality of the research on homeschooling. This is instructive for it provides information on two essential questions: What counts as outcomes? That is, what gets assessed in studies? And how much stock can we place in the available body of evidence? Unfortunately, the storyline that gets crafted from answers to these questions is thinly developed at best and less than trustworthy at worst, although some of the chapters of the narrative are better than others—that is, they provide informative if not scientifically reliable data.

Given this overarching research grounding, we then interrogate the literature to distill what is known about the impact of homeschooling across an array of outcomes: the social fabric of the nation, schools, costs, families, and children. On the last topic, we explore what is known (and how well it is known) on academic achievement, social development, and success after completing homeschooling.

❖ THE QUALITY OF THE EXISTING RESEARCH BASE

> *The soundness of a particular world view can be seen in whether or not it operates as well in practice as it does in the planning session. When it comes to judging the effectiveness and legitimacy of home schooling, it is natural to want empirical evidence. (Parker, 1992, p. 65)*

~◦ᵛ◦~

> *Finally, some careful "proof-in-the-pudding" studies need to be conducted to learn if there are important positive or negative developmental consequences for children who remain home for a significant portion of their formal education. (Groover & Endsley, 1988, p. 24)*

~◦ᵛ◦~

An Assessment of Research Evidence

> *Comprehensive empirical evidence is lacking. (Kunzman, 2005, p. 4)*

~◦ᵛ◦~

> *Research on home schooling is in its infancy and what little research currently exists is either of poor quality or is capable of reaching only very limited conclusions. (Reich, 2005, p. 115)*

~◦ᵛ◦~

> *It will take more research—and better research methods—to gain a deeper understanding of the advantages and limitations of home schooling. (Blok, 2004, p. 49)*

~◦ᵛ◦~

As Medlin (2000, p. 118) informs us, the summative narrative of research in homeschooling parallels the chronicle found in many new domains of study:

> no guiding theory, inadequate experimental design, poorly defined research questions, untried and weak measures, unorthodox

treatment and presentation of data, and conclusions based on sub-jective judgments. Even a cursory look at the research reveals that many studies are qualitative descriptions of so few participants that the results cannot be generalized. Many are surveys that rely exclusively on parental reports but offer no idea of how reliable those reports may be. Many test only home-schooled children without comparing them to children attending conventional schools, making it very difficult to know what the results might mean. Further, all home school research is correlational (because researchers have no way to control the type of schooling children experience), samples are usually self-selected (because researchers cannot require home schooling families to participate), and how-ever carefully researchers try to match their home-schooled and traditionally schooled groups, there are probably still important differences between the two.

Reinforcing many of these points and adding some additional insights, Belfield (2004a, p. 10) exposes two major problems that plague research that compares the impact of homeschooling against other types of school-ing, especially public schooling:

> The first is the common concern over the endogeneity of school choice, that is different types of families choose the type of school that their children attend, and little can be inferred about the impacts of schools for students who do not attend them. The sec-ond is the need to distinguish the absolute performance of home-schoolers from the treatment effect of home-schooling. Given the above median resources of many home-schooling families, aca-demic performance should be even if home-schooling itself is not differentially effective. Full controls for family background are needed, however, to identify a treatment effect.

Blok (2004) also reminds us that the body of empirical work on the impacts of homeschooling is rather thin. And an assortment of analysts have pointed out that most of the research that has been undertaken has been conducted by investigators with a good deal of interest in shaping results into positive stories—advocacy groups whose defined mission is to promote the cause of homeschooling (Houston & Toma, 2003; Kunzman, 2005; Reich, 2005). The conclusion at present is that research on the impacts of homeschooling leaves a good deal to be desired. Most troubling is that we know almost nothing about the causal links in the homeschool theory of action and their connections to various outcomes (Ray, 2009b).

Much of what we do know about homeschooling is anecdotal in nature (Houston, 1999). Stories of individual children who have demonstrated remarkable achievements in academic competitions of varied sorts or in higher education are especially prevalent. On the other side of the ledger, negative stories are sometimes spotlighted to confirm the dangers of homeschooling. While for many these stories are proof of the impact of homeschooling, for 25 years now scholars have been reminding us that stories and anecdotes, personal experiences, and folklore in the area of homeschooling lack the authority of scientific evidence (M. L. Stevens, 2001; J. Taylor, 1986a).

As we attempt to move beyond anecdotes and stories, we find that rigorous empirical research on the effects of homeschooling remains scarce (Houston, 1999; M. L. Stevens, 2001). We learn that studies on homeschooling effects suffer from major, interconnected problems that significantly limit the degree of certainty we can draw from research reports. Problems with samples and with controls are particularly troublesome. On the first issue, analysts have routinely urged caution in accepting findings at face value because of the nonrepresentativeness of the samples employed in almost all homeschool research (Kaseman & Kaseman, 1999; Kunzman, 2005), or as Mitchell Stevens (2001, p. 13) succinctly captures the problem, "the paucity of solid systematic data results from a lack of adequate sampling frames." Weak sampling frames mean that samples are almost never drawn on a representative group of homeschoolers (Houston, 1999; Kaseman & Kaseman, 1999), but rather that studies employ highly selective samples (K. Bauman, 2002; Winstanley, 2009). Self-selection and sampling bias have been and continue to be the norm in the study of homeschool effects (Lines, 2000b; Ray & Wartes, 1991). Nonrepresentativeness means, of course, that findings cannot be generalized to the homeschool population. Even in these studies with nonrepresentative samples, return rates often fall below acceptable standards (Dahlquist, York-Barr, & Hendel, 2006; M. L. Stevens, 2001) and we rarely see efforts to examine nonresponders (Wright, 1988). (For good treatment of these problems in context of Rudner's classic 1999 study, see Kaseman & Kaseman, 1999; Welner & Welner, 1999.)

Concomitantly, researchers are quick to point out that the claimed benefits of homeschooling rest on shaky ground because studies rarely control for other explanatory variables in the causal effects equation (Blok, 2004; Ray, 2000c), either through random assignment or other less powerful methods that can help eliminate alternative explanations for effects (Collom, 2005; Kunzman, 2005). In particular, analysts decry the absence of controls for socioeconomic variables such as income, occupation, and education (Dahlquist et al., 2006); previous achievement (Ice & Hoover-Dempsey, 2011); marital status (Burns, 1999); and parental support and commitment (Barwegen, Falciani, Putnam, Reamer, & Stair, 2004; Hertzel, 1997). Because these conditions are linked to student learning, they need to be accounted for in homeschool effects research. Without appropriate controls it is impossible to establish whether outcomes are the result of the treatment (i.e., homeschooling) or other factors (e.g., family income; Belfield, 2005). Or as Lines (1995, p. 3) nicely penned it, without controls, research does not allow us to "determine whether the *same* children would perform better or worse in a public classroom or in a home-schooling arrangement."

> The question aptly raised is whether any cause and effect relationship exists vis-à-vis home school education. . . . To date, no controlled studies exist that shed significant light on the important question. . . . Until some type of study is conducted, using control and experimental groups, the question likely will be left for speculative—rather than concrete—answers. (Wilhelm & Firman, 2009, pp. 310–311)

Other difficulties are visible in the portfolio of research on homeschool outcomes. For example, in studies of effects on homeschool youngsters, comparisons to national norms are traditional. While not without informative power, this strategy leaves a good deal to be desired. We also very rarely hear from children in homeschool families about their perceptions of homeschool work and their assessments of outcomes (Mayberry, Knowles, Ray, & Marlow, 1995; Schemmer, 1985). Testing conditions in some homes are problematic (Basham, Merrifield, & Hepburn, 2007). Practical problems arise in getting information to establish effects (Belfield, 2005). For example, almost all of the data available because children are enrolled in public schools are missing for homeschool children (Isenberg, 2007). There are very few longitudinal studies. And almost all of the issues we surfaced in Chapter 1 associated with gathering demographic data (e.g., preference for anonymity) hold when conducting research on the effects of homeschooling (Kunzman, 2005; M. L. Stevens, 2001).

What Counts as Evidence of Success

> *Home schoolers of the future should judge their success not by the degree to which they surpass the struggling government schools, but how closely they come to obtaining for their children the full potential of home schooling itself. (Farris & Woodruff, 2000, pp. 242–243)*

> *Lifestyle changes are much more important benefits of homeschooling than the grandest of academic achievement. (Dobson, 2001, p. 4)*

> *The problem is this: Nothing has been done to assess any outcomes related to the movement's primary, self-selected objective. (Cizek, 1993, p. 2)*

Perhaps the most puzzling finding in the area of homeschooling effects is that almost every potential domain of impact that defines the intervention from parents' perspectives is ignored while researchers chase down data on whether homeschool children can answer two or three more questions correctly on standardized tests than their public school peers. At the *macro level*, this is the case because the impacts of homeschooling as a broad social movement are generally not investigated. In addition, while there is a fair amount of conceptual work on the issue of the impact of homeschooling on the social fabric of the nation, especially by those who foresee potential negative consequences (e.g., Apple, 2007; Lubienski, 2000; Reich, 2005), with the exception of work from scholars such as Gaither (2008) and Mitchell Stevens (2001) there is scant guidance in the literature about how to think about operationalizing and measuring societal impacts.

At the *mid level* this absence of attention to core outcomes occurs because most of the reasons parents provide for homeschooling (i.e., the essential values of the movement discussed in detail in Chapter 5) are simply ignored (Cizek, 1993; Klicka, 1995). The goals of building strong families, preventing the litany of social problems attributed to public education from infecting children, and learning values are almost never tested in any scientific manner (for exceptions, see Parker, 1992; Ray, 2004a). If one were to draw a central conclusion from those who study homeschooling, it would be that the primary goal of this movement is to ratchet up academic achievement in mathematics and reading. The fact that this is patently inaccurate seems to escape the attention of most researchers plying their skills in this area. In short, what counts as evidence of success in public schools has de facto become the measure of progress in homeschools, at least for researchers.

At the *micro level*, the neglect of outcomes at the heart of the homeschooling community occurs because when scholars focus on academic outcomes they confine themselves to the most basic elements of the achievement algorithm, measures of performance on basic skills in two or three areas (e.g., mathematics, reading). Most of the academic outcomes pursued by homeschooling families, such as learning for understanding, developing habits of inquiry, and learning across content areas, never appear in research studies on the effects of homeschooling (Mayberry et al., 1995).

In short, what Ray and Wartes (1991) refer to as the major agenda of public education has become the platform for assessing the productivity of homeschools. Other outcomes that are more important to the homeschool community and to the larger society receive very little empirical attention (Lines, 2000a).

❖ HOMESCHOOLING EFFECTS: BROAD MEASURES

The growing appeal of homeschooling to all sorts of people has led to many, often contradictory, claims about its broader significance.
(Gaither, 2008, p. 224)

~◠⦙◠~

In assessing home education research, it seems reasonable to follow [this] approach: First identify the goals of home education, then assess the extent to which progress toward the goals is evident. (Cizek, 1993, p. 1)

~ↄ⭒ↄ~

Two well-established pathways are available to follow in examining the impacts of homeschooling. First, we can turn to the designs developed to assess privatization initiatives in general. For example, Murphy (1996) assesses privatization strategies such as homeschooling around five criteria: efficiency, quality, choice, equity, and community. The second design evaluates homeschooling on categories of impact (e.g., socialization). In this chapter, we feature the second design and weave in essential ideas from the privatization pathway as appropriate. We divide the impact of homeschooling into two major categories: effects on broad measures and effects on children. In the first bin, we include outcomes in four areas: society writ large, public schooling, costs, and family. In the second bin, we review findings on three outcomes: academic achievement; social development; and postschool success, especially college attendance and graduation.

Impact on the Social Fabric

It seems clear that both parents and children have profound interests at stake in the shape of a homeschooling education. But the outcome matters to broader society as well, both in terms of having economically self-sufficient members and citizens committed to a healthy democracy.
(Kunzman, 2009a, p. 11)

~ↄ⭒ↄ~

How will the common social reality be affected by the unique perspective of the home school families? That big question remains to be answered.
(Smedley, 1992, p. 14)

~ↄ⭒ↄ~

Most academic studies of home schooling have focused on questions about the academic performance or socialization of home schooled children and adolescents. While these are certainly important questions, they do not offer much guidance in determining the democratic potential of the movement. What is necessary therefore is an examination of the home schooling movement with particular focus on questions of democracy and political struggles. (Riegel, 2001, pp. 92–93)

~ↄ⭒ↄ~

A few homeschool analysts, both advocates and those with more skeptical mindsets, have forged theories of action about the potential effects of home-based education on the social fabric of the country, often expressed in terms of the common good and the well-being of the democratic state (Apple, 2000b; Kunzman, 2009a). There seems to be consensus on all sides that the homeschooling movement is likely to have an important impact beyond what happens in individual homes and with specific children (Apple, 2000a; Bates, 1991; Riegel, 2001). There is also widespread agreement that effects on the public weal need to be considered in assessing the overall impact of homeschooling (Belfield, 2005). As discussed above, while we sometimes find well-developed analyses of the logic of action in the literature, research on the question of homeschooling's impact on society writ large is almost nonexistent. Operationalization needed to begin empirical work is also scarce. We are left, therefore, with an ideologically defined landscape with little evidence to test claims and counter claims.

Since this is an empirical review, it is not our intention to delve into the theories of logic that power various perspectives on how homeschooling is linked, positively and negatively, to what Apple (2000a) refers to as the health of the public sphere. Suffice it to say that one side, often anchored by economists, concludes that community can be built through individualization, freedom of choice, and market forces (Belfield, 2005; Murphy, 1996). Analysts here also attempt to cast doubt on claims by opponents of homeschooling that the common school experience is essential for the development and maintenance of the public good (Hardenbaugh, 2005). They view exit from public schooling as an attack on public monopoly, not a lack of commitment to the common good (Murphy, 1999).

The other side, opponents and the skeptics, sees things quite differently. Their theories lead them to the conclusion that homeschooling, by failing to grow the social networks in schools that glue society together (Apple 2000b; Lubienski, 2000; Reich, 2005), undermines the public good (Apple, 2000a; Luke, 2003) and reinforces old and grows new inequalities (Apple, 2005). The crux of the equity argument in terms of homeschooling has been laid out by Lubienski (2000), Apple (2000a), and others: Making schooling private may enhance educational quality for some but will surely diminish quality for others. The pathway that leads from homeschooling to inequality is characterized by reduced concern for and commitment to the larger democratic society by homeschool parents. According to Apple, for example, homeschooling is defined by an anti-democratic logic and impoverishes the public good. For critics, homeschooling represents a retreat from the public sphere (Riegel, 2001). These analysts hold that social justice is diminished by homeschooling (Apple, 2000a; Lubienski, 2000).

If we have not been sufficiently clear to this point, we restate critical insights here. Research provides little evidence about the impact of homeschooling on the larger public sphere. More accurately, there is remarkably little attention to this important outcome in the homeschool literature. The one study that directs an empirical spotlight to the issue suggests that the ground on which critics stand may be a little less firm than they believe. Operationalizing the public good in terms of civic involvement, Smith and Sikkink (1999) conclude that homeschoolers are not isolated, disengaged citizens. Employing regression analysis with National Household Education Survey data and providing a strong set of controls, these researchers found that homeschooling families are significantly more likely than public school families "to participate in public life through a broad range of activities" (p. 18). Their assessment is that "there appears to be something about homeschooling that increases families' participation in mostly non–school related civic activities in the public square" (p. 18). Indeed, they conclude "that the challenges, responsibilities and practices that home educators normally entail for their participants may actually help reinvigorate America's civic culture and the participation of her citizens in the public square" (p. 20).

Impact on Schools

> *What it portends for our current system of school is still unknown.*
> *(K. Bauman, 2002, p. 14)*

~◦◦◦~

> *The growing number of students being educated at home affects the public*
> *education system in a number of ways. (Lips & Feinberg, 2008, p. 5)*

~◦◦◦~

> *We suspect that those families who have taken it upon themselves to*
> *provide education at home may have something important to offer those*
> *working to change public education. (J. D. Marshall & Valle, 1996, p. 2)*

~◦◦◦~

As Wartes (1990) reminded us in the early years of the homeschooling movement, one potential effect of homeschooling could be its shaping influence on public education, an impact that has been rehypothesized for 20 years (McKeon, 2007; Muntes, 2006). The literature here, as is the case with most of the broad-based outcomes, provides some suggestions and some initial clues but very little empirical evidence (K. Bauman, 2002; Lines, 2004; Mayberry, 1989a). Meighan (1995) and others suggest that information from the homeschooling movement offers important insights about both the overhaul of the public education system and the reform of individual schools (Cooper & Sureau, 2007; Dahlquist et al., 2006). Similar arguments have been amassed by scholars for the larger field of privatization generally (Murphy, 1996) and for specific strategies such as vouchers and charter schools (Murphy, Gilmer, Weise, & Page, 1998; Murphy & Shiffman, 2002). With homeschooling in particular, analysts foresee potential impacts in public schools across an array of areas, including staffing, curriculum, organizational structure, and resources (K. Bauman, 2002; Cooper & Sureau, 2007).

It is useful to think through the pathways by which homeschooling could shape conventional schooling. Three avenues stand out: withdrawal impacts, lighthouse effects, and competitive effects. It is suggested that when parents, especially the deeply involved parents one often sees in the homeschooling movement, pull away from public schools social capital is diminished (Wilhelm & Firman, 2009). It is also obvious that the funding associated with each homeschooled child will no longer be available to the public schools (Sutton & Bogan, 2005). This, in turn, could influence educational quality (Nemer, 2002). Relatedly, a reduced commitment to public education (Dahlquist et al., 2006; Riegel, 2001) and a reduced willingness to support taxes for schools (Apple, 2005; Hill, 2000) suggests that homeschooling leads to less financial support for public education (Apple, 2000a; Houston & Toma, 2003). In short, it is argued that withdrawal to the home is also accompanied by a reduction of political capital and material resources for public schools (Riegel, 2001).

Other analysts who think about lighthouse effects suggest that the "good stuff" that makes homeschooling effective will find its way into public education, thus ratcheting up the quality of conventional schools (Lines, 2000b; Luke, 2003; Ray, 2010)—both individual schools and the system of public education (Mayberry, 1993). Here it is suggested that homeschooling will be an incubator of good practices that can be adopted and adapted by public school educators (Hardenbaugh, 2005; Holt, 1983). Currently, there is very little empirical data about the robustness of either the withdrawal or the spillover pathways. Information from other privatization efforts, however, would lead one to be less than sanguine about the power of spillover effects (Murphy & Shiffman, 2002).

Some preliminary data on cooperative relationships is beginning to be woven into a tentative finding. Specifically, there is some evidence that competition from homeschooling is encouraging public schools to develop new institutional forms (K. Bauman, 2002; Jackson, 2007; Mayberry et al., 1995). Noteworthy here has been the creation of new schools to serve homeschooled children and the development of more flexible public schools that permit homeschoolers to complete their education in multiple venues, at home and in the public school (K. Bauman, 2002; Hill, 2000; Knowles, 1989). Meighan (1995) refers to the latter phenomenon as *flexi-schooling.*

Before leaving our discussion of the impact of homeschooling on conventional schools, it is important to recall that previously enrolled private school children are overrepresented among homeschoolers (Lines, 2000b; Wartes, 1987). Thus, as Lines (2004) reminds us, the competitive effects of homeschooling are likely to fall heavily on private schools as well as public schools.

In a similar vein, homeschooling has the potential to influence institutions of higher education in America (Gaither, 2008; Prue, 1997; Ray, 2005), especially around admissions criteria. At a minimum, preliminary data suggest that homeschooling is encouraging these institutions to broaden their admissions procedures (Prue, 1997).

Costs

The home schooler's agenda, if anything, will reduce the tax price of schooling. (Cibulka, 1991, p. 107)

✦

Homeschools save taxpayers education monies. (Wenders & Clements, 2007, p. 17)

✦

Little attention has been given to the financial impact of homeschooling on public school districts. (Ray & Weller, 2003, p. 24)

✦

To date, only limited attention has been directed to the costs, or what Cibulka (1991) describes as the fiscal appeal, of homeschooling. As with most everything in homeschooling, both proponents and opponents have a point of view on the cost issue. Critics see homeschooling as pulling resources from public school districts, specifically the per-pupil allotment that no longer flows to the coffers of the district (Apple, 2007). Supporters, on the other hand, argue that there are considerable cost savings, or a reduced tax burden on taxpayers, when children leave (or do not to enter) public schools (Belfield, 2005; Lyman, 1998; Ray & Weller, 2003). Going even further, Wenders and Clements (2007) maintain that homeschooling not only saves taxpayers money but leads to greater spending on public schools (see also Ray & Weller, 2003).

As with many things in the area of homeschooling, the inside story on costs is a little more complex than it appears at first blush. The issue of what gets counted in the calculations is especially nettlesome and, as Luebke (1999) reminds us, the true impact depends a good deal on whom you ask and what one considers evidence. However, more so than with other impacts, there are meaningful data to inform the discussion. What the data suggest is that the idea that homeschoolers are taking money out of the pockets of schools (Apple, 2005) does not hold up well. On the theory side here, it is important to remember that public schools enjoy no entitlement to student enrollment (Wenders & Clements, 2007). Indeed, critics of the entitlement perspective see it as a return to the architecture of public monopoly that dominated education throughout the 20th century (Murphy, 1999).

On the empirical side, researchers have explored two approaches to the cost impact of homeschooling. Some reviewers extrapolate tax savings that materialize by not having students in public school classrooms. For example, at the state level figures on tax savings have been provided by

Wenders and Clements (2007) in Nevada, Sutton and Bogan (2005) in Florida, Luebke (1999) in Wisconsin, and Ray and Weller (2003) in Oregon. At the national level, these tax savings have been calculated at $3.7 billion to $6.1 billion in 1996–1997 (Ray, 1997b) and $4.4 billion to $9.9 billion in 2003 (Lips & Feinberg, 2008). Other reviewers examine real expenses to uncover the financial impact of homeschooling on school districts. The two studies that have examined this issue reveal that in addition to providing tax savings, homeschooling reduces educational costs for school districts (Thompson, 1994; Wenders & Clements, 2007).

Other costs that could make homeschooling less of a net gain receive almost no analysis in the literature, however. To begin with, there are real costs to families because of labor income forgone to allow one parent to remain at home for schooling purposes (Houston & Toma, 2003; Parker, 1992). Relatedly, there is the cost of tax revenue missed because homeschooling parents elect not to participate in the paid labor market.

Impact on Families

Parents who educate their children at home do so at considerable cost.
(J. D. Marshall & Valle, 1996, p. 11)

~◠⚬◠~

Although it is stated in different ways, the general message of these mothers' words is clear; staying home is best for the kids, valuable enough to trump other valuables like income, comfort, and career.
(M. L. Stevens, 2001, p. 87)

~◠⚬◠~

Research and theory also suggest that home schooling is associated with, if not causes, strong and healthy families. (Ray, 2000a, p. 288)

~◠⚬◠~

We reported in Chapter 5 that building healthy families is one of the four driving factors for homeschooling. Unfortunately, there is almost no direct research on the topic. There is, at best, some indirect evidence in some of the case studies of homeschooling. Given its place in the pantheon of motivations for home-based education, this is actually a jarring conclusion. Considerable research is needed to address the oft-stated logic of action that homeschooling (a) prevents the generational gap between children and their parents; (b) builds healthy relationships among siblings; and (c) establishes a nurturing family environment—that is, allows families to knit together strong bonds, including successful marriages (Farris & Woodruff, 2000; Mayberry, 1993; J. Webb, 1989).

Researchers also have been less than diligent and hardly systematic in exploring how homeschooling impacts the ongoing activities of families.

As we discussed in earlier chapters, there is abundant evidence that mothers assume primary and often near total responsibility for homeschooling work, both in individual families and in the larger homeschooling support structure (M. L. Stevens, 2001). The fact that many parents have reconfigured their lifestyles to engage in the task of educating their children is discussed in the literature but not systematically investigated (Colfax & Colfax, 1988). Based on empirical evidence, we uncover three things about family lifestyle changes, but again little about the core issue of building relationships, which is not even operationalized in the literature. First, homeschooling requires a major commitment of time (Aurini & Davies, 2005; M. Martin, 1997; M. L. Stevens, 2001) and much hard work (Green & Hoover-Dempsey, 2007; Kunzman, 2009b; Williams, Arnoldson, & Reynolds, 1984). For example, Parker (1992) reported severe time pressures in 11% of his sample and distinct time pressures in another 62%. Second, homeschooling often requires a significant financial sacrifice, primarily the income forgone to keep the mother at home (Lyman, 2000; M. L. Stevens, 2001), although there is no information on how many of these women would be full-time homemakers in the absence of homeschooling. Third, homeschooling has the potential to limit the careers of mothers who do stay at home (Aurini & Davies, 2005; Lyman, 2000), what Mitchell Stevens (2001) refers to as costs to homeschooling mothers in terms of career opportunities. Or as Perry and Perry (2000) assert, it represents a career change.

There is a very small window in the literature onto the frustrations and satisfactions that parents experience from homeschooling, and those insights are often refracted (Divoky, 1983; Green & Hoover-Dempsey, 2007). The most important work was undertaken by Gladin (1987) a quarter century ago. On the frustration side of the ledger, Gladin concludes that the greatest angst arises from the difficult assignment of balancing homemaking and hometeaching activities. But again, we do not know how this frustration compares to that of mothers balancing careers and homemaking. Williams and colleagues (1984) also surface the frustration of competence among some homeschooling mothers. On the asset side of the balance book, Gladin uncovered eight factors that cluster into three bundles: seeing children develop; spending time with children, including deepening sibling relations; and taking control and fulfilling God's mandate (Klicka, 1995; Sheffer, 1995). Sheffer (1995) and Williams and associates add a fourth satisfaction: using homeschooling as an avenue of personal learning and development, especially the invigoration of full-time motherhood.

❖ HOMESCHOOLING EFFECTS ON CHILDREN

Our exploration of the effects of homeschooling on children attends to three outcomes: academic achievement, social development, and posthomeschooling success. We remind the reader that our discussion of the limitations of the research in the area of homeschooling has particular relevance at this stage of the analysis.

Academic Achievement

The question of how homeschool students compare academically with their public school peers remains a matter of dispute. (Kunzman, 2005, p. 4)

Home education has not achieved its present level of ascendancy without some scrutiny. The first issue to be researched has to do with academic performance. (McCulloch, Slocum, Kolegue, & Montaudo, 2006, p. 1)

Of all the home schooling issues, undoubtedly the one receiving the most publicity centers on the academic achievement of home schooled youth. (Calvery, Bell, & Vaupel, 1992, p. 3)

A Caveat

To begin with, the implicit assumption in the research that measures of academic performance are the keystone elements in the debate over the value of homeschooling needs to be thrown open to scrutiny (Hill, 2000; Kaseman & Kaseman, 1999). Three concerns emerge. First, analysts from both sides of the homeschooling community portrayed in Chapter 3 soundly reject the notion of the primacy of achievement scores in understanding the impact of homeschooling (Farenga, 1997; Klicka, 1995). Other, more important goals (e.g., inculcation of values), it is argued, should hold center stage in explorations of whether homeschooling works. Relatedly, many others maintain that the door to homeschooling should not open and close in response to test scores. It is a right that transcends test results (Kaseman & Kaseman, 1999). Its warrant rests on a higher power, not government-anchored measures of outcomes. The final concern is that focusing on achievement results puts the burden of proof for the legitimacy of homeschooling on homeschoolers, rather than those who are opposed to the practice (Hill, 2000). It also pulls homeschools into the orbit of public education. Given our earlier discussion of the near absence of evaluation of the family-preferred outcomes of homeschooling, the critique over emphasis on academic achievement merits considerably more ink.

Lay of the Land

For the time being, let us place our concern for the proper place of achievement scores in evaluating homeschooling in abeyance. Instead, let us direct the analytic spotlight to what we know about the academic performance of homeschooled youngsters. One group of scholars concludes that we know almost nothing about the impact of homeschooling on academic performance (Lips & Feinberg, 2008; Reich, 2005). Their conclusion is based on the fact that the extant research base (discussed above) lacks the scientific foundations to distill any reliable findings (E. Frost & Morris, 1988; Reich, 2005). Absent comparative data and controlled studies, we simply are unable to draw any firm conclusions (Dahlquist et al., 2006). That is, the current research base of descriptive analyses and case studies precludes forming generalizations about the cognitive growth of homeschooled youngsters. Even when these children test well, there is simply no way to determine that the homeschooling intervention is responsible for the results (Reich, 2005).

Other analysts, while acknowledging the limitations of the research, argue that there are no data to suggest that homeschooling is harmful to the academic achievement of children (Lines, 2000a; Luebke, 1999). That is, they find that academic test results suggest that homeschooling students are not disadvantaged by home-based education (Belfield, 2005; Blok, 2004; Knowles, Marlow, & Muchmore, 1992).

Still another cluster of reviewers maintain that the cumulative body of evidence suggests that real academic benefits flow to homeschool children (Luebke, 1999; Ray & Wartes, 1991). They hold that indirect evidence signals a positive link between homeschooling and academic performance (Basham et al., 2007; Ray, 1997b).

Comparisons With National Norms

Analysts who link homeschooling and positive academic achievement almost always compare the performance of homeschooled youngsters to national norms (Collom, 2005; M. L. Stevens, 2001; Wenger & Hodari, 2004). They find that homeschool students who take standardized tests usually do quite well when compared to traditionally schooled peers as a group (Calvery et al., 1992; Lines, 1991; Ray, 2001a, 2001b). For example, Delahooke (1986) compared homeschool achievement with test norms of private school children. She found similar levels of performance. Wartes (1987, 1988) reported that homeschoolers scored between the 65th to 68th percentile on national norms in his studies in Washington. In a study in Alabama, Rakestraw (1988) found that homeschooled children scored about the same as public school students. Frost (1988) and Frost and Morris (1988) discovered that homeschooled youngsters in Illinois performed better than public school children in every subject area other than mathematics.

Ray (2001a, 2001b) reached similar conclusions in his landmark 1990 national study, reporting that homeschooled children achieved at or above the 80th percentile in all subjects on standardized tests. Ray's subsequent investigations (1997b, 2010) reinforced his earlier conclusions. For example, in his 1997 study

> the students scored, on the average, at the following percentiles on standardized achievement tests: (a) total reading, 87th, (b) total language, 80th, (c) total math, 82nd, (d) total listening, 85th, (e) science, 84th, (f) social studies, 85th, (g) study skills, 81st, (h) basic battery (typically, reading, language, and mathematics), 85th, and (i) complete battery (all subject areas in which student was tested), 87th. (Ray, 1997b, p. 54)

In his 2010 study he found homeschool achievement reported in national percentiles as follows: total reading, 89th; total language, 84th; total mathematics, 84th; science, 86th; social studies, 84th; and composite, 86th.

In another hallmark national study, Rudner (1999) documented achievement test scores for homeschoolers between the 76th and 91st percentile across all 12 grades. He noted that homeschoolers in grades 1–4 were a full year above their private and public school peers on standardized tests and about 4 years above them in the 8th grade. Parker (1992) followed a similar approach using reports of homeschooling parents. He found that these parents reported considerable academic success. Schemmer (1985) calculated growth of homeschool students from one year to the next, reporting that these students performed well but in some cases did not achieve 12 months' growth. In a small-scale study in which growth over time (one semester) was measured, Duvall and associates (Duvall, 2005; Duvall, Delquadri, & Ward 2004; Duvall, Ward, Delquadri, & Greenwood 1997) found that homeschooled special needs children demonstrated more growth than public school peers in reading and written language and about equal growth in mathematics. Wenger and Hodari (2004) compared the scores of homeschool recruits into the military against students educated in public and private schools on the Armed Forces Qualification Test. They found that the homeschoolers performed about the same as the public school graduates.

In addition, an assortment of scholars have conducted reviews of studies of the impact of homeschooling on children's academic performance. All of these reviews report that homeschooling children almost always do as well as children in public schools and generally a good deal better, in terms of comparisons with national norms (Blok, 2004; Galloway & Sutton, 1995; Knowles et al., 1992; M. L. Stevens, 2001).

Scholars also have compared college entrance examination scores of homeschoolers to national norms for those tests. Rudner (1999) reported that homeschoolers had a composite ACT score of 22.8, while the national norm was 21.0, a score that placed homeschooled children in the 65th percentile of all ACT test takers. In an earlier study, Oliveira, Watson, and

Sutton (1994) found no significant differences on ACT scores. Dovie Gray (1998) reported a similar conclusion for SAT scores. In a more sophisticated study (Belfield, 2005), investigators found that homeschooled students enjoyed a strong advantage over public school peers on the SAT even after controlling for 21 relevant independent variables, with all of the advantage coming from the verbal scores (Belfield, 2004b). Ray (2004b) also reported that the homeschooled youngsters in his study outperformed public school colleagues on college entrance examinations. They scored 568 in verbal and 532 in mathematics on the SAT, compared to averages of 501 and 510, respectively.

Other Windows on Achievement

While almost all judgments about the academic performance of homeschoolers rely on comparisons with public school students using national norms on standardized tests, there are a few exceptions. Klugewicz and Carraccio (1999) asked pediatricians to estimate the academic position of their homeschooled patients. Fifty-eight percent of them judged homeschoolers to be average, while 30% were assessed as above and 12% as below average.

Contextual Issues

Researchers have also invested energy in exploring the effect of environmental or background factors (e.g., family income) on the achievement of homeschooled children. In particular, they have been interested in determining how powerful these contextual variables are in homeschools vis-à-vis the homes of public school children. They have also been engaged in investigating the impact of these variables on student achievement within homeschools. To presage the more detailed analysis that follows, and keeping in mind the state of research in the areas of homeschooling, the bulk of the evidence to date suggests that (a) most of these contextual factors have weaker relationships to academic performance than is the case in public schools (Basham et al., 2007; Ray, 1997b) and (b) these background factors, by and large, are not significant determinants of academic achievement of homeschooled children (Collom & Mitchell, 2005).

In their treatments of *household income*, analysts have uncovered two important findings. To begin with, there is evidence that low-income children in homeschools often achieve at or above national norms while low-income children in public schools on average score considerably below national norms (Ray, 2004b, 2009a). That is, there is a less pronounced relationship between family income and student learning in homeschools than in public schools (Blok, 2004; Ray, 1997b; Wartes, 1990). At the same time, although there is some difference of opinion, it does appear that family income still matters. That is, across homeschools there is a significant difference in the cognitive performance of youngsters based on family income (Ray, 2010; Rudner, 1999). Higher income is associated with higher test scores, and the differences are larger for youngsters in higher grades (Rudner, 1999).

Turning to *parental education,* we arrive at parallel conclusions. Homeschooling appears to tamp down the negative effects of low levels of parental education on student performance (Basham et. al., 2007). More specifically, the children of poorly educated parents score higher on achievement tests in homeschools than they do in public schools (Basham et al., 2007; Ray, 2000c). Looking at the topic with another lens, Ray (1997b) found that homeschool parents with low levels of education routinely have children who reach national norms on achievement tests. He provided the following data on the issue:

> For public school students a parent's education level *does* affect their children's performance. In eighth grade math, public school students whose parents are college graduates score at the 63rd percentile, whereas students whose parents have less than a high school diploma score at the 28th percentile. Remarkably, students taught at home by mothers who never finished high school score a full 55 percentile points higher than public school students from families of comparable educational backgrounds. (Ray, 1997a, p. 4)

Rudner (1999, p. 25), in turn, encapsulated his findings as follows:

> It is worthy to note that, at every grade level, the mean performance of home school students whose parents do not have a college degree is much higher than the mean performance of students in public schools. Their percentiles are mostly in the 65th to 69th percentile range.

Concomitantly, when researchers focus solely on homeschool families, the bulk of the evidence points to only a weak to moderate relationship between parents' educational levels and measures of academic performance (Collom, 2005; Ray, 2010; Rudner, 1999), although some researchers and reviewers suggest no relationship (Lines, 2000b; Mayberry et al., 1995; Moore & Moore, 1994). For example, in his comprehensive study Rudner (1999) found that homeschool children with college-educated parents performed better in every grade than those with parents who had less than a college degree.

Turning to other contextual variables, researchers provide some evidence on the public–homeschool comparison front, but very limited information on the across-homeschools front. On the first topic, as was the case for income, there is preliminary evidence that homeschooling depresses the negative effects of *race* visible in the public schools (Collom, 2005). For example, and remembering the research limitations examined above, Ray (1997a) found only minimal difference between African American and white students in reading and mathematics in homeschools, but large differences in scores in those two subjects by race in public schools. Investigators also have shown that widely seen *gender* differences in public school achievement scores may be muted by homeschooling. Wartes (1990) was the first scholar to document this compression in achievement variability by gender. Later studies by Rudner (1999) and Ray (2010) confirm Wartes's initial results.

Religion is a critical theme in the homeschool literature, but we know almost nothing about its place in the student achievement equation. *Motivations* in general are also a critical piece of the homeschooling story, but here too there is almost no information available when we explore the chapters on achievement in the book on homeschools. Collom (2005) reported that reading and language scores were higher for children in homes that were motivated to homeschool because of their criticism of public education, while lower scores were recorded for children of parents who homeschooled for family reasons, although Collom reminds us that the latter finding could be explained by the high number of special needs children in homes motivated by family needs.

Other contextual variables address conditions in the homeschool program. For example, Wartes (1990) examined the amount of *religious content* in the homeschool experience. He found no relationship with student achievement. Wartes (1988, 1990) also documented no meaningful relationship between *grade level* and academic achievement in homeschools, although Rudner's (1999) later and more methodologically sophisticated study suggests otherwise, that student cognitive development does vary with grade level in homeschools. Rudner's landmark study also shed some light on Parker's (1992) suggestive finding that there exists a positive relationship between *length of time homeschooling* and student achievement. Rudner discovered that students who had been schooled at home for their entire schooling experience posted higher achievement scores than youngsters who had attended public and private schools as well. Ray (2010) and others have also begun to provide some initial insights on other dimensions of homeschooling and student achievement. In his most recent comprehensive analysis, he uncovered no differences in achievement scores between children *engaged with full-package curriculums* and other homeschool students. Wartes's (1990) work extends this finding to the *structure of schooling* more generally as well as to *hours of formal schooling*. Ray's investigation unearthed a positive relationship between *money spent on homeschooling* and student learning. A number of scholars over the last quarter century have explored the link between homeschool parents' (past or current) *certification as a teacher* and student achievement. The consistent conclusion from this work is that there is no relationship between parental certification and student performance on standardized achievement tests (Basham et al., 2007; Ray, 2010; Wartes, 1990).

The Take Away Message on Student Achievement

After all the information on student achievement is arrayed and reviewed, a number of key conclusions can be distilled. First, we know more than some analysts suggest we do. Important empirically grounded clues are visible, and tentative hypotheses are being formed. At the same time, we know a lot less than advocates of homeschooling would have us believe. Second, there is a growing body of evidence that reveals how homeschool students are performing academically compared to national norms on standardized tests. Third, there is a fair amount of suggestive evidence that homeschooling can tamp down the effects found in public schools of family socioeconomic variables. Or as Collom (2005, p. 329) so nicely captures it, "the two great divides that public school children face—race and class—are inconsequential for student achievement among home-educated children." Fourth, until scholars employ more rigorous research designs, we will continue to be unable to speak with any degree of certainty about the contribution of homeschooling to the cognitive development of children. Given the methodologies in play to date, alternative explanations for generally higher achievement scores cannot be evaluated. Finally, we want to revisit our cardinal caveat: There are a number of valid reasons why it is inappropriate to privilege academic achievement in the algorithm we craft to assess the impact of homeschooling.

Social Development

> *In addition to academic concerns, the socialization of home-schooled children has been a primary consideration.*
> *(Rakestraw & Rakestraw, 1990, p. 72)*

~◠◡◠~

> *The issue of socialization and, related to it, the development of self-esteem in home schooled children is perhaps the greatest concern of educators, courts, and laypeople alike. (Tillman, 1995, p. 1)*

The Storyboard

> *Contrasting views about homeschooling continue, especially regarding questions of socialization. (Dahlquist et al., 2006, p. 361)*

~◠◡◠~

> *Critics see homeschoolers as isolationists, atomistic, and even undemocratic. (Lines, 2000a, p. 83)*

~◠◡◠~

*Like everything else they have done, homeschoolers are redefining the
debate about socialization. They question whether school-based socialization
is preferable to family-based socialization. (Lyman, 2000, p. 56)*

～⌒⋮⌒～

The topic of the social development of youngsters is consistently
reported to be a critical outcome measure of homeschooling, often ranked
first in importance but almost never less than second (Arai, 1999; Lyman,
2000; Ray & Wartes, 1991). Those who are apprehensive about the socialization of homeschool youngsters put forth a theory of action that runs as
follows. Schools are a critical caldron in which important social skills are
formed and social norms are learned (Guterson, 1992; Kelley, 1991).
Homeschooling, it is asserted, limits the exchanges by which skills (e.g.,
conflict resolution) and norms (e.g., respect for others) are developed
(Gladin, 1987; Gorder, 1990; Shyers, 1992). As a consequence, a variety of
negative outcomes materialize (e.g., poor ability to cope in larger society).
The claim is made that by limiting socialization to the family, children may
be harmed, that lack of exposure to and interaction with peers at school
can negatively impact social development, including self-worth and social
skills (Delahooke, 1986; Medlin, 2000). The fear is that absent the socializing experiences of traditional schooling, homeschoolers will not be as
socially well adjusted as their conventionally educated peers; they could
become social misfits (Romanowski, 2001; Sheffer, 1995). As Guterson
(1992, p. 4) captures the sentiment, they could "be like caterpillars who
never become butterflies, crawling along down the labyrinths of adult life
and blinking unhappily at the shrubbery."

Embedded in this logic in action are a variety of more specific concerns. There is the worry that absent traditional schooling homeschooled
children will become socially isolated (Farris & Woodruff, 2000; Gaither,
2008; Medlin, 2000) and the homeschool movement will produce an army
of social isolates (Delahooke, 1986; S. Gray, 1993; M. L. Stevens, 2001).
There is also the concern that too great a reliance on one institution for
socialization, the family, could lead to indoctrination (Apple, 2000a, 2000b;
Reich, 2005). An assortment of analysts in their reviews have expressed
apprehension about the potential negative effects of homeschooling in the
area of friendship development (S. Gray, 1993; Knowles & Muchmore,
1995; M. Martin, 1997). They sometimes paint a "picture of home school
students as lonely children who don't get a chance to interact with their
peers" (Dalaimo, 1996, p. 15). Critics worry about identity formation
(Belfield, 2004b). There is a generalized angst from some that homeschoolers will not develop needed social skills (Delahooke, 1986; Medlin, 2000).
Nor, it is argued, will they learn essential social norms (Arai, 1999). Still
another often-noted worry is that these children will suffer from a lack of
exposure to people from all walks of life and to the diversity of perspectives one finds in public schools (Lyman, 2000; Medlin, 1998; Reich, 2002),

what Romanowski (2001) refers to as different viewpoints and distinctive ways of life. They may have, it is maintained, a limited horizon of experience (Kunzman, 2009a; Reich, 2002). Because of these deficiencies, it is further asserted, homeschooled graduates may lack the capacity to be productive members of society, to fit into the real world (Kelley, 1991, Knowles & Muchmore, 1995)—to adapt to the tough realities of life beyond their families, particularly the competitive culture of the workplace (Arai, 1999). It is also postulated that these youngsters will be more likely to withdraw from civic engagements (Apple, 2000b; Lubienski, 2000; Reich, 2002).

Proponents of homeschooling, you will not be surprised to learn, have a different perspective on the social development of homeschooled youngsters (Farris & Woodruff, 2000), and, as we will see below, considerably more empirical evidence to bolster their position.

> Home schooling parents, not surprisingly, disagree on every point. They describe conventional schools as rigid and authoritarian institutions where passive conformity is rewarded, where peer interactions are too often hostile or derisive or manipulative, and where children must contend with a dispiriting ideological and moral climate. Home schooling parents argue that this kind of environment can stifle children's individuality and harm their self-esteem. They say it can make children dependent, insecure, or even antisocial. They believe it can undermine their efforts to teach their children positive values and appropriate behavior. Finally, they insist that it is unlikely to cultivate the kind of rewarding and supportive relationships that foster healthy personal and moral development. (Medlin, 2000, p. 109)

They maintain that a healthy family provides a better caldron in which to brew positive social development than the public school (Belfield, 2004a; S. Gray, 1998; Moore & Moore, 1981). They caution us that the robust portrait of socialization unfolding in America's schools is somewhat of an illusion (Hill, 2000; Holt, 1981), carrying as much negative freight as benefits (Farris & Woodruff, 2000; Gorder, 1990; Jaycox, 2001). Proponents also remind us that there is a good deal more to the day than the few hours of "school time" and argue that most homeschoolers are socially engaged during this extended time (Duvall, 2005; Groover & Endsley, 1988; Perry & Perry, 2000). Proponents also define "variety" differently, suggesting that what is lost in engagement with peers in school is more than compensated for with abundant contacts with other peers and adults (Dalaimo, 1996; Jaycox, 2001). They argue that if the formation of positive social skills is the goal, then socialization with adults trumps socialization with peers (Farris & Woodruff, 2000; Meighan, 1995). They contend that extensive peer socialization, which we have already seen is viewed suspiciously by all sides of the homeschool community (Holt, 1981; Moore, 1982), is actually likely to be harmful (Boone, 2000; J. Taylor, 1986a; J. Webb, 1989).

The Evidence

The findings provide no basis to question the social development of homeschooled children. (Lines, 2000a, p. 82)

⌁

Research shows that home-educated children are healthy in terms of psychological and emotional health. (Ray, 2000a, p. 276)

⌁

A number of researchers help us think through the rather messy concept of social development/socialization. One group assists by providing definitions. For example, Brim and Wheeler (cited in Kelley, 1991, p. 2) define socialization as the "process by which persons acquire the knowledge, skills, and dispositions that make them more or less able members of society." McNeil (also cited in Kelley, 1991, p. 2), in turn, "defines socialization as the process by which the child learns the ways of society and how to best function as a part of it." Another cluster of analysts decompose socialization into its core elements; they provide frameworks for navigating through the research, examining the impacts of homeschooling on young persons. Ray (2005), for example, discusses socialization around three domains: social, emotional, and psychological development. Medlin (2000, p. 110) also unpacks socialization into three components: "participating in daily routines of one's communities, acquiring the [needed] rules of behavior and systems of beliefs and attitudes, and functioning effectively as members of society." Medlin provides us with a second framework as well, categorizing socialization as social activity, social influence, and social experience. Based on the work of pioneers in the field, we present the empirical evidence on the impact of homeschooling on the social development of children around three constructs: social engagement, self-concept, and social skills. Before we begin, however, it is instructive to remind the reader that (a) the body of research, although larger than in most of the impact domains of homeschooling, is still relatively small (Guterson, 1992) and (a) all of the research limitations we have surfaced throughout the book are evident in the scholarship on the socialization effects of homeschooling (Belfield, 2004b; Kunzman, 2005; Medlin, 2000).

Social Engagement

The results show that these home schoolers are not isolated but active, contributing members of society, even in childhood. (Tillman, 1995, p. 5)

⌁

Social engagement as an outcome is assessed in three spheres of the homeschool literature: engagement of families (parents), engagement of children being homeschooled, and engagement of homeschool graduates. We report on homeschool graduates below when we take up the topic of posthomeschooling success. We touched on the engagement of home-school families in the earlier section on the impact on the social fabric, documenting that, in general, homeschool families are at least as involved, if not more involved, civically as the general public (Isenberg, 2002; Ray, 2004a; Smith & Sikkink, 1999). Here we review what is known about the socialization impact on youngsters when they are being homeschooled.

We start with the social isolation hypothesis that is batted back and forth by critics and proponents of homeschooling. Here is what we can comfortably say based on the evidence. Homeschooling does impact the calculus of interpersonal relationships for homeschoolers. This is hardly surprising, given their absence from groups of peers in formal school settings (Chatham-Carpenter, 1994). At the same time, nearly every research study conducted to date finds that these youngsters are not socially isolated (Arai, 1999; Ray, 2004a; Van Galen, 1991). Or as Chatham-Carpenter (1994) puts it, they are not at risk socially when "riskness" is assessed by the total number of social contacts.

The average homeschool youngster interacts with a large number of persons on a daily basis. He or she is part of both an extensive and diverse social network (McCulloch et al., 2006; Ray, 2009b), although generally less extensive than the network maintained by the average public school child (Chatham-Carpenter, 1994). There is also some evidence that closeness of connections varies by school type, with public schoolers having more close contacts than homeschoolers (Chatham-Carpenter, 1994). Also, not unex-pectedly, homeschool students spend more time with siblings and adults than they do with public school peers (Allie-Carson, 1990). Consistent with what we reported above, homeschooling is likely to restructure the social world of the student, promoting more mixed-age than same-age engagements (Chatham-Carpenter, 1994; Ensign, 1997; Ray, 2009a). The basis for peer connections also changes for homeschoolers, from proximity to common interests. At the same time, fewer peer contacts (i.e., 11 versus 20 for public school youngsters in Chatham-Carpenter's 1994 study) do not translate into an insufficient number of peer connections (Chatham-Carpenter, 1994; Montgomery, 1989). Indeed, studies routinely document robust peer linkages for homeschoolers (Groover & Endsley, 1988; Wartes, 1987). Although in short supply, the data that are available also suggest that homeschooled students are not isolated from cultural diversity (Medlin, 1998). Homeschoolers on average are engaged with persons of diverse socioeconomic backgrounds, ages, religions, and ethnicities (Medlin, 1998, 2000).

Researchers help us see that these out-of-home relations are fostered through the social and civic activities in which homeschool youngsters par-ticipate. For the last 30 years, they have documented that homeschoolers are involved in a wide variety of religious, social, sporting, co-curricular, government, work, educational, and service activities outside the home (Basham et al., 2007; Montgomery, 1989; Tillman, 1995). Homeschoolers are engaged at least to the same extent as their conventionally schooled peers, and often more so (Delahooke, 1986; Duvall et al., 2004; Medlin, 2000).

Self-Concept

Any substantial educational movement must also be evaluated for its effect upon self-concept. (J. Taylor, 1986a, p. 13)

The weight of evidence to date is that the self-concept (and self-esteem) of home educated students is comparable to, and usually stronger than, that of children in conventional schools. (Ray, 1997b, p. 12)

Researchers consistently find that on various measures of self-concept and self-esteem, homeschoolers score as well as or better than age mates in other forms of schooling (Medlin, 2000). There is also a line of analysis that reveals that self-concept and socialization are tightly linked (Romanowski, 2001; J. Taylor, 1986b), connected in a recursive manner. It is generally held that socialization can be measured by self-concept, or that socialization is a core element in the formation of self-concept—that self-concept is a reflection of socialization (Kelley, 1991; J. Taylor, 1986a).

On the definitional front, Kelley (1991) reviews an assortment of meanings for self-concept. An especially clear and useful definition has been provided by Woolfolk (cited in Kelley, 1991, p. 4): "how people view themselves physically, emotionally, socially, and academically; all self-perceptions taken together." Another was penned by John Wesley Taylor (1986a, p. 14): "a construct defined as an individual's perception of himself, of what he perceives others to think of him and what he himself would wish to be."

Keeping in mind the caveat we have introduced and reinforced throughout these chapters (i.e., the limited body of high-quality research studies), almost all of the evidence amassed over the last 30 years leads to the conclusion that homeschoolers do not suffer from poor self-concepts. Their self-concepts are as strong as, or stronger than, those of peers in public and private schools (Ray, 2009b). Among the studies and reviews that focus on self-concept, a few are considered foundational. The seminal work of Ray (1997b, 2000c, 2009b) and Medlin (1998, 2000) falls into this category.

One of the early landmark studies was conducted by John Wesley Taylor (1986a). Using the Piers-Harris Children's Self-Concept Scale (PHCSCS), he discovered that the self-concepts of homeschooled youngsters were significantly higher than those of their peers in public schools. Indeed, he reported that over half of the home-educated children scored above the 90th percentile on the composite scale. Only 10% scored below the 50th percentile. Not surprisingly, he also found that the homeschool students performed well on each of the six subscales of the PHCSCS—behavioral, intellectual, physical, anxiety, popularity, and happiness—with somewhat lower scores on the popularity scale. Within the homeschool group, he found that socioeconomic status matters. Specifically, higher socioeconomic status was significantly related to higher self-concept. He also discovered that self-concept decreases for homeschoolers as they increase in age and by grade. His overall conclusion was that a positive self-concept is a benefit of homeschooling.

Kitchen's (1991) analysis, although hampered by limited sample size, supports Taylor's findings. Kitchen documented that homeschooled children scored better than conventionally schooled age mates on three of four dimensions (personal security, academic competence, familial acceptance) and on the summative dimension of the Self-Esteem Index. The only area in which they trailed their peers was in the area of peer popularity, the area where homeschoolers scored the lowest in John Wesley Taylor's (1986a) study as well. Shyers (1992), like Taylor, used the PHCSCS to measure the self-concept of homeschoolers. His conclusion was that there was equivalence between homeschooled children and traditionally schooled youngsters. Lee (1994) also documented that homeschooled youngsters did not lag behind other children on a measure of self-worth. Using the Harter Self-Perception Profile for Children, he reported no significant difference between home and public school children in self-esteem. Parker (1992) and Sheffer (1995) also reported positive self-concept for homeschoolers, although without comparative data.

A moving-forward hypothesis then seems evident. For a number of reasons that we explain in Chapter 8, home-based education appears at least as capable of nurturing self-concept as conventional schools. It is distinctly possible that homeschoolers perform even better in this area than their peers do in traditional schools. As John Wesley Taylor (1986a) and other scholars over the years have consistently pointed out, critics should be cautious about placing bets against homeschooling on the socialization rationale in general and the self-concept rationale in particular.

Social Skills

> *In reviewing these results, one would conclude that home-schooled children are as socially well adjusted as school pupils, if not more so.*
> *(Blok, 2004, p. 48)*

~◌⋮◌~

> *Literature also indicated that home schooled children tend to develop social skills superior to their conventionally schooled peers. (Kelley, 1991, p. 3)*

~◌⋮◌~

The third dimension of our social development framework attends to how well homeschool children develop the social skills essential to the intercourse of life. As we revealed above in our discussion of the socialization storyboard, there is a recurring concern in the literature that because of their isolation homeschooled children will not develop the skills they need to engage effectively with others, that they will be stifled socially. The empirical evidence available to date suggests that at a minimum this concern is likely overblown and more likely is without foundation (Dahlquist et al., 2006; Medlin, 2000).

To be sure, "social skills" covers a good deal of ground. One aspect is maturity. We learn from the research that homeschoolers are as mature as, or more mature than, children in public schools (Saunders, 2010; Smedley, 1992). We also discover that they demonstrate good leadership skills (Montgomery, 1989) and are rated high on measures of ability to interact with others, both peers and adults (Wartes, 1987)—communication skills and daily living skills (Ray & Wartes, 1991; Smedley, 1992; J. Webb, 1989). They do not appear to be socially anxious (J. Taylor, 1986a). Homeschooled youngsters measure well against their peers on indices of confidence, assuredness, and well-adjustedness (Lee, 1994; Tillman, 1995). There is also evidence that homeschoolers demonstrate fewer behavioral problems than traditionally schooled peers (Delahooke, 1986; Lee, 1994; Shyers, 1992). They tend to be trustful and noncynical in nature (McCulloch et al., 2006). They are generally a happy group (Taylor, 1986a). They score about the same as conventionally schooled peers on measures of social acceptance (Lee, 1994; J. Webb, 1989). Overall, they demonstrate appropriate prosocial behavior and social responsibility (Shyers, 1992; Wartes, 1987).

Posthomeschooling Success: Long-Term Impacts

The measure of the success or failure of the home school movement lies in the success or failure of the adults who have been home schooled.
(Galloway & Sutton, 1995, p. 1)

⁓⌒⚬⌒⁓

Much regarding the future of the population of students being homeschooled has been theorized, but little has been researched.
(Saunders, 2010, p. 96)

⁓⌒⚬⌒⁓

Educators continue to argue that the conventional educational system is better than home education in preparing children for life.
(Kitchen, 1991, p. 8)

⁓⌒⚬⌒⁓

For a variety of reasons—the general lack of research on homeschooling, the recency of the movement, the difficulty of engaging the work—research on the impacts of homeschooling on "graduates," or what Knowles and Muchmore (1995) refer to as the long-term effects of homeschooling, is in very short supply. While there is no shortage of theories on what Galloway and Sutton (1995) call the products of homeschools, few data are available to inform that discussion. When the data points that have been produced over the last quarter century are compiled, the emerging narrative conveys a story of homeschoolers who (a) are reasonably successful adults and (b) are holding their own vis-à-vis conventionally schooled youngsters (Cochran, 1995; Knowles & Muchmore, 1995; Ray, 2000a). That narrative, as told by Julie Webb (1989), comprises four chapters: further education, employment, social ability, and community engagement. Ray (2004a) arrays the data in two chapters: general and civic involvement. Cochran (1995), in turn, packages product data into three broad chapters: employment, education, and social adjustment. Below, we build from these frameworks, placing posthomeschool graduation into four broad categories: college preparation, access, and success; success in the workforce and the military; participation in the community; and satisfaction with education and life and economic benefits.

College Preparation, Access, and Success

Parents and policy makers have the right to ask, Does homeschooling equip students to function effectively in colleges and universities?
(Luebke, 1999, p. 27)

~✦~

Empirical research on homeschoolers and their experiences at a college or university is scarce. (Sorey & Duggan, 2008, p. 24)

~✦~

Current evidence indicates that homeschoolers' college academic performance is comparable to that of traditionally educated students.
(Wood, 2003, p. 3)

~✦~

While there is more research on this posthomeschool outcome than on most others, the empirical portfolio is still relatively thin (Cogan, 2010; Saunders, 2010). On the issue of *preparation,* evidence has been generated in two areas: perceptions of significant actors in the chronicle and test scores. In the first area, when asked, college admission officers have assessed homeschoolers as being academically and socially prepared to handle the rigors of college life (Prue, 1997; Sorey & Duggan, 2008), and at least as well prepared as graduates of public high schools (Jenkins, 1998).

In the second area, test scores, researchers find that homeschoolers demonstrate academic preparedness equal to graduates of public schools on measures of verbal, writing, and critical thinking skills (Galloway & Sutton, 1995; Oliveira et al., 1994). Two investigators have found that homeschool students score as well as or better than their public school peers on college entrance examinations, both the ACT and the SAT (Cogan, 2010; Ray & Weller, 2003). Early indications are that homeschooled youngsters apply to and are admitted to postsecondary education in proportions similar to their conventionally educated peers (Lips & Feinberg, 2008; Ray, 1997b). They are enrolling in some of the nation's most distinguished institutions of higher education as well (Basham et al., 2007; Gaither, 2008; Marean, Ott, & Rush, 2005).

So far, the research shows that once enrolled, homeschooled students in colleges and universities are performing as well as public school graduates (Ray, 2009b), remembering that the body of evidence is small (Cogan, 2010; D. W. Gray, 1998; Prue, 1997). As with preparedness, the data on *success* is of two types, perceptual and harder indicators. On the perceptual side of the ledger, researchers such as Jenkins (1998), Ray (2005), and Sorey and Duggan (2008) reveal that college admissions officers report that homeschooled youngsters are as successful as (or better than) public school graduates. Harder measures of student success also dot the impact literature. Turning first to earned grades, findings of equivalence are present here as well (D. W. Gray, 1998; Galloway & Sutton, 1995; Oliveira et al., 1994). The operational hypothesis at this point in time is as follows: There are few, if any, meaningful differences in retention and academic performance in college between homeschooled students and peers from public schools (Saunders, 2010).

Sutton and Galloway (2000) assessed additional domains of success beyond academic achievement. They bundled 40 discrete indicators of success into five broad impact categories: achievement, leadership, professional aptitude, social behavior, and physical activity. They reported equivalence between homeschoolers and public school graduates on all the domains. Their interpretation follows:

> Implications from the nonsignificant results are mixed for home schools. First and foremost, the fact that neither the public school nor the private school groups significantly outperformed the home school group is noteworthy. . . . Conversely, however, the inability of the home school group to outperform their private and public school counterparts academically suggests that home school students are not generalizing their exceedingly high K–12 achievement scores to the college level. (p. 143)

Research on postsecondary graduation rates of homeschooled students is very limited. We have a few empirical starting points (Cogan, 2010; Ray, 2004b) but no body of evidence.

Success in the Workforce and the Military

Exceedingly little information is available in the literature about the further employment careers of home-educated people. (J. Webb, 1989, p. 128)

∽Ↄᵻↄ∼

By most measures, homeschool [military] recruits fail to match the performance of traditional high school graduates.
(Wenger & Hodari, 2004, p. 45)

∽Ↄᵻↄ∼

We begin our discussion here with a recurring theme: A very thin data base from which to draw conclusions dominates this impact domain. In one early study, Knowles and Muchmore (1995) reported that homeschooled adults tended to move into entrepreneurial and professional positions. In his comprehensive study, Ray (2004a) documented remarkably high levels of satisfaction with their jobs among homeschooled adults, with 61.4% being very satisfied and 34.5% expressing moderate satisfaction.

We were able to uncover only one robust examination of the success of homeschooled graduates in the military. While the investigators are careful to specify the limitations of their study, especially in terms of the small and likely nonrepresentative sample of homeschoolers who enter the armed services, their conclusions, nonetheless, reflect poorly on homeschoolers. Specifically, compared to public school graduates, Wenger and Hodari (2004) documented that homeschoolers (a) have significantly higher attrition rates, (b) are less likely to enter the military at an advanced pay grade (a measure of quality), (c) are more likely to be admitted on a waiver (another measure of quality), (d) are more likely to exit the military for negative reasons, and (e) are not viewed as high quality at the time they leave the armed forces.

Participation in the Community

Most of the concerns about and objections to homeschooling are worries about whether homeschooled children will grow up to be good citizens. (Arai, 1999, p. 2)

∽Ↄᵻↄ∼

The research base on adults who were home educated is growing; thus far it indicates that they participate in local community services more frequently than does the general population. (Ray, 2009b, p. 3)

∽Ↄᵻↄ∼

Consistent with the findings on the socialization of homeschooling youngsters and the social and civic engagement of their parents (Lines,

2000a), available research finds that homeschooled adults also participate in community-based activities at rates much higher than those found in the general population (Ray, 2005). Two studies, in particular, open a window on this issue. In the mid-1990s, Knowles and Muchmore (1995) reported that homeschooled adults were not disengaged socially or civically. In a comprehensive analysis of the issue a decade later, Ray (2004a) documented that homeschooled adults were indeed heavily involved in community life at the local and national levels and were more civically involved than the general population of adults. He found that compared to public school graduates, homeschooled adults were more likely to vote; be involved in ongoing community service; be part of an organization; write, telephone, or sign petitions; and participate in a protest or boycott.

Satisfaction With Education and Life and Economic Benefits

There are some clues in the empirical literature that youngsters who complete their education at home enjoy higher life satisfaction ratings than peers who graduate from public schools (Basham et al., 2007). In a similar vein, there is evidence that they view their homeschooling experiences quite positively (Knowles & Muchmore, 1995; Ray, 2004a). Again, these data are in line with the limited findings on satisfaction when students are engaged in the homeschooling experience (Duvall et al., 1997; Jackson, 2007). One good but indirect measure of satisfaction is a willingness and commitment of homeschooled adults to homeschool their own children (J. Webb, 1989). Using this measure, we learn that homeschooled adults are very satisfied with the education they received (Meighan, 1995; Ray, 2004a).

While we know that homeschooling decisions are rarely made on the basis of cost-benefit calculations, there are no available studies on economic benefits to homeschool graduates (Aurini & Davies, 2005).

❖ CONCLUSION

In this chapter, we examined the impact of homeschooling, the outcomes of the movement. We began with a review of the quality of the research on homeschooling, noting several times that the existing data base severely limits the conclusions that can be drawn about the effects of homeschooling. We also took the research community to task for their myopic view of outcomes worth assessing, especially the infatuation with academic achievement results at the expense of reasons why homeschooling occurs in families. We reviewed broad measures of outcomes first and then turned our attention to what can be said about the outcomes of homeschooling on participants in and graduates of homeschooling, both children and adults.

8

Hunches

Explanations for Positive Effects

In short, it is very difficult to identify what it is about the provision of home-schooling that should lead to better or worse academic performance. (Belfield, 2005, p. 169)

～◠◡◠～

Regarding the cause of these children's high academic achievement, however, there is little consensus and the problem has not been thoroughly investigated. (Ray, 1997b, p. 99)

～◠◡◠～

❖ THE CONTEXT

The theoretical evidence is limited. (Belfield, 2005, p. 169)

～◠◡◠～

In the previous chapter, we investigated the impact of homeschooling on society and students. There and across earlier chapters we uncovered clues about the causal chains in these impact equations. Here we pull together these explanations for the positive influence of homeschools on the academic and social learning of youngsters. We begin with a few important explanatory and cautionary notes.

First, the logic model we construct does not warrant a conclusion of uniform positive effects. As we have seen throughout earlier chapters, generalized conclusions do not apply to all homeschools. Second, it is instructive to remember that key elements in the causal chain (e.g., flexibility over curriculum) that are often positively charged can accept negatives charges as well. Or as Kunzman (2009a) reminds us, variables can be employed in the service of learning or can hinder growth. Third, there is an implicit theory in the homeschool literature that leaves much to be desired. It runs as follows: If you take responsibility away from some entity that may not be performing adequately (e.g., the school) and give it to someone else (e.g., the home), conditions and outcomes will improve. Fourth, as with most dimensions of homeschooling we have explored so far, "believing is seeing" (Lotto, 1983). Alternative understandings and counterfactuals are routinely ignored in explaining the effects of homeschooling. Fifth, as we have taken care to note throughout, family background characteristics remain important elements in the success equation (Lips & Feinberg, 2008). It is distinctly possible that absent indicators of high socioeconomic status, explanations for homeschooling success may be much less relevant. Sixth, there are limited theoretical foundations for understanding how homeschools influence academic and social learning. Most of what we do know comes not from work in homeschools but from general theories of learning. Seventh, and most important, there are almost no empirical studies that specifically explore the question of *how* homeschooling impacts student learning.

With these cautionary notes in mind, it is possible to begin to build an incipient logic model about the linkages between the practice of homeschooling and student achievement and social development. The planks for such a theory of action have been suggested by analysts as far back as Holt (1981) and Moore (1982) and as recently as Ray (2010). Colfax and Colfax (1988) propose that homeschools are more effective than public schools because they often offer advantages in four areas: they allow for more control, they are more efficient, they nurture autonomy, and they promote creativity. Other analysts throw the spotlight on the schooling process. For example, Ray (2009a, p. 4) maintains that homeschools promote "practices, relationships, and environments" that lead to academic and social learning. More concretely still, a variety of reviewers suggest that homeschools work because they promote conditions (e.g., learning time, parental involvement) that are linked to learning outcomes, and they do so more vigorously than do public schools (Belfield, 2004a; Duvall, Ward, Delquadri, & Greenwood, 1997; Ray, 2000a).

❖ A THEORY OF ACTION

Parental Involvement

When parental involvement in children's education is high, students are more likely to become academically successful and reach their potential.
(Romanowski, 2001, p. 80)

When we look at high test scores for a home school student, we are seeing, among other things, the fruits of a highly motivated, active, and interested parent participating in the life of the child.
(Lubienski, 2000, p. 223)

If there is a beginning point in the logic of action for homeschooling's impact, it is most likely parental involvement (see Figure 8.1). It is also the keystone variable in the success algorithm. It includes the massive amounts of time and energy that parents invest in the education of their children (Dahlquist, York-Barr, & Hendel, 2006). Equally important, it encompasses personal accountability for the academic and social development of children (V. Taylor, 2005).

Figure 8.1   The Influence of Homeschooling on Student Learning: A Logic Model

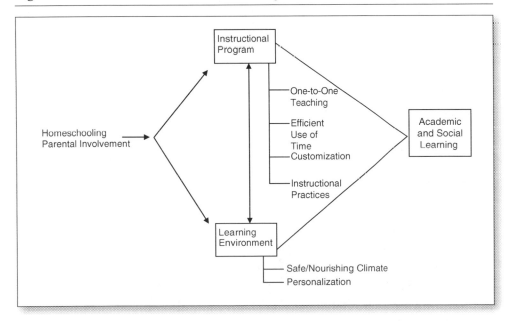

Instructional Program

> *Home schools, when compared to special education programs, provided*
> *equal if not more advantageous instructional environments for children*
> *with learning disabilities. (Duvall et al., 1997, p. 165)*

⌒◦⌒

One–to–One Instruction

> *An important part of the educational effectiveness of home*
> *instruction is the proved tutorial method that it embodies.*
> *(Whitehead & Bird, 1984, pp. 98–99)*

⌒◦⌒

> *Another element that might explain home educated students' academic*
> *success is tutoring. Many home educated children are essentially tutored.*
> *That is, they have private instructors, their parents, in a one-to-one or*
> *small group instructional setting. (Ray, 1997b, p. 94)*

⌒◦⌒

Many reviewers have expressed concern (or documented the concerns of others) about the professional competence of parents to effectively instruct their children in the home (Gaither, 2008; Gladin, 1987; Luke, 2003). Those apprehensions center on pedagogical skills (Duvall, 2005; Romanowski, 2001) and curricular content knowledge (Kunzman, 2009a; M. Martin, 1997; Mirochnik & McIntire, 1991), logical worries given the centrality of quality instruction and rigorous curriculum in the school effects research. At the same time, the literature on homeschooling consistently suggests that this mode of schooling promotes high amounts of one-to-one instruction (Lange & Liu, 1999; Lyman, 1998; Mayberry, 1989b). It also bundles evidence, generally in domains other than homeschools, that this one-to-one design is an especially effective strategy for promoting student learning (Blok, 2004; Duvall, 2005; Whitehead & Bird, 1984). That is, bringing student–teacher ratios to very low levels is good for the social and academic development of youngsters (Belfield, 2004a; Moore, 1982).

What is especially interesting in the homeschooling literature is the deeply embedded but rarely surfaced assumption that extensive one-to-one engagement is more important than pedagogical technique, the belief that personalized time can trump instructional expertise when the student–teacher ratio is extremely low (Duvall, Delquadri, & Ward, 2004; Duval et al., 2007). There is no work from the homeschool literature that examines what would be possible on the learning front if the one-to-one format and pedagogical expertise were combined.

Efficient Use of Time

Use of instruction time is considerably more efficient at home than it is in schools. (Blok, 2004, p. 49)

⁓ᴑᵛᴑ⁓

This alone—academically engaged time—may be the major factor accounting for homeschoolers' high scores on standardized testing. (Hertzel, 1997, p. 78)

⁓ᴑᵛᴑ⁓

Time is universally judged to be a critical pattern in the learning mosaic. Analysts consistently suggest that homeschoolers are successful because they receive more of this critical commodity than do their peers in public and private schools (Parker, 1992). They also maintain that time is used more effectively in homeschools, that there is greater efficiency in learning (Meighan, 1995).

To begin with, the logic and the very limited data that are available hold that homeschooled children spend more time engaged in learning than their peers even when their "school days" are shorter (Holt, 1981; Ray, 1997b). That is, they receive more academic learning time (Duvall et al., 1997, 2004). There is also a sense that time is used more productively in the one-to-one format we described above than in the traditional classroom. Less time, it is argued, is lost (Ray, 1997b) as lessons are aligned with the individual needs of the homeschooled child (Duvall et al., 1997) and "time-consuming activities (or nonactivities) are trimmed" (Parker, 1992, p. 55), activities such as test preparation. Down time is much less of a problem (Parker, 1992). And for some families homeschooling is a year-round experience (Gorder, 1990).

Customization

Homeschooling offers opportunities to take different, more individualized approaches to instruction and curriculum in order to capitalize on students' interests and learning preferences and community learning opportunities. (Jaycox, 2001, p. 3)

⁓ᴑᵛᴑ⁓

Homeschooling provides instructional differentiation that is taboo in many public schools, and that is often impossible within the physical confines of schools of any type. (Erickson, 2005, p. 22)

⁓ᴑᵛᴑ⁓

There is a recurring theme in the literature that the instructional program in homeschools works because it fosters a high degree of customization of learning experiences. The starting point, it is held, is that considerable flexibility is permissible in homeschools (S. Gray, 1993; Meighan, 1995; Romanowski, 2001). This flexibility, it is argued, is translated into more individualistic as opposed to collective approaches to learning (Ray, 2004b; V. Taylor, 2005).

Customization, analysts suggest, can and does play out across an array of dimensions in homeschools. Commonly, it is reported that customization permits parents to tailor programs of study, especially the curriculum, to the experiences, culture, needs, and interests of their children (M. Martin, 1997; McKeon, 2007; Ray, 2000a, 2009a). It is asserted that the lockstep, same-for-everyone approach that dominates classes with large numbers of students can be discarded in homeschools (Blok, 2004; Parker, 1992; Romanowski, 2001). Customization also allows the instructional program to be tailored to the appropriate level of challenge (Ensign, 1998). Relatedly, pacing can be manipulated much more easily for a single child or small cluster of students (i.e., in homeschools) than it can in classes of youngsters (Jackson, 2007; Kunzman, 2009a; Lyman, 2000). Strategies such as ability grouping and tracking come off the table in homeschools (Gorder, 1990; V. Taylor, 2005). Customization can also open the door to greater use of natural and experiential learning opportunities (Dahlquist et al., 2006; Knowles, Muchmore, & Spaulding, 1994; Parker, 1992). Homeschooling, reviewers regularly claim, also permits customization of content and method to fit the learning style of the child, something that is much more difficult to accomplish in traditional schools (Mayberry, 1993; McKeon, 2007).

Instructional Practices

Researchers and educators find that homeschooling lends itself, systematically, to several practices found to be desirable in classroom schooling. (Ray, 2005, p. 15)

∼◠❖◠∽

Immediate feedback on assignments can be done with great success in the homeschool setting, whereas it is a greater challenge to give immediate feedback in the traditional school setting with a larger student/teacher ratio. (Hertzel, 1997, p. 71)

∼◠❖◠∽

A variety of reviewers also suggest that homeschooling promotes academic and social learning by providing structures that encourage good instructional practices to flourish. For example, we know that feedback to students is essential for growth. Analysts routinely claim that it is easier to provide meaningful feedback in the one-on-one situations that define homeschooling than in large classes found in conventional schools (Hertzel, 1997; Whitehead & Bird, 1984). Homeschooling, it is suggested by some, also makes it easier to integrate subject matter (Parker, 1992; Scheps, 1998).

More extensive, two-way dialogue between adults and children is possible in homeschools. More specifically, as Duvall and colleagues (2004) document, homeschooling has the potential to encourage active academic responses. The structure of homeschools also makes it more difficult for a child to coast or hide in the crowd (Parker, 1992). Supporters also argue that in homeschools it is easier for parents to teach using direct (authentic) experiences. Finally, some research finds that homeschooling is a good way to encourage student ownership of learning (Sheffer, 1995).

Learning Environment

Research on successful home schools has revealed that parents, often without knowledge of the effective learning environment literature, have constructed learning environments that promote the type of norms, values, and relationships research has demonstrated to positively affect academic achievement. (Mayberry, 1993, p. 61)

Safe and Nourishing Climate

[Another] element that might explain the high academic achievement of the home educated deals with social interaction. To put it simply, the home educated do not have to deal with the constant distractions that are attendant to a peer group. (Ray, 1997b, p. 97)

Throughout the literature on homeschooling there is a theme that good things happen to children because they find themselves in more productive learning environments than those often found in the average public school (Mayberry, 1993; Montgomery, 1989). On the one hand, this means the development of a climate that is safe and orderly, a nonthreatening culture in which the academic work of school can unfold (Mayberry, 1993; Ray, 2009a). Particularly important here, analysts inform us, is the elimination of the negative peer culture sometimes seen in conventional schools (Medlin, 2000; Parker, 1992; J. Taylor, 1986a). In its stead, one often finds a supportive culture that grows from committed families and loving parents (Gustavsen, 1981; Moore & Moore, 1981; Romanowski, 2001).

Personalization

Homeschooling does foster a stronger, more influential connection among families and offers a chance for parents and teens to relate at a deeper level than usual simply because they spend so much time together.
(Boone, 2000, p. 29)

The emotional bond between the parent and the child provides another reason why this kind of schooling is so effective. (Gorder, 1990, p. 31)

~⌒⌒~

On a second front, a positive learning environment is made possible by the nurturing relationships that seem to be more easily forged in homeschools. Homeschools, it is argued, need not develop the institutional scaffolding and impersonality that define conventional schools (Medlin, 2000; Smith & Sikkink, 1999). The key here is the development in homeschools of a highly personalized climate in which the child is known, cared for, and respected more deeply than is possible in models of collective schooling (Moore, 1982; Ray, 1997b). Holt (1981, 1983), for example, consistently maintained that the absence of the "professional distance" found in conventional schools sets the stage for enhanced learning among homeschoolers. On the positive side of the story ledger, research confirms that these personalized environments are key in the student learning equation (Murphy, Beck, Crawford, & Hodges, 2001) and that such climates define homeschools (Wartes, 1988). Teachers in the home are more likely to know children well (Holt, 1981). They maintain more personal connections than are found in conventional schools (Moore, 1982). There is significant potential for the forging of strong bonds between children and parents. Or as Ray (1997b, 2000a) has regularly reminded us, it is easier for positive social capital to accumulate in homeschools than in other forms of schooling.

❖ CONCLUSION

In this final chapter, we took a look behind the curtain to see what might explain the positive effects of homeschools on the academic and social learning of children. We proposed a theory of action beginning with parental involvement that in turn leads to productive instructional programs and learning environments for children. We close with a caveat. Our model is speculative at best. Theory built from material from homeschools is quite limited, and research that examines reasons for the positive outcomes of homeschools is in very short supply.

References

Allie-Carson, J. (1990). Structure and interaction patterns of home school families. *Home School Researcher, 6*(3), 11–18.

Anderson, V. E., & Gruhn, W. T. (1962). *Principles and practices of secondary education* (2nd ed.). New York, NY: Ronald.

Apostoleris, N. H. (1999, April). *The development of children's motivation in the homeschool setting.* Paper presented at the Biennial Meeting of the Society for Research in Child Development, Albuquerque, NM.

Apple, M. (2000a). Away with all teachers: The cultural politics of home schooling. *International Studies in Sociology of Education, 10*(1), 61–80.

Apple, M. (2000b). The cultural politics of home schooling. *Peabody Journal of Education, 75,* 256–271.

Apple, M. (2005). Away with all teachers: The cultural politics of home schooling. In B. S. Cooper (Ed.), *Home schooling in full view* (pp. 75–95). Greenwich, CT: Information Age.

Apple, M. (2007). Who needs teacher education? Gender, technology, and the work of home schooling. *Teacher Education Quarterly, 34*(2), 111–130.

Arai, B. (1999). Homeschooling and the redefinition of citizenship. *Education Policy Analysis Archives, 7*(27), 1–15.

Arai, B. (2000). Reasons for home schooling in Canada. *Canadian Journal of Education, 25,* 204–217.

Armon, J. (1990). Is home schooling for everyone? In A. Pederson & P. O'Mara (Eds.), *Schooling at home: Parents, kids, and learning* (pp. 218–224). Santa Fe, NM: John Muir.

Aurini, J., & Davies, S. (2005). Choice without markets: Homeschooling in the context of private education. *British Journal of Sociology of Education, 26,* 461–474.

Barker, P. (1990). The home schooled teenager grows up. In A. Pederson & P. O'Mara (Eds.), *Schooling at home: Parents, kids, and learning* (p. 20). Santa Fe, NM: John Muir.

Barwegen, L., Falciani, N., Putnam, S., Reamer, M., & Stair, E. (2004). Academic achievement of homeschool and public school students and student perception of parent involvement. *School Community Journal, 14*(1), 39–58.

Basham, P., Merrifield, J., & Hepburn, C. (2007). *Home schooling: From the extreme to the mainstream.* Vancouver, British Columbia, Canada: Fraser Institute.

Bates, V. (1991). Lobbying for the Lord: The new Christian right home-schooling movement and grassroots lobbying. *Review of Religious Research, 33,* 3–17.

Bauman, K. (2002). Home schooling in the United States: Trends and characteristics. *Education Policy Analysis Archives, 10*(26), 1–21.

Bauman, P. C. (1996). Governing education in an antigovernment environment. *Journal of School Leadership, 6,* 625–643.

Beers, D., & Ellig, J. (1994). An economic view of the effectiveness of public and private schools. In S. Hakim, P. Seidenstat, & G. W. Bowman (Eds.), *Privatizing education and educational choice: Concepts, plans, and experiences* (pp. 19–38). Westport, CT: Praeger.

Belfield, C. (2004a). *Home-schooling in the US* (Occasional Paper No. 88). New York, NY: Columbia University, Teachers College, National Center for the Study of Privatization in Education.

Belfield, C. (2004b). Modeling school choice: A comparison of public, private-independent, private-religious, and home-schooled families. *Education Policy and Analysis Archives, 12*(30), 1–16.

Belfield, C. (2005). Home schoolers: How well do they perform on the SAT for college admissions? In B. S. Cooper (Ed.), *Home schooling in full view* (pp. 167–177). Greenwich, CT: Information Age.

Bell, P., & Cloke, P. (1990). Concepts of privatization and deregulation. In P. Bell & P. Cloke (Eds.), *Deregulation and transport: Market forces in the modern world* (pp. 3–27). London, UK: David Fulton.

Bennett, J. T., & DiLorenzo, T. J. (1987). The role of tax-funded politics. In S. H. Hanke (Ed.), *Prospects for privatization. Proceedings of the Academy of Political Science* (Vol. 36, No 3; pp. 14–23). Montpelier, VT: Capital City Press.

Bennett, J. T., & Johnson, M. H. (1980). Tax reduction without sacrifice: Private-public production of public services. *Public Finance Quarterly, 8,* 363–396.

Berliner, D. (1997). Educational psychology meets the Christian right: Differing views of children, schooling, teaching, and learning. *Teachers College Record, 98,* 381–416.

Bielick, S. (2008). *1.5 million homeschooled students in the United States in 2007.* Washington, DC: National Center for Education Statistics.

Bielick, S., Chandler, K., & Broughman, S. (2001). Homeschooling in the United States: 1999. *Education Statistics Quarterly, 3*(3), 1–13.

Blok, H. (2004). Performance in home schooling: An argument against compulsory schooling in the Netherlands. *International Review of Education, 50,* 39–52.

Boone, J. (2000). Homeschool alumni. *Paths of Learning: Options for Families & Communities, 3,* 25–30.

Boyer, W. (2002). Exploring home schooling. *International Journal of Early Childhood, 34*(2), 19–29.

Brazer, H. E. (1981). On tax limitation. In N. Walzer & D. L. Chicoine (Eds.), *Financing state and local governments in the 1980s* (pp. 9–34). Cambridge, MA: Oelgeschlager, Gunn & Hain.

Buchanan, J. M. (1987). *Economics: Between predictive science and moral philosophy.* College Station: Texas A&M University Press.

Bulkley, K. E. (1998). *Telling stories: The political construction of charter schools* (Unpublished doctoral dissertation). Stanford University, Palo Alto, CA.

Burns, J. (1999). *The correlational relationship between homeschooling demographics and high test scores* (Unpublished manuscript). Northeastern State University, Broken Arrow, OK.

Butler, S. (1991). Privatization for public purposes. In W. T. Gormley (Ed.), *Privatization and its alternatives* (pp. 17–24). Madison: University of Wisconsin Press.

Cai, Y., Reeve, J., & Robinson, D. (2002). Home schooling and teaching style: Comparing the motivating styles of home school and public school teachers. *Journal of Educational Psychology, 94,* 372–380.

Callahan, R. E. (1962). *Education and the cult of efficiency.* Chicago, IL: University of Chicago Press.

Calvery, R., Bell, D., & Vaupel, C. (1992, November). *The difference in achievement between home schooled and public schooled students for grades four, seven, and ten in Arkansas.* Paper presented at the annual meeting of the Mid-South Research Association, Knoxville, TN.

Carper, J. (2000). Pluralism to establishment to dissent: The religious and educational context of home schooling. *Peabody Journal of Education, 75,* 8–19.

Carroll, B. J., Conant, R. W., & Easton, T. A. (1987). Introduction. In B. J. Carroll, R. W. Conant, & T. A. Easton (Eds.), *Private means, public ends: Private business in social service delivery* (pp. ix–xiii). New York, NY: Praeger.

Caruana, V. (1999). Partnering with homeschoolers. *Educational Leadership, 57*(1), 58–60.

Chatham-Carpenter, A. (1994). Home versus public schoolers: Differing social opportunities. *Home School Researcher, 10*(1), 15–24.

Cibulka, J. (1991). State regulation of home schooling: A policy analysis. In J. Van Galen & M. Pittman (Eds.), *Homeschooling: Political, historical, and pedagogical perspectives* (pp. 101–120). Norwood, NJ: Ablex.

Cibulka, J. G. (1996). Afterword: Interpreting the religious impulse in American schooling. *Education and Urban Society, 28,* 378–387.

Cizek, G. (1993). The mismeasure of home schooling effectiveness (a commentary). *Home School Researcher, 9*(3), 1–4.

Clements, A. (2002, March). *Variety of teaching methodologies used by homeschoolers: Case studies of three homeschooling families.* Paper presented at the Annual Meeting of the Eastern Educational Research Association, Sarasota, FL.

Cochran, C. (1995). *The home school movement in the U.S.: Georgia as a test case, 1979–1984* (Unpublished doctoral dissertation). Emory University, Atlanta, GA.

Cogan, M. F. (2010). Exploring academic outcomes of homeschooled students. *Journal of College Admission, 208,* 18–25.

Colfax, D. (1990). Beyond the classroom. In A. Pederson & P. O'Mara (Eds.), *Schooling at home: Parents, kids, and learning* (pp. 191–199). Santa Fe, NM: John Muir.

Colfax, D., & Colfax, M. (1988). *Homeschooling for excellence.* New York, NY: Warner Books.

Collom, E. (2005). The ins and outs of homeschooling: The determinants of parental motivations and student achievement. *Education and Urban Society, 37,* 307–335.

Collom, E., & Mitchell, D. (2005). Home schooling as a social movement: Identifying the determinants of homeschoolers' perceptions. *Sociological Spectrum, 25,* 273–305.

Committee for Economic Development. (1994). *Putting learning first: Governing and managing the schools for high achievement.* New York, NY: Author.

Consortium on Productivity in the Schools. (1995). *Using what we have to get the schools we need.* New York, NY: Columbia University, Teachers College, Institute on Education and the Economy.

Cooper, B. S. (2005). Preface: An introduction to homeschooling. In B. S. Cooper (Ed.), *Home schooling in full view* (pp. ix–xix). Greenwich, CT: Information Age.

Cooper, B. S., & Sureau, J. (2007). The politics of homeschooling: New developments, new challenges. *Educational Policy, 21,* 110–131.

Cremin, L. A. (1955). The revolution in American secondary education, 1893–1918. *Teachers College Record, 56,* 295–308.

Cremin, L. A. (1961). *The transformation of the school: Progressivism in American education 1876–1957.* New York, NY: Vintage.

Cronin, T. E. (1989). *Direct democracy: The politics of initiative, referendum, and recall.* Cambridge, MA: Harvard University Press.

Dahlquist, K., York-Barr, J., & Hendel, D. D. (2006). The choice to homeschool: Home educator perspectives and school district options. *Journal of School Leadership, 16,* 354–385.

Dahrendorf, R. (1995, Summer). A precarious balance. Economic opportunity, civil society, and political liberty. *The Responsive Community,* 13–39.

Dalaimo, D. (1996). Community home education: A case study of a public school–based home schooling program. *Educational Research Quarterly, 19*(4), 3–22.

De Alessi, L. (1987). Property rights and privatization. In S. H. Hanke (Ed.), *Prospects for privatization. Proceedings of the Academy of Political Science* (Vol. 36, No. 3; pp. 24–35). Montpelier, VT: Capital City Press.

Delahooke, M. (1986). *Home educated children's social/emotional adjustment and academic achievement: A comparative study* (Unpublished doctoral dissertation). California School of Professional Psychology, Los Angeles, CA.

Divoky, D. (1983). The new pioneers of the home-schooling movement. *Phi Delta Kappan, 64,* 395–398.

Dobson, L. (2001). *The first year homeschooling your child: Your complete guide to getting off to the right start.* Roseville, CA: Prima.

Donahue, J. D. (1989). *The privatization decision: Public ends, private means.* New York, NY: Basic Books.

Dowity, T., & Cowlishaw, K. (2002). *Home educating our autistic spectrum children: Paths are made by walking.* London, UK: Jessica Kingsley.

Downs, A. (1967). *Inside bureaucracy.* Boston, MA: Little, Brown.

Dudek & Company. (1989). *Privatization and public employees: The impact of city and county contracting out on government works* (Report No. NCEP-RR-88-07). Washington, DC: U.S. National Commission for Employment Policy.

Duvall, S. F. (2005). The effectiveness of homeschooling students with special needs. In B. S. Cooper (Ed.), *Home schooling in full view* (pp. 151–166). Greenwich, CT: Information Age.

Duvall, S., Delquadri, J., & Ward, D. (2004). A preliminary investigation of the effectiveness of homeschool instructional environments for students with attention-deficit/hyperactivity disorder. *School Psychology Review, 33,* 140–158.

Duvall, S., Ward, D. L., Delquadri, J., & Greenwood, C. (1997). An exploratory study of home school instructional environments and their effects on the basic skills of students with learning disabilities. *Education and Treatment of Children, 20,* 150–172.

Elmore, R. F. (1993). School decentralization: Who gains? Who loses? In J. Hannaway & M. Carnoy (Eds.), *Decentralization and school improvement* (pp. 35–54). San Francisco, CA: Jossey-Bass.

Ensign, J. (1997). *Homeschooling gifted students: An introductory guide for parents.* Reston, VA: Council for Exceptional Children, ERIC Clearinghouse on Disabilities and Gifted Education.

Ensign, J. (1998, April). *Defying the stereotypes of special education: Homeschool students.* Paper presented at the Annual Meeting of the American Educational Research Association, San Diego, CA.

Erickson, D. A. (2005). Homeschooling and the common school nightmare. In B. S. Cooper (Ed.), *Home schooling in full view* (pp. 21–44). Greenwich, CT: Information Age.

Fager, J., & Brewster, C. (2000). *Making positive connections with homeschoolers.* Washington, DC: U.S. Department of Education, Office of Educational Research and Improvement.

Farenga, P. (1990). Home schoolers and college. In A. Pederson & P. O'Mara (Eds.), *Schooling at home: Parents, kids, and learning* (pp. 208–217). Santa Fe, NM: John Muir.

Farenga, P. (1998). Homeschooling: Creating alternatives to education. *Bulletin of Science, Technology & Society, 18,* 127–133.

Farris, M., & Woodruff, S. (2000). The future of home schooling. *Peabody Journal of Education, 75,* 233–255.

Finn, C. E., Manno, B. V., & Vanourek, G. (2000). *Charter schools in action: Renewing public education.* Princeton, NJ: Princeton University Press.

Fitzgerald, R. (1988). *When government goes private: Successful alternatives to public services.* New York, NY: Universe Books.

Florestano, P. S. (1991). Considerations for the future. In R. L. Kemp (Ed.), *Privatization: The provision of public services by the private sector* (pp. 291–296). Jefferson, NC: McFarland.

Frost, E., & Morris, R. (1988). Does home-schooling work? Some insights for academic success. *Contemporary Education, 59,* 223–227.

Frost, G. (1988). The academic success of students in home schooling. *Illinois School Research and Development, 24*(3), 111–117.

Fuller, B., Elmore, R. F., & Orfield, G. (1996). Policy-making in the dark: Illuminating the school choice debate. In B. Fuller, R. F. Elmore, & G. Orfield (Eds.), *Who chooses? Who loses? Culture, institutions, and the unequal effects of school choice* (pp. 1–21). New York, NY: Teachers College Press.

Fusarelli, L. D. (1999). Reinventing urban education in Texas: Charter schools, smaller schools, and the new institutionalism. *Education and Urban Society, 31,* 214–224.

Gaither, M. (2008). *Homeschool: An American history.* New York, NY: Palgrave MacMillan.

Galloway, R., & Sutton, J. (1995). Home schooled and conventionally schooled high school graduates: A comparison of aptitude for and achievement in college English. *Home School Researcher, 11*(1), 1–9.

Gatto, J. T. (1992). *Dumbing us down: The hidden curriculum of compulsory schooling.* Philadelphia, PA: New Society.

Gladin, E. (1987). *Home education: Characteristics of its families and schools* (Unpublished doctoral dissertation). Bob Jones University, Greenville, SC.

Glanzer, P. L. (2008). Rethinking the boundaries and burdens of parental authority over education: A response to Rob Reich's case study of homeschooling. *Educational Theory, 58*(1), 1–16.

Glenn, C. L. (2005). Homeschooling: Worldwide and compulsory state education. In B. S. Cooper (Ed.), *Home schooling in full view* (pp. 45–68). Greenwich, CT: Information Age.

Gorder, C. (1990). *Home schools: An alternative.* Tempe, AZ: Blue Bird.

Gormley, W. T. (1991). Two cheers for privatization. In W. T. Gormley (Ed.), *Privatization and its alternatives* (pp. 307–318). Madison: University of Wisconsin Press.

Gottfried, P. (1993). *The conservative movement* (Rev. ed.). New York, NY: Twayne.

Gray, D. W. (1998). *A study of the academic achievements of home-schooled students who have matriculated into postsecondary institutions* (Unpublished doctoral dissertation). University of Sarasota, Sarasota, FL.

Gray, S. (1993). Why some parents choose to home school. *Home School Researcher, 9*(4), 1–12.

Green, C., & Hoover-Dempsey, K. (2007). Why do parents homeschool? A systematic examination of parental involvement. *Education and Urban Society, 39,* 264–285.

Groover, S., & Endsley, R. (1988). *Family environment and attitudes of homeschoolers and non-homeschoolers* (Unpublished master's thesis). University of Georgia, Athens, GA.

Gustavsen, G. (1981). *Selected characteristics of home schools and parents who operate them* (Unpublished doctoral dissertation). Andrews University, Berrien Springs, MI.

Guterson, D. (1992). *Family matters: Why homeschooling makes sense.* New York, NY: Harcourt Brace Jovanovich.

Hadeed, H. (1991). Home schooling movement participation: A theoretical framework. *Home School Researcher, 7*(2), 1–9.

Hanke, S. H. (1985). The theory of privatization. In S. M. Butler (Ed.), *The privatization option: A strategy to shrink the size of government* (pp. 1–14). Washington, DC: Heritage Foundation.

Hanke, S. H., & Dowdle, B. (1987). Privatizing the public domain. In S. H. Hanke (Ed.), *Prospects for privatization: Proceedings of the Academy of Political Science* (Vol. 36, No. 3; pp. 114–123). Montpelier, VT: Capital City Press.

Hanna, L. G. (2011). Homeschooling education: Longitudinal study of methods, materials, and curricula. *Education and Urban Society, 43*(3), 1–23.

Hanson, E. M. (1991). *School-based management and educational reform: Cases in the USA and Spain.* East Lansing, MI: National Center for Research on Teacher Learning. (ERIC Document Reproduction Service No. ED336832.)

Hardenbaugh, N. (2005). Through the lens of homeschooling: A response to Michael Apple and Rob Reich. In B. S. Cooper (Ed.), *Home schooling in full view* (pp. 97–108). Greenwich, CT: Information Age.

Hardin, H. (1989). *The privatization putsch.* Halifax, Nova Scotia, Canada: Institute for Research on Public Policy.

Hartnett, M. K. (2005). *Choosing home: Deciding to homeschool with Asperger's syndrome.* London, UK: Jessica Kingsley.

Hassel, B. C. (1999). *The charter school challenge: Avoiding the pitfalls, fulfilling the promise.* Washington, DC: Brookings Institute.

Hegener, M., & Hegener, H. (1997). *The homeschool reader: Collected articles from Home Education Magazine, 1984–1994.* Tonasket, WA: Home Education Press.

Henry, S. (1997). Homeschooling is for everyone. In M. Hegener & K. Hegener (Eds.), *The homeschool reader: Collected articles from* Home Education Magazine, *1984–1994* (pp. 24–30). Tonasket, WA: Home Education Press.

Hertzel, J. (1997). Literacy in the homeschool setting. In P. H. Dreyer (Ed.), *Literacy: Building on what we know* (pp. 60–81). Claremont, CA: Claremont Reading.

Hilke, J. C. (1992). *Competition in government-financed services.* New York, NY: Quorum Books.

Hill, P. T. (1994). Public schools by contract: An alternative to privatization. In S. Hakim, P. Seidenstat, & G. W. Bowman (Eds.), *Privatizing education and educational choice: Concepts, plans, and experiences* (pp. 75–90). Westport, CT: Praeger.

Hill, P. T. (2000). Home schooling and the future of public education. *Peabody Journal of Education, 75,* 20–31.

Hill, P. T., & Bonan, J. (1991). *Decentralization and accountability in public education.* Santa Monica, CA: Rand.

Hill, P. T., Pierce, L. C., & Guthrie, J. W. (1997). *Reinventing public education: How contracting can transform America's schools.* Chicago, IL: University of Chicago Press.

Hirsch, W. Z. (1991). *Privatizing government services: An economic analysis of contracting out by local governments.* Los Angeles: University of California, Institute of Industrial Relations.

Holland, O. (2005). *Teaching at home: A new approach to tutoring children with autism and Asperger syndrome.* London, UK: Jessica Kingsley.

Holt Associates. (1999). *GWS back issues, Volume One, Issues 1–12 (August 1977–December 1979).* Cambridge, MA: Author.

Holt, J. (1964). *How children fail.* Lanham, MD: Pitman.

Holt, J. (1967). *How children learn.* Lanham, MD: Pitman.

Holt, J. (1972). *Freedom and beyond.* New York, NY: Dutton.

Holt, J. (1981). *Teach your own: A hopeful path for education.* New York, NY: Delacorte Press.

Holt, J. (1983). Schools and home schoolers: A fruitful partnership. *Phi Delta Kappan, 64,* 391–394.

Holt, J. (1997). Answers to a mother's questions. In M. Hegener & K. Hegener (Eds.), *The Homeschool reader: Collected articles from* Home Education Magazine, *1984–1994* (pp. 37–40). Tonasket, WA: Home Education Press.

Hood, C. (1994). *Explaining economic policy reversals.* Buckingham, UK: Open University Press.

Houston, R. (1999). *The economic determinants of home education* (Unpublished doctoral dissertation). University of Kentucky, Lexington, KY.

Houston, R., & Toma, E. (2003). Home schooling: An alternative school choice. *Southern Economic Journal, 69,* 920–935.

Hula, R. C. (1990a). Preface. In R. C. Hula (Ed.), *Market-based public policy* (pp. xiii–xiv). New York, NY: St. Martin's Press.

Hula, R. C. (1990b). Using markets to implement public policy. In R. C. Hula (Ed.), *Market-based public policy* (pp. 3–18). New York, NY: St. Martin's Press.

Ice, C. L., & Hoover-Dempsey, K. V. (2011). Linking parental motivations for involvement and student proximal achievement outcomes in homeschooling and public schooling settings. *Education and Urban Review, 43,* 339–369.

Isenberg, E. (2002). *Home schooling: School choice and women's time use.* New York, NY: Columbia University, Teachers College, National Center for the Study of Privatization in Education.

Isenberg, E. (2007). What have we learned about homeschooling? *Peabody Journal of Education, 82,* 387–409.

Ismael, J. S. (1988). Privatization of social services: A heuristic approach. In J. S. Ismael & Y. Vaillancourt (Eds.), *Privatization and provincial social services in Canada* (pp. 1–11). Edmonton, Alberta, Canada: University of Alberta Press.

Jackson, G. (2007). Home education transitions with formal schooling: Student perspectives. *Issues in Educational Research, 17,* 62–84.

Jaycox, R. (2001). *Rural home schooling and place-based education.* Charleston, WV: ERIC Clearinghouse on Rural Education and Small Schools.

Jenkins, T. (1998). *The performance of home schooled students in community colleges* (Unpublished doctoral dissertation). Texas A&M University–Commerce, Commerce, TX.

Jeub, C. (1994). Why parents choose home schooling. *Educational Leadership, 52*(1), 50–52.

Jones, P., & Gloeckner, G. (2004). A study of admission officers' perceptions of and attitudes toward homeschool students. *Journal of College Admission, 185,* 12–21.

Kaseman, L., & Kaseman, S. (1999, July–August). HSLDA study: Embarrassing and dangerous. *Home Education Magazine.* Retrieved from http://homeedmag.com/home-education-magazine/

Katz, M. B. (1971). From voluntarism to bureaucracy in American education. *Sociology of Education, 44,* 297–332.

Katz, M. B. (1992). Chicago school reform as history. *Teachers College Record, 94,* 56–72.

Kelley, S. (1991). Socialization of home schooled children: A self-concept study. *Home School Researcher, 7*(4), 1–12.

Kerman, K. (1990). Home schooling day by day. In A. Pederson & P. O'Mara (Eds.), *Schooling at home: Parents, kids, and learning* (pp. 17–18). Santa Fe, NM: John Muir.

Kirschner, J. (1991). The shifting roles of family and school as educator: A historical perspective. In J. Van Galen & M. Pittman (Eds.), *Homeschooling: Political, historical, and pedagogical perspectives* (pp. 137–158). Norwood, NJ: Ablex.

Kitchen, P. (1991). Socialization of home school children versus conventional school children. *Home School Researcher, 7*(3) 7–13.

Kleist-Tesch, J. M. (1998). Homeschoolers and the public library. *Journal of Youth Services in Libraries, 11,* 231–241.

Klicka, C. J. (1995). *The right choice: The incredible failure of public education and the rising hope of home schooling: An academic, historical, practical, and legal perspective.* Gresham, OR: Noble.

Klicka, C. J. (2004). *Academic statistics on homeschooling.* Purcelville, VA: Home School Legal Defense Association.

Kliebard, H. M. (1995). *The struggle for the American curriculum 1893–1958* (2nd ed.). New York, NY: Routledge.

Klugewicz, S., & Carraccio, C. (1999). Home schooled children: A pediatric perspective. *Clinical Pediatrics, 38,* 407–411.

Knowles, J. G. (1988). Parents' rationales and teaching methods for homeschooling: The role of biography. *Education and Urban Society, 21,* 69–84.

Knowles, J. G. (1989). Cooperating with home school parents: A new agenda for public schools? *Urban Education, 23*, 392–411.

Knowles, J. G. (1991). Parents' rationales for operating home schools. *Journal of Contemporary Ethnography, 20*, 203–230.

Knowles, J. G., Marlow, S. E., & Muchmore, J. A. (1992). From pedagogy to ideology: Origins and phases of home education in the United States. *American Journal of Education 100*, 195–235.

Knowles, J. G., & Muchmore, J. A. (1995). Yep! We're grown up home-schooled kids—and we're doing just fine, thank you. *Journal of Research on Christian Education, 4*(1), 35–56.

Knowles, J. G., Muchmore, J. A., & Spaulding, H. W. (1994). Home education as an alternative to institutionalized education. *The Education Forum, 58*, 238–243.

Kolderie, T. (1994, February). Charter schools: States begin to withdraw the "exclusive." *Network News & Views*, 103–108.

Koos, L. (1927). *The American secondary school.* Boston, MA: Ginn.

Krug, E. A. (1964*). The shaping of the American high school.* New York, NY: Harper & Row.

Kunzman, R. (2005). *Homeschooling in Indiana: A closer look* (Education Policy Brief Vol. 3, No. 7). Bloomington: Indiana University, Center for Evaluation and Education Policy.

Kunzman, R. (2009a). Understanding homeschooling: A better approach to regulation. *Theory and Research in Education, /*, 311–330.

Kunzman, R. (2009b). *Write these laws on your children: Inside the world of conservative Christian homeschooling.* Boston, MA: Beacon Press.

Lange, C., & Liu, K. K. (1999). *Homeschooling: Parents' reasons for transfer and the implications for educational policy.* Minneapolis, MN: National Center on Educational Outcomes.

Lee, W. J. (1994). *The socialization of home-schooled and public-schooled children* (Unpublished doctoral dissertation). University of La Verne, La Verne, CA.

Leppert, M., & Leppert, M. (2001). *Homeschooling almanac 2002–2003.* Roseville, CA: Prima.

Lewis, D. A. (1993). Deinstitutionalization and school decentralization: Making the same mistake twice. In J. Hannaway & M. Carnoy (Eds.), *Decentralization and school improvement* (pp. 84–101). San Francisco, CA: Jossey-Bass.

Lines, P. M. (1987). An overview of home education. *Phi Delta Kappan, 68*, 510–517.

Lines, P. M. (1991). Home instruction: The size and growth of the movement. In J. Van Galen & M. Pittman (Eds.), *Homeschooling: Political, historical, and pedagogical perspectives* (pp. 9–42). Norwood, NJ: Ablex.

Lines, P. M. (1995). Home schooling. *ERIC Digest, No. 95.* Eugene: University of Oregon, ERIC Clearinghouse on Educational Management.

Lines, P. M. (1999). *Homeschoolers: Estimating numbers and growth.* Washington, DC: U.S. Department of Education, National Institute on Student Achievement, Curriculum, and Assessment.

Lines, P. M. (2000a). Homeschooling comes of age. *The Public Interest, 140*, 74–85.

Lines, P. M. (2000b). When home schoolers go to school: A partnership between families and schools. *Peabody Journal of Education, 75*, 159–186.

Lines, P. M. (2004). Enrolled home study partners with public schools. *Education Digest, 69*(6), 43–46.

Lips, D., & Feinberg, E. (2008). *Homeschooling: A growing option in American education*. Washington, DC: Heritage Foundation.

Little Hoover Commission. (1996). *The charter movement: Education reform school by school*. Sacramento, CA: Author. Retrieved from http://www.lhc.ca.gov/studies/138/report138.pdf

Lotto, L. S. (1983). Believing is seeing. *Organizational Theory Dialogue, 3*(1), 6–26.

Loveless, T., & Jasin, C. (1998). Starting from scratch: Political and organizational challenges facing charter schools. *Educational Administration Quarterly, 34,* 9–30.

Lubienski, C. (2000). Whither the common good? A critique of home schooling. *Peabody Journal of Education, 75,* 207–232.

Luebke, R. V. (1999). *Homeschooling in Wisconsin: A review of current issues and trends.* Milwaukee: Wisconsin Policy Research Institute.

Luke, C. (2003). Home schooling: Learning from dissent. *Canadian Journal of Educational Administration and Policy, 25.* Retrieved from http://www.umanitoba.ca/publications/cjeap/

Lyman, I. (1998). Homeschooling: Back to the future? *Policy Analysis, 294,* 1–15.

Lyman, I. (2000). *The homeschooling revolution.* Amherst, MA: Bench Press International.

Marean, J., Ott, M., & Rush, M. (2005). Home schooled students and the Ivy League: Gaining admissions to highly selective universities in the United States. In B. S. Cooper (Ed.), *Home schooling in full view* (pp. 179–197). Greenwich, CT: Information Age.

Marlow, S. (1994). Educating children at home: Implications for assessment and accountability. *Education and Urban Society, 26,* 438–460.

Marshall, J. D., & Valle, J. P. (1996). Public school reform: Potential lessons from the truly departed. *Education Policy Analysis Archives, 4*(12), 1–15.

Marshall, R., & Tucker, M. (1992). *Thinking for a living: Work, skills, and the future of the American economy.* New York, NY: Basic Books.

Martin, B. (1993). *In the public interest? Privatization and public sector reform.* London, UK: Zed Books.

Martin, M. (1997). *Homeschooling: Parents' reactions.* Retrieved from http://www.eric.ed.gov/PDFS/ED415984.pdf

Mathews, D. (1996). *Is there a public for public schools?* Dayton, OH: Kettering Foundation Press.

Mayberry, M. (1989a). Characteristics and attitudes of families who home school. *Education and Urban Society, 21,* 32–41.

Mayberry, M. (1989b). Home-based education in the United States: Demographics, motivations, and educational implications. *Educational Review, 41,* 171–180.

Mayberry, M. (1992). Home-based education: Parents as teachers. *Continuing Higher Education Review, 56,* 48–58.

Mayberry, M. (1993). Effective learning environments in action: The case of home schools. *School Community Journal, 3*(1), 61–68.

Mayberry, M., & Knowles, G. (1989). Family unity objectives of parents who teach their children: Ideological and pedagogical orientations to homeschooling. *Urban Review, 21,* 209–225.

Mayberry, M., Knowles, G., Ray, B., & Marlow, S. (1995). *Home schooling: Parents as educators.* Thousand Oaks, CA: Corwin.

McCulloch, D., Slocum, S., Kolegue, C., & Montaudo, S. (2006). Cynicism, trust, and internal-external locus of control among home educated students. *Academic Leadership, 4*(4). Retrieved from http://www.academicleadership.org

McCurdy, K. (1997). Why homeschool? In M. Hegener & K. Hegener (Eds.), *The homeschool reader: Collected articles from* Home Education Magazine, *1984–1994* (pp. 15–16). Tonasket, WA: Home Education Press.

McDowell, S., & Ray, B. (2000). The home education movement in context, practice, and theory: Editors' introduction. *Peabody Journal of Education, 75,* 1–7.

McDowell, S., Sanchez, A., & Jones, S. (2000). Participation and perception: Looking at home schooling through a multicultural lens. *Peabody Journal of Education, 75,* 124–146.

McGree, K. (1995). Charter schools: Early learnings. In *Insights on Education Policy and Practice* (No. 5). Austin, TX: Southwest Educational Development Laboratory.

McKeon, C. C. (2007). *A mixed methods nested analysis of homeschooling styles, instructional practices, and reading methodologies* (Doctoral dissertation). Retrieved from http://www.eric.ed.gov/PDFS/ED504128.pdf

Medlin, R. G. (1998). For homeschooled children, the social contacts are diverse. *Homeschooling Today, 7*(5), 51–52.

Medlin, R. G. (2000). Home schooling and the question of socialization. *Peabody Journal of Education, 75,* 107–123.

Meighan, R. (1995). Home-based education effectiveness: Research and some of its implications. *Educational Review, 47,* 275–287.

Miller, J. R., & Tufts, C. R. (1991). A means to achieve "more with less." In R. L. Kemp (Ed.), *Privatization: The provision of public services by the private sector* (pp. 97–109). Jefferson, NC: McFarland.

Mirochnik, D. A., & McIntire, W. G. (1991). *Homeschooling: Issues for administrators.* (Occasional Paper Series, No. 12). Orono: University of Maine.

Montgomery, L. (1989). The effect of home schooling on the leadership skills of home schooled students. *Home School Researcher, 5*(1), 1–10.

Moore, R. (1982). Research and common sense: Therapies for our homes and schools. *Teachers College Record, 84,* 355–377.

Moore, R., & Moore, D. (1981). *Home grown kids: A practical handbook for teaching your children at home.* Waco, TX: Word Books.

Moore, R., & Moore, D. (1994). *The successful homeschool family handbook: A creative and stress-free approach to homeschooling.* Camas, WA: Moore Foundation.

Muntes, G. (2006). Do parental reasons to homeschool vary by grade? Evidence from the National Household Educational Survey. *Home School Researcher, 16*(4), 11–17.

Murnane, R. J., & Levy, F. (1996). *Teaching the new basic skills: Principles for educating children to thrive in a changing economy.* New York, NY: Free Press.

Murphy, J. (1991). *Restructuring schools: Capturing and assessing the phenomena.* New York, NY: Teachers College Press.

Murphy, J. (1996). *The privatization of schooling: Problems and possibilities.* Newbury Park, CA: Corwin.

Murphy, J. (1999). New consumerism: The emergence of market-oriented governing structures for schools. In J. Murphy & K. S. Louis (Eds.), *The handbook of research on school administration.* San Francisco, CA: Jossey-Bass.

Murphy, J. (2000). Governing America's schools: The shifting playing field. *Teachers College Record, 102,* 57–84.

Murphy, J. (2006). The evolving nature of the American high school: A punctuated equilibrium model of institutional change. *Leadership and Policy in Schools, 5*(4), 285–324.

Murphy, J. (2010). *The educator's handbook for understanding and closing achievement gaps.* Thousand Oaks, CA: Corwin.

Murphy, J., Beck, L. G., Crawford, M., & Hodges, A. (2001). *The productive high school: Creating personalized academic communities.* Thousand Oaks, CA: Corwin.

Murphy, J., Gilmer, S., Weise, R., & Page, A. (1998). *Pathways to privatization in education.* Norwood, NJ: Ablex.

Murphy, J., & Meyers, C. V. (2008). *Turning around failing schools: Leadership lessons from the organizational sciences.* Thousand Oaks, CA: Corwin.

Murphy, J., & Shiffman, C. (2002). *Understanding and assessing charter schools.* New York, NY: Teachers College Press.

Nathan, J. (1996). *Charter schools: Creating hope and opportunity for American education.* San Francisco, CA: Jossey-Bass.

Nemer, K. M. (2002). *Understudied education: Toward building a homeschooling research agenda* (Occasional Paper). New York, NY: Columbia University, Teachers College, National Center for the Study of Privatization in Education.

Newlon, J. H. (1934). *Educational administration as social policy.* New York, NY: Scribner.

Niskanen, W. A. (1971). *Bureaucracy and representative government.* Chicago, IL: Aldine-Atherton.

Niskanen, W. A. (1994). *Bureaucracy and public economics.* Brookfield, VT: Edward Elgar.

Oliveira, P. C. M. de, Watson, T. G., & Sutton, J. P. (1994). Differences in critical thinking skills among students educated in public schools, Christian schools, and home schools. *Home School Researcher, 10*(4), 1–8.

Pack, J. R. (1991). The opportunities and constraints of privatization. In W. T. Gormley (Ed.), *Privatization and its alternatives* (pp. 281–306). Madison: University of Wisconsin Press.

Parker, R. D. (1992). *Inside home schools: A portrait of eighty-four Texas families and the schools in their homes* (Unpublished master's thesis). Texas Tech University, Lubbock, TX.

Payne, J. L. (1995). *Profiting from education: Incentive issues in contracting out.* Washington, DC: Education Policy Institute.

Pearson, R. C. (1996). *Homeschooling: What educators should know.* Retrieved from http://www.eric.ed.gov/PDFS/ED402135.pdf

Perry, J., & Perry, K. (2000). *The complete guide to homeschooling.* Los Angeles, CA: Lowell House.

Peterson, D. (2009). You can homeschool your child with special needs. *Exceptional Parent, 39*(5), 38–39.

Pines, B. Y. (1985). Foreword. In S. M. Butler (Ed.), *The privatization option: A strategy to shrink the size of government* (p. v). Washington, DC: Heritage Foundation.

Pirie, M. (1988). *Privatization.* Hants, UK: Wildwood House.

Pitman, M., & Smith, L. (1991). Culture acquisition in an intentional American community: A single case. In J. Van Galen & M. Pittman (Eds.), *Homeschooling: Political, historical, and pedagogical perspectives* (pp. 77–98). Norwood, NJ: Ablex.

President's Commission on Privatization. (1988). *Privatization: Toward more effective government*. Washington, DC: U.S. Government Printing Office.

Princiotta, D., & Bielick, S. (2006). *Homeschooling in the United States: 2003*. Washington, DC: National Center for Education Statistics.

Princiotta, D., Bielick, S., & Chapman, C. (2004). *1.1 million homeschooled students in the United States in 2003*. Washington, DC: National Center for Education Statistics.

Prue, I. (1997). *A nation-wide survey of admissions personnel's knowledge, attitudes, and experiences with home schooled applicants* (Unpublished doctoral dissertation). University of Georgia, Athens, GA.

Putnam, R. D. (1995). Bowling alone: America's declining social capital. *Journal of Democracy, 6*(1), 65–77.

Pyles, L. (2004). *Homeschooling the child with Asperger syndrome: Real help for parents anywhere on any budget*. London, UK: Jessica Kingsley.

Rakestraw, J. (1988). Home schooling in Alabama. *Home School Researcher, 4*(4), 1–6.

Rakestraw, J., & Rakestraw, D. (1990). Home schooling: A question of quality, an issue of rights. *Educational Forum, 55*, 67–77.

Ramsey, J. B. (1987). Selling the New York City subway: Wild-eyed radicalism or the only feasible solution. In S. H. Hanke (Ed.), *Prospects for privatization. Proceedings of the Academy of Political Science* (Vol. 36, No. 3; pp. 93–103). Montpelier, VT: Capital City Press.

Ray, B. (1997a). *Home education across the United States: Family characteristics, student achievement, and longitudinal traits*. Salem, OR: Home School National Defense Fund.

Ray, B. (1997b). *Strengths of their own: Home schoolers across America*. Salem, OR: National Home Education Research Institute.

Ray, B. (2000a). Home schooling for individuals' gain and society's common good. *Peabody Journal of Education, 75*, 272–293.

Ray, B. (2000b). *Homeschooling teaching strategies*. Retrieved from http://www.eric.ed.gov/PDFS/ED501189.pdf

Ray, B. (2000c). Home schooling: The ameliorator of negative influences on learning? *Peabody Journal of Education, 75*, 71–106.

Ray, B. (2001a). *Home education research fact sheet*. Salem, OR: National Home Education Research Institute.

Ray, B. (2001b). *Home schooling achievement*. Purcellville, VA: Home School Legal Defense Association. Retrieved from http://www.hslda.org/docs/study/comp2001/HomeSchoolAchievement.pdf

Ray, B. (2004a). *Home educated and now adults: Their community and civic involvement, views about homeschooling, and other traits*. Salem, OR: National Home Education Research Institute.

Ray, B. (2004b). Homeschoolers on to college: What research shows us. *Journal of College Admission, 185*, 5–11.

Ray, B. (2005). A homeschool research story. In B. S. Cooper (Ed.), *Home schooling in full view* (pp. 1–19). Greenwich, CT: Information Age.

Ray, B. (2008). *Home centered learning annotated bibliography* (17th ed.). Salem, OR: National Home Education Research Institute.

Ray, B. (2009a). *Home education reason and research: Common questions and research-based answers about homeschooling*. Salem, OR: National Home Education Research Institute.

Ray, B. (2009b). *Research facts on homeschooling: General facts and trends.* Salem, OR: National Home Education Research Institute.

Ray, B. (2010). Academic achievement and demographic traits of homeschool students: A nationwide study. *Academic Leadership Live, 8*(1). Retrieved from http://www.academicleadership.org/

Ray, B. (2011). *2.04 million homeschool students in the United States in 2010.* Salem, OR: National Home Education Research Institute.

Ray, B., & Eagleson, B. (2008). State regulation of homeschooling and homeschoolers' SAT scores. *Academic Leadership Live: The Online Journal, 6*(3).

Ray, B., & Wartes, J. (1991). The academic achievement and affective development of home-schooled children. In J. Van Galen & M. Pittman (Eds.), *Homeschooling: Political, historical, and pedagogical perspectives* (pp. 43–62). Norwood, NJ: Ablex.

Ray, B., & Weller, N. (2003). Homeschooling: An overview and financial implications for public schools. *School Business Affairs, 69*(5), 22–26.

Reese, W. J. (1995). *The origins of the American high school.* New Haven, CT: Yale University Press.

Reich, R. (2002). The civic perils of homeschooling. *Educational Leadership, 59*(7), 56–59.

Reich, R. (2005). Why homeschooling should be regulated. In B. S. Cooper (Ed.), *Home schooling in full view* (pp. 109–120). Greenwich, CT: Information Age.

Reinhaller, N., & Thomas, G. (1996). Special education and home schooling: How laws interact with practice. *Rural Special Education Quarterly, 15*(4), 11–17.

Ressler, C. (1997). The most meaningful lesson. In M. Hegener & K. Hegener (Eds.), *The homeschool reader: Collected articles from* Home Education Magazine, *1984–1994* (pp. 49–55). Tonasket, WA: Home Education Press.

Richards, C. E., Shore, R., & Sawicky, M. B. (1996). *Risky business: Private management of public schools.* Washington, DC: Economic Policy Institute.

Richardson, S., & Zirkel, P. (1991). Home schooling law. In J. Van Galen & M. Pittman (Eds.), *Homeschooling: Political, historical, and pedagogical perspectives* (pp. 159–200). Norwood, NJ: Ablex.

Riegel, S. (2001). The home schooling movement and the struggle for democratic education. *Studies in Political Economy, 65,* 91–116.

Roach, V. (1988). Home schooling in an era of educational reform. *School Business Affairs, 54*(11), 10–14.

Rofes, E. E. (1998). *What are the effects of charter laws and charter schools on school districts? A study of eight states and the District of Columbia* (Unpublished doctoral dissertation). University of California, Berkeley, CA.

Romanowski, M. (2001). Common arguments about the strengths and limitations of home schooling. *The Clearing House, 75*(2), 79–83.

Ross, R. L. (1988). *Government and the private sector: Who should do what?* New York, NY: Crane Russak.

Rudner, L. M. (1999). Achievement and demographics of home school students: 1998. *Education Policy Analysis Archives, 7.* Retrieved from http://epaa.asu.edu/ojs/

Rungeling, B., & Glover, R. W. (1991). Educational restructuring—the process for change? *Urban Education, 25,* 415–427.

Russo, C. J. (2006). Conflicts over directing the education of children: Who controls, parents or school officials? *Journal of Education, 186*(2), 27–40.

Sarason, S. B. (1995). *Parental involvement and the political principle: Why the existing governance structure of schools should be abolished.* San Francisco, CA: Jossey-Bass.

Saunders, M. (2010). Previously homeschooled college freshmen: Their first year experiences and persistence rates. *Journal of College Student Retention, 11,* 77–100.

Savage, P. (1990). In love with learning. In A. Pederson & P. O'Mara (Eds.), *Schooling at home: Parents, kids, and learning* (pp. 16–17). Santa Fe, NM: John Muir.

Savas, E. S. (1982). *Privatizing the public sector: How to shrink government.* Chatham, NJ: Chatham House.

Savas, E. S. (1985). The efficiency of the private sector. In S. M. Butler (Ed.), *The privatization option: A strategy to shrink the size of government* (pp. 15–31). Washington, DC: Heritage Foundation.

Savas, E. S. (1987). *Privatization: The key to better government.* Chatham, NJ: Chatham House.

Schemmer, B. A. S. (1985). *Case studies of four families engaged in home education* (Unpublished doctoral dissertation). Ball State University, Muncie, IN.

Scheps, S. (1998). *The librarian's guide to homeschooling resources.* Chicago, IL: American Library Association.

Seldon, A. (1987). Public choice and the choices of the public. In C. K. Rowley (Ed.), *Democracy and public choice* (pp. 122–134). New York, NY: Columbia University Press.

Shanker, A. (1988a, March 31). National Press Club speech. Washington, DC.

Shanker, A. (1988b). Restructuring our schools. *Peabody Journal of Education, 65,* 88–100.

Shanker, A. (1988c, July 17). Where we stand: A charter for change (cont'd). *The New York Times,* p. E9.

Sheehan, M. (2002). Dancing with Monica: Personal perceptions of a home-school mom. *Roeper Review, 24*(4), 191–196.

Sheffer, S. (1995). *A sense of self: Listening to homeschooled adolescent girls.* Portsmouth, NH: Boynton/Cook.

Shyers, L. (1992). A comparison of social adjustment between home and traditionally schooled students. *Home School Researcher, 8*(3), 1–8.

Sizer, T. R. (1964). *Secondary schools at the turn of the century.* New Haven, CT: Yale University Press.

Sizer, T. R. (1984). *Horace's compromise: The dilemma of the American high school.* Boston, MA: Houston Mifflin.

Smedley, T. C. (1992). Socialization of home school children. *Home School Researcher, 8*(3), 9–16.

Smith, C., & Sikkink, D. (1999). Is private school privatizing? *First Things, 92,* 16–20. Retrieved from http://www.firstthings.com

Snauwaert, D. T. (1993). *Democracy, education, and governance: A developmental conception.* Albany: State University of New York Press.

Somerville, S. (2005). Legal rights for homeschool families. In B. S. Cooper (Ed.), *Home schooling in full view* (pp. 135–149). Greenwich, CT: Information Age.

Sorey, K., & Duggan, M. (2008). Homeschoolers entering community colleges: Perceptions of admission officers. *Journal of College Admission, 200,* 22–28.

Spring, J. (1990). *The American school 1642–1990: Varieties of historical interpretation of the foundations and developments of American education* (2nd ed.). New York, NY: Longman.

Starr, P. (1987). The limits of privatization. In S. H. Hanke (Ed.), *Prospects for privatization. Proceedings of the Academy of Political Science* (Vol. 36, No. 3; pp. 124–137). Montpelier, VT: Capital City Press.

Starr, P. (1991). The case for skepticism. In W. T. Gormley (Ed.), *Privatization and its alternatives* (pp. 25–36). Madison: University of Wisconsin Press.

Stevens, E. (1997a). Finding reasons to write. In M. Hegener & K. Hegener (Eds.), *The Homeschool reader: Collected articles from* Home Education Magazine, *1984–1994* (pp. 66–68). Tonasket, WA: Home Education Press.

Stevens, M. L. (2001). *Kingdom of children: Culture and controversy in the homeschooling movement.* Princeton, NJ: Princeton University Press.

Stevens, M. L. (2003). The normalisation of homeschooling in the USA. *Evaluation and Research in Education, 17,* 90–100.

Sutton, L., & Bogan, Y. (2005). School choice: The fiscal impact of home education in Florida. *AASA Journal of Scholarship & Practice, 2*(2), 5–9.

Sutton, L., & Galloway, R. (2000). College success of students from three high school settings. *Journal of Research in Development and Education, 33*(3), 137–146.

Taylor, J. (1986a). *Self-concept in home-schooling children* (Doctoral dissertation). Available from ProQuest Dissertations and Theses database. (UMI No. DA8624219.)

Taylor, J. (1986b). Self-concept in home-schooling children. *Home School Researcher, 2*(2), 1–3.

Taylor, V. (2005). Behind the trend: Increases in homeschooling among African American families. In B. S. Cooper (Ed.), *Home schooling in full view* (pp. 121–133). Greenwich, CT: Information Age.

Taylor-Hough, D. (2010). *Are all homeschooling methods created equal?* Retrieved from http://www.eric.ed.gov/PDFS/ED510702.pdf

Thayer, F. C. (1987). Privatization: Carnage, chaos, and corruption. In B. J. Carroll, R. W. Conant, & T. A. Easton (Eds.), *Private means, public ends: Private business in social service delivery* (pp. 146–170). New York, NY: Praeger.

Thom, S. (1997). Expert advice. In M. Hegener & K. Hegener (Eds.), *The homeschool reader: Collected articles from* Home Education Magazine, *1984–1994* (pp. 43–46). Tonasket, WA: Home Education Press.

Thompson, J. (1994, March). *The impact of structural costs on home schooling decisions in rural and non-rural districts.* Paper presented at the annual meeting of the American Educational Finance Association, Nashville, TN.

Tillman, V. D. (1995). Home schoolers, self-esteem, and socialization. *Home School Researcher, 11*(3), 1–6.

Tullock, G. (1965). *The politics of bureaucracy.* Washington, DC: Public Affairs Press.

Tullock, G. (1988). *Wealth, poverty, and politics.* New York, NY: Basil Blackwell.

Tullock, G. (1994a). Public choice: The new science of politics. In G. L. Brady & R. D. Tollison (Eds.), *On the trail of homo economicus* (pp. 87–100). Fairfax, VA: George Mason University Press.

Tullock, G. (1994b). Social cost and government policy. In G. L. Brady & R. D. Tollison (Eds.), *On the trail of homo econonomicus* (pp. 65–85). Fairfax, VA: George Mason University Press.

Tushman, M. L., & Romanelli, E. (1985). Organizational evolution: A metamorphosis model of convergence and reorientation. In L. L. Cummings & B. M. Straw (Eds.), *Research in organizational behavior* (pp. 171–222). Greenwich, CT: JAI Press.

Tyack, D. B. (1974). *The one best system: A history of American urban education.* Cambridge, MA: Harvard University Press.

Tyack, D. (1992). Can we build a system of choice that is not just a "sorting machine" or a market-based "free-for-all"? *Equity and Choice, 9*(1), 13–17.

Tyack, D. (1993). School governance in the United States: Historical puzzles and anomalies. In J. Hannaway & M. Carnoy (Eds.), *Decentralization and school improvement* (pp. 1–32). San Francisco, CA: Jossey-Bass.

Van Galen, J. (1991). Ideologues and pedagogues: Parents who teach their children at home. In J. Van Galen & M. Pittman (Eds.), *Homeschooling: Political, historical, and pedagogical perspectives* (pp. 63–76). Norwood, NJ: Ablex.

Van Galen, J., & Pittman, M. (1991). Introduction. In J. Van Galen & M. Pittman (Eds.), *Homeschooling: Political, historical, and pedagogical perspectives* (pp. 1–5). Norwood, NJ: Ablex.

Van Horn, C. E. (1991). The myths and realities of privatization. In W. T. Gormley (Ed.), *Privatization and its alternatives* (pp. 261–280). Madison: University of Wisconsin Press.

Vickers, J., & Yarrow, G. (1988). *Privatization: An economic analysis.* Cambridge, MA: MIT Press.

Vinovskis, M. A. (1985). *The origins of public schools: A reexamination of the Beverly High School controversy.* Madison: University of Wisconsin Press.

Wallace, N. (1990). Home schooling's unique structure. In A. Pederson & P. O'Mara (Eds.), *Schooling at home: Parents, kids, and learning* (pp. 18–19). Santa Fe, NM: John Muir.

Wartes, J. (1987). *Report from the 1986 homeschool testing and other descriptive information about Washington's homeschoolers.* Woodinville, WA: Washington Homeschool Research Project.

Wartes, J. (1988). The Washington home school project: Quantitative measures for informing policy decisions. *Education and Urban Society, 21,* 42–51.

Wartes, J. (1990). *The relationship of selected input variables to academic achievement among Washington's homeschoolers.* Woodinville, WA: Washington Homeschool Research Project.

Webb, D. L. (1997). Home-schools and interscholastic sports: Denying participation violates United States Constitutional due process and equal protection rights. *Journal of Law and Education, 26*(3), 123–132.

Webb, J. (1989). The outcomes of home-based education: Employment and other issues. *Educational Review, 41,* 121–133.

Wells, A. S., Grutzik, S. C., Carnochan, S., Slayton, J., & Vasudeva, A. (1999). Underlying policy assumptions of charter school reform: The multiple meanings of a movement. *Teachers College Record, 100,* 513–535.

Wells, A. S., Lopez, A., Scott, J., & Holme, J. J. (1999). Charter school as postmodern paradox. Rethinking social stratification in an age of deregulated school choice. *Harvard Educational Review, 69,* 172–204.

Welner, K. M. (2002). *Exploring the democratic tensions within parents' decisions to homeschool* (Occasional Paper). New York, NY: Columbia University, Teachers College, National Center for the Study of Privatization in Education.

Welner, K. M., & Welner, K. G. (1999). Contextualizing homeschooling data: A response to Rudner. *Education Policy Analysis Archives, 7*(13). Retrieved from http://epaa.asu.edu/ojs/

Wenders, J., & Clements, A. (2007). An analysis of the economic impact of home and private schooling in Nevada. *Home School Researcher, 17*(2), 13–35.

Wenger, J., & Hodari, A. (2004). *Final analysis of evaluation of homeschool and challenge program recruit.* Alexandria, VA: CNA.

Whitehead, J., & Bird, W. (1984). *Home education and constitutional liberties: The historical and constitutional arguments in support of home instruction.* Westchester, IL: Crossway Books.

Wilhelm, G., & Firman, M. (2009). Historical and contemporary developments in home school education. *Journal of Research on Christian Education, 18,* 303–315.

Williams, D., Arnoldson, L. M., & Reynolds, P. (1984, April). *Understanding home education: Case studies of home schools.* Paper presented at the Annual Meeting of the American Educational Research Association, New Orleans, LA.

Willing, M. H. (1942). From 1890 to 1930 American educators changed the purpose and practice of high schools. In P. B. Jacobson, R. Lindquist, G. N. Mackensie, H. Spears, & B. L. Johnson (Eds.), *General education in the American high schools* (pp. 41–81). Chicago, IL: Scott Foresman.

Winstanley, C. (2009). Too cool for school? Gifted children and homeschooling. *Theory and Research in Education, 7,* 347–362.

Wise, A. E. (1989). Professional teaching: A new paradigm for the management of education. In T. J. Sergiovanni & J. H. Moore (Eds.), *Schooling for tomorrow: Directing reforms to issues that count* (pp. 301–310). Boston, MA: Allyn & Bacon.

Wood, P. (2003). *Homeschooling and higher education.* Washington, DC: ERIC Clearinghouse on Higher Education, Institute for Education Policy Studies.

Worsnop, R. L. (1992). Privatization. *CQ Researcher, 2,* 977–1000.

Wraga, W. G. (1994). *Democracy's high school: The comprehensive high school and educational reform in the United States.* Lanham, MD: University Press of America.

Wright, C. (1988). Home school research: Critique and suggestions for the future. *Education and Urban Society, 21,* 96–113.

Index

A Beka Publications curriculum, 115, 116
Ability grouping, 158
Academic achievement, 140, 153
    certification of home-teachers and,
        139–140
    college entrance examinations and,
        136–137
    contextual variables in, 137–140
    financial investment in homeschooling
        and, 139
    full-package curricula, use of, 139
    gender differences and, 139
    higher education, measures of success
        and, 149
    higher education, preparation for,
        148–149
    household income and, 137–138
    impacts of homeschooling and, 39, 47,
        134–140
    length of time of homeschooling and, 139
    national norms, comparisons with,
        135–137
    parent motivation and, 139
    parental education levels and, 138
    race, effects of, 138–139
    religious-based homeschooling and, 139
    special needs students and, 136, 139
    See also Impact of homeschooling;
        Positive effects of homeschooling
Achievement tests, 119–120, 126, 134–135
    certification of home-teachers and,
        139–140
    college entrance examinations,
        136–137, 149
    national norms and, 135–137
    See also Academic achievement;
        Standardized testing
Advanced Training Institute International
    curriculum, 115

Alpha Omega curriculum, 115
Apple, M., 59, 60, 66, 68, 70, 98, 128
Arai, B., 150
Armed Forces Qualification Test, 136
Arnoldson, L. M., 85, 101, 116, 118, 133
Assessments. *See* Achievement tests;
        Standardized testing
Athletic program participation, 47
Aurini, J., 9, 68, 121

Basham, P., 9, 17, 46, 119
Bates, V., 11, 69
Bauman, K., 20, 21, 129
Bauman, P. C., 61
Belfield, C., 4, 27, 59, 109, 123, 153
Bell, D., 134
Bennett, J. T., 64
Bielick, S., 17, 117
Bird, W., 38, 44, 156
Blok, H., 122, 123, 146, 157
Bob Jones University Press, 116
Bob Jones University Press Testing and
        Evaluation Services, 120
Bogan, Y., 132
Boone, J., 159
Boyer, W., 86
Broughman, S., 17

Cai, Y., 23, 100
California Achievement Tests, 120
Calvert School curriculum, 115, 116
Calvery, R., 134
Carnochan, S., 69
Carraccio, C., 137
Carroll, B. J., 64
Chandler, K., 17
Charlotte Mason method, 114
Charter schools, 2–3, 11, 51, 129
Chatham-Carpenter, A., 144

Christian fundamentalism, 22–23
  academic achievement and, 139
  child inherent goodness/sinfulness
      and, 35
  conservative national political turn
      and, 69–70
  homeschool support associations
      and, 42–43
  homeschooling movement and, 32, 33,
      34–35, 69
  morally conservative counter revolution
      and, 69
  parental authority vs. child freedom
      and, 35
  secularism, family values and, 35
  support association goals and, 43
  See also Homeschooling origins; Parent
      motivation; Support group networks
Christian Liberty Academy curriculum,
    115, 116
Cibulka, J. G., 44, 64, 131
Cizek, G., 87, 125, 127
Clements, A., 87, 131, 132
Clonlara School curriculum, 115
Cochran, C., 30, 75, 148
Colfax, D., 105, 154
Colfax, M., 105, 154
College entrance examinations,
    136–137, 149
Collom, E., 9, 11, 12, 39, 82, 84, 86, 108,
    139, 140
Community-based opportunities, 117, 119,
    150–151
Compulsory education movement, 31, 38
Computer-based home education, 115,
    117, 118
Conant, R. W., 64
Conservative ideology, 2, 22–23, 24, 32–33,
    34–35, 42, 69–70, 72
  See also Christian fundamentalism
Consortium on Productivity in the
    Schools, 94
Context of homeschooling movement,
    53–55
  antigovernment political/social
      movements and, 60–61, 62, 72–73
  bureaucratic government agencies,
      decreasing faith in, 64–65, 69
  centralized control, larger state role and,
      56, 57–58, 60, 64–66, 68
  choice, ideology of, 69, 72
  conservative Christian ideology, spread
      of, 69

  conservative national political turn and,
      69–70, 72
  corporate bureaucratic model of
      governance and, 57–58, 60
  democratic professionalism, rise of, 69
  direct democracy, populist perspective
      and, 68–69
  educational establishment and,
      58, 67, 69
  educational governance/management,
      need for reform of, 66–68, 70
  1800–1890 social/economic factors
      and, 55–56
  1890–1970 social/economic factors and,
      56–58
  government domination, struggle
      against, 60–68
  government downsizing/rightsizing
      and, 71, 73
  government employees, bureaucratic
      imperialism/goal displacement
      and, 65–66
  government-controlled schooling,
      discontent with, 64–66
  individualism, principles of, 72
  liberal democratic state and, 56–57,
      59–60, 62–63, 68
  local-control/self-governance and, 56,
      59–60, 62, 68, 69, 73
  market economy, schooling-economy
      connections and, 55, 57
  new contemporary economic
      foundations and, 70–73
  new contemporary social/cultural/
      political foundations and, 68–70
  1970-present social/economic factors
      and, 58–73
  occupational specialization and, 57
  parental control and, 59–60, 69
  postindustrial/postmodern society and,
      57, 61, 63, 68–73
  privatization movement and, 61–62,
      70–73
  professional expertise and, 58, 60, 65, 67,
      69
  public sector economic policy, taxpayer
      revolt and, 63–64
  social harmony, public education
      and, 55
  sociopolitical/economic calculus and,
      54–55
  unions, decline of, 69, 72
  urbanized/industrialized society and, 57

value preferences, state intrusiveness and, 62
See also Homeschooling origins; Legalization initiatives; Parent motivation; Support group networks
Cooper, B. S., 44
Cooperative schooling approach, 48–49, 51, 114, 115
Correspondence schools, 114, 115
Cremin, L. A., 57
Cronin, T. E., 68
Current Population Survey, 9
Curriculum. See Homeschooling practices
Cyber schools, 51

Dahlquist, K., 39, 77, 108, 140
Dalaimo, D., 141
Data collection, 11–12
Davies, S., 9, 68, 121
De Alessi, L., 63, 65, 70
Deinstitutionalization, 38
Delahooke, M., 135
Delquadri, J., 106, 136, 156, 159
Demographic data, 14, 15–16
    family income status, 18–19
    family size, 25
    homeschooling vs. non-homeschooling parent education levels and, 17–18
    marital status, 21–22
    parent education levels, 16–18
    parent motivation to homeschool and, 82–83
    parent occupational status, 19–20
    parental age, 22
    political viewpoints, 24
    race/ethnicity, 20–21, 82, 138–139
    regional geographic distribution, 24–25
    religious affiliations, 22–23
    schooling-related demographics, 26–27
    student data, 26–27
    urban vs. rural distribution, 25
Dewey, J., 33
DiLorenzo, T. J., 64
Distance learning, 117
Divoky, D., 90, 97
Dobson, L., 79, 83, 125
Dual enrollment, 50 (table), 51
Duggan, M., 148, 149
Duvall, S., 106, 136, 156, 159

Eagleson, B., 46, 59
Early childhood movement, 34

Easton, T. A., 64
Emotional harm, 98
Endsley, R., 122
Environmental factors. See Context of homeschooling movement; Homeschooling origins; Legalization initiatives; Parent motivation; Support group networks
Erickson, D. A., 157
Experiential learning opportunities, 117, 158, 159
Extended curriculum, 116–119
Extracurricular activities, 47, 49

Families, 2, 3
    data collection, cooperation with, 12
    extended families and, 118–119
    homeschooling, core definitions of, 4–6
    impacts of homeschooling on, 132–133
    income status of, 18–19
    marital cohesiveness and, 21–22
    parent education levels and, 16–18
    parent occupational status and, 19–20
    religious affiliations and, 22–23
    research on homeschooling, resistance to, 14
    school as substitute for, 31, 35
    size of, 25
    stay-at-home moms and, 19–20, 22
    See also Demographic data; Homeschooling; Homeschooling practices; Parent motivation; Positive effects of homeschooling; Support group networks
Family Centered Learning Alternatives curriculum, 115
Farris, M., 37, 44, 47, 125
Feinberg, E., 5, 129
Field trips, 43, 117, 119
Finn, C. E., 67
Firman, M., 125
Fitzgerald, R., 73
Free market economy, 55
Frost, E., 135
Frost, G., 135

Gaither, M., 5, 29, 33, 40, 48, 59, 61, 67, 68, 101, 126
Galloway, R., 19, 147, 148, 149
Gladin, E., 4, 16, 18, 23, 26, 107, 108, 111, 112, 116, 117, 118, 133
Gorder, C., 60, 91, 160
Government oversight, 2, 12, 54

domains of regulation and, 46
illegality/legality of homeschooling
and, 36, 37, 38, 44–47
independent home-based education
and, 50 (table), 51
political support of homeschooling
and, 38
regulatory environment and, 46–47
schooling, provision of, 38, 60–68
See also Context of homeschooling
movement; Legalization initiatives;
Public education
Gray, D. W., 137
Gray, S., 17, 75, 95
Green, C., 80, 86, 100, 106
Greenwood, C., 136, 156
Groover, S., 122
Grutzik, S. C., 69
Gustavsen, G., 16, 18, 22, 40, 84, 108,
112, 119
Guterson, D., 5, 11, 36, 41, 141

Hadeed, H., 5
Hanna, L. G., 110
Hanson, E. M., 67
Hassel, B. C., 60
Hendel, D. D., 39, 77, 108, 140
Hepburn, C., 9, 17, 46, 119
Hertzel, J., 78, 85, 98, 108, 157, 158
Hill, P. T., 66, 69
Historic context. *See* Context of
homeschooling movement;
Homeschooling origins
Hodari, A., 1, 10, 136, 150
Holistic approach, 117
Holt, J., 32, 33, 34, 36, 38, 41, 84, 91, 97, 98,
154, 160
Home School Legal Defense Association
(HSLDA), 40, 45, 47
Homeschooling, 1–4
American education system and, 2–3
charter schools and, 11
conventional schooling, rejection of, 5–6
core definitions of, 4–6
data collection on, 11–12
empirical knowledge base on, 12–14
expanding enrollment growth in, 7–10,
8–9 (table)
growth rates of, 10–11
hybrid collaborative models of, 4, 6, 27,
47, 48–49, 51
media coverage of, 39
postmodern society and, 2

prevalence of, 7–12, 8–9 (table)
privatization framework, dimensions
of, 6–7
public acceptance of, 37
resource availability for, 37, 40
socialization and, 3, 39
success of, 39, 47
support group networks for, 37, 39,
40–44
synonyms for, 5
technologies and, 39
voluntary nature of, 5–6
See also Academic achievement; Context
of homeschooling movement;
Demographic data; Families;
Homeschooling origins;
Homeschooling practices; Impact of
homeschooling; Models of
homeschooling; Parent motivation;
Positive effects of homeschooling
Homeschooling origins, 29–30
Christian conservative fundamentalism
and, 32–33, 34–35
compulsory public schooling stage
and, 31
diversity, proliferation of homeschool
families and, 38–39
early movement student data, 26
expanding enrollment growth and,
7–10, 8–9 (table)
foundations of homeschooling, 30–35
grassroots-inspired movement and, 33
illegality/legality of homeschooling
and, 36, 37, 45
legal rights, expansion of, 37, 38,
44–47
legitimacy of homeschooling, growth of,
36–37, 38
liberal progressive left roots and, 32,
33–34, 38
mainstream, movement toward, 35–39
models of homeschooling and, 47–51, 50
(table)
modern homeschooling era and, 31–35,
48–51
normalization of homeschooling and,
37–39
parental control, demand for, 33
pre-compulsory public schooling stage
and, 31
stages of development and, 30–32
support group networks and, 37, 39,
40–44

See also Context of homeschooling
  movement; Demographic data;
  Homeschooling; Homeschooling
  practices
Homeschooling practices, 105
  apprenticeships/mentors and, 117
  classical education approach and, 114
  community-based opportunities and,
    117, 119
  computer-based home education
    approach and, 115, 117, 118
  content focus and, 112, 113
  cooperative schooling approach and,
    114, 115
  correspondence schools and, 114, 115
  curricular materials, options in, 110–111,
    113–116
  curricular packaging systems and,
    113–116
  distance learning and, 117
  eclectic approach and, 114
  expenditures on materials and, 111
  extended curriculum and, 116–119
  extended family and, 118–119
  family-based businesses/cottage
    industries, participation in, 117
  field trips and, 43, 117, 119
  holistic approach to education and, 117
  household management, participation
    in, 117
  income, loss of, 111, 132
  instructional activities and, 109–110
  instructional aids/supplemental
    resources and, 112–113
  instructional time and, 108–109
  interest-driven learning and, 113, 117
  life experience-based learning and, 117,
    158, 159
  public library use and, 113
  public school resources and, 113, 114
  race and, 107
  religious interest and, 106–107, 110, 111
  school-at-home approach and, 114–115
  selection of curricular materials and,
    111, 112–113
  service learning activities and, 43, 117,
    119
  socialization and, 3, 39, 99, 118–119
  standardized testing and, 49, 82, 113,
    119–120
  state teacher certification and, 108
  structured-to-unstructured instruction
    continuum and, 111–112

  teaching role and, 107–108, 109
  teaching-learning work, variability in,
    106–107, 109–110
  television viewing habits and, 118
  traditional boxed curriculum and, 114
  umbrella organizations and, 114
  unschooling approach and, 114–115
  See also Academic achievement;
    Demographic data; Homeschooling;
    Homeschooling origins; Impact of
    homeschooling; Positive effects of
    homeschooling
Hood, C., 61, 62
Hoover-Dempsey, K., 80, 86, 100, 106
Houston, R., 80, 81, 82, 83, 91
Hula, R. C., 61
Humanistic orientation, 33, 69, 85, 90, 91,
  92, 96

Illich, I., 33
Impact of homeschooling, 121–122
  academic achievement outcomes and,
    134–140
  child well-being/psychological health,
    147
  child-based impacts, 133–147
  civic involvement and, 129, 142, 144, 150
  college entrance examinations and, 136–
    137
  community-based activities,
    participation in, 150–151
  cost issues and, 131–132
  economic benefits and, 151
  existing research on, 122–126
  families, impact on, 132–133
  flexi-schooling, development of, 130
  higher education, experiences with,
    148–149
  income, loss of, 111, 132
  life satisfaction and, 151
  military service and, 150
  national norms, comparisons with,
    135–137
  out-of-home relations and, 144–145
  posthomeschooling success, long-term
    impacts and, 147–151
  public school system, impacts on,
    129–131
  self-concept/self-esteem and,
    145–147
  social development/socialization and,
    140–145, 150
  social engagement and, 143–145, 150

social fabric/public sphere, impacts on, 127–129, 144
social skill development and, 146–147
special needs students and, 136, 139
spillover effects and, 130
success, evidence of, 125–126
workforce, successful participation in, 150
See also Academic achievement; Context of homeschooling movement; Homeschooling practices; Legalization initiatives; Positive effects of homeschooling; Support group networks
Independent homeschooling, 50 (table), 51
Industrial revolution, 57
Integrative principle, 89, 90
Interest-driven learning, 113, 117
Iowa Test of Basic Skills, 119, 120
Isenberg, E., 10, 80, 81, 86
Ismael, J. S., 71

Jaycox, R., 157
Jenkins, T., 149
Jeub, C., 85
Jones, S., 82

Katz, M. B., 68, 69
Kelley, S., 143, 145, 146
Kitchen, P., 146, 147
Kleibard, H. M., 57
Klicka, C., 47, 66, 90, 91, 93
Klugewicz, S., 137
Knowles, J. G., 16, 18, 20, 22, 23, 24, 30, 40, 41, 45, 53, 54, 58, 72, 76, 77, 79, 80, 85, 90, 93, 99, 104, 111, 117, 148, 150, 151
Kohl, H. R., 33
Kolegue, C., 134
KONOS curriculum, 115
Koos, L., 57
Kunzman, R., 46, 48, 70, 76, 102, 107, 122, 127, 134, 154

Lange, C., 18, 86, 97, 100
Lee, W. J., 146
Legalization initiatives, 44
athletic program participation and, 47
constitutional cases and, 45
deregulation/loosened regulatory environment and, 47
First/Fourteenth Amendment rights and, 45
high regulation states and, 47
legal defense associations, 40, 43
low regulation states and, 46, 47
medium regulation states and, 46, 47
normalization of homeschooling and, 44–45
political debate, various interests in, 46
state law/mandates and, 45, 46
state regulatory framework and, 45–47
support group efforts and, 47
See also Context of homeschooling movement; Homeschooling origins; Support group networks
Levy, F., 94
Lewis, D. A., 61
Liberal democratic state, 56–57, 59–60, 62–63, 68
Liberal progressive ideology, 32
homeschool associations and, 42
homeschool movement origins and, 32, 33–34, 38
See also Unschooling movement
Lines, P. M., 5, 9, 20, 32, 106, 110, 116, 124, 130, 140, 143
Lips, D., 5, 129
Liu, K. K., 18, 86, 97, 100
Localism, 38
Lotto, L. S., 12
Lubienski, C., 70, 75, 128, 155
Luebke, R. V., 54, 131, 132, 148
Lyman, I., 5, 32, 40, 79, 86, 113, 141

Manno, B. V., 67
Market-based education systems, 3, 38, 48, 55
Marlow, S. E., 16, 18, 20, 22, 23, 24, 30, 40, 41, 45, 53, 54, 72, 76, 79, 80, 87, 90, 91, 99, 117
Marshall, J. D., 79, 129, 132
Martin, B., 62, 72
Martin, M., 89
Mayberry, M., 15, 16, 18, 20, 22, 23, 24, 40, 45, 53, 54, 58, 59, 72, 76, 77, 79, 80, 85, 99, 100, 104, 117, 159
McCulloch, D., 134
McDowell, S., 36, 82
McGuffey Readers, 116
McIntire, W. G., 4
McKeon, C. C., 23, 112, 114
Media reporting, 39
Medlin, R. G., 13, 122, 142, 143, 145
Meighan, R., 129, 130
Merrifield, J., 9, 17, 46, 119
Mirochnik, D. A., 4
Mitchell, D., 39, 84, 86
Models of homeschooling, 47–48

blended model and, 50 (table), 51
distrust of, 49
dual enrollment category, 51
extracurricular activities and, 47, 49
homeschool cooperatives and, 49
hybrid collaborative model and,
    48–49, 51
ideological rifts and, 48
independent home-based education
    category and, 51
limited public school support and, 49
mom schools and, 49
public school education, alternatives to,
    48
pure homeschool model and, 49, 50
    (table)
pure traditional public schooling and,
    50 (table), 51
standardized testing and, 49
See also Homeschooling; Homeschooling
    origins; Homeschooling practices;
    Legalization initiatives
Montaudo, S., 134
Moore, D., 40, 99
Moore, R., 32, 34, 35, 40, 93, 94, 99, 154
Moral imperative, 88–89
Morris, R., 135
Muchmore, J. A., 30, 41, 77, 90, 148, 150, 151
Muntes, G., 22, 47, 80
Murnane, R. J., 94
Murphy, J., 127

Nathan, J., 66
National Association for the Legal Defense
    of Alternative Schools, 40
National Center for Educational Statistics
    (NCES), 6, 16, 98
National Home Education Research
    Institute (NHERI), 9, 15–16, 19–20, 23,
    41, 47, 86, 115
National Household Education Survey
    (NHES), 9, 10, 12, 17, 20, 22, 86, 113,
    117, 129
Natural learning opportunities, 158
Neill, A. S., 33
Nemer, K. M., 9, 35, 53
Niskanen, W. A., 64, 65

Occupational specialization, 57
Oliveira, P. C. M. de, 136
Origins. See Homeschooling origins

Pack, J. R., 64, 71
Parent motivation, 75–76

academic challenge, insufficiencies of,
    96, 139
academic deficiencies in schools and,
    93–97
complexity, overlapping rationales and,
    79
contextual considerations and, 80–83
dysfunctional socialization and, 99
evangelical beliefs/values, centrality of,
    89–90
family cohesion, promotion of, 103–104
family-based motivation and, 100–104
household characteristics and, 82–83
independent thinking/creativity, stifling
    of, 97
integrative principle and, 89, 90
moral imperative and, 88–89
parent-child bond and, 101
pedagogical insufficiencies and, 95–96
physical/emotional harm, protection
    from, 98
prime motivation, 76–77
push and pull dynamics and, 77–78, 78
    (figure)
religious family life and, 88–90
religious-based motivations and, 87–92
responsibility for education and, 100–
    101, 155, 155 (figure)
school environmental conditions and,
    81–82
school quality, measures of, 81
schooling characteristics and, 80–82
secularization of public schools and,
    90–92
shifting motivations and, 79–80
social stigmatization and, 103
social/environmental problems in
    school and, 97–99
sources of motivation and, 77
special circumstances and, 101–102
special needs children and, 83, 87,
    102–103
structure of academic programs and,
    96–97
student/community characteristics and,
    83
typologies of motivation and, 84–87
values clarification perspective and, 92
See also Families; Positive effects of
    homeschooling; Support group
    networks
Parker, R. D., 19, 20, 40, 85, 100, 105, 108,
    109, 111, 112, 113, 119, 122, 133, 139,
    146, 157

Pearson, R. C., 7
Pedagogy. *See* Academic achievement;
    Homeschooling practices; Parent
    motivation
Peer socialization, 142–143, 144
Perry, J., 5, 10, 133
Perry, K., 5, 10, 133
Pestalozzi, J. H., 33
Physical harm, 98
Piers-Harris Children's Self-Concept Scale
    (PHCSCS), 145–146
Pines, B. Y., 72
Pirie, M., 71
Political conservatism, 24, 43, 69–70, 72
Positive effects of homeschooling, 153–154
    active learning and, 159
    autonomy/creativity, promotion of, 154
    customized instruction and, 157–158
    efficiencies and, 154, 157
    generalized conclusions, dangers in, 154
    instructional practices and, 158–159
    instructional programs and, 156–159
    integrated content spheres and, 158
    learning environment and, 159–160
    logic of action, impact of homeschooling
        and, 155–160, 155 (figure)
    natural/experiential learning
        opportunities and, 158, 159
    one-to-one instruction and, 156, 158
    parental involvement and, 154, 155
    personalized environment and, 159–160
    positive social capital, accumulation of,
        160
    safe/nurturing climate and, 159, 160
    schooling process and, 154
    success, evidence of, 125–126
    time use efficiencies and, 157
    See also Academic achievement; Impact
        of homeschooling
President's Commission on
    Privatization, 62
Princiotta, D., 117
Private school designation, 12
Private school withdrawals, 26
Privatization movement, 2, 6–7, 38, 61–62,
    70–73
Professionalism, 54, 56, 58, 60, 65, 69
Progressive ideology, 32, 33–34
    See also Liberal progressive ideology;
        Unschooling movement
Public education:
    academic deficiencies in, 93–97
    administrative experts, school
        management and, 58, 67, 69

bureaucratic governance infrastructure,
    reform of, 66–68
centralized vs. local control and, 56,
    57–58
characteristics of, 50 (table), 51
charter schools and, 2–3, 11
client sensitivity and, 48
compulsory education movement and,
    31, 38
conservative Christian ideology and, 35
corporate bureaucratic model of
    governance and, 57–58, 60
1800–1890 social/economic context and,
    55–56
1890–1970 social/economic context and,
    56–58
entrepreneurial focus and, 48
hospitable environment for
    homeschoolers and, 37, 48–49
market orientation and, 3, 38, 48, 55, 57
opposition to homeschooling and,
    36–37, 39, 48
postindustrial world, global competition
    and, 57
public opinion and, 38, 39
reform, elusive goal of, 94–95
school choice movement and, 2, 48
school climate, family values and, 35
scientific management method and, 58
secularization of, 90–92
socialization, illusion of, 142–143
See also Context of homeschooling
    movement; Models of
    homeschooling

Rakestraw, D., 30, 99, 140
Rakestraw, J., 30, 99, 108, 111, 135, 140
Ramsey, J. B., 65
Ray, B., 1, 5, 7, 10, 16, 17, 18, 19, 20, 22, 23,
    24, 25, 26, 36, 40, 45, 46, 53, 54, 59, 72,
    76, 79, 80, 86, 99, 107, 108, 109, 110,
    111, 112, 113, 115, 116, 117, 118, 119,
    121, 126, 131, 132, 135, 136, 137, 138,
    139, 143, 145, 148, 149, 150, 151, 153,
    154, 156, 158, 159, 160
Reese, W. J., 55, 56
Reeve, J., 23, 100
Regulatory environment. *See* Government
    oversight; Legalization initiatives
Reich, R., 9, 10, 12, 46, 122
Religious-based homeschooling, 12, 22–23,
    27, 79
    See also Christian fundamentalism
Ressler, C., 101

Reynolds, P., 85, 101, 116, 118, 133
Richardson, S., 66
Riegel, S., 99, 127
Robinson, D., 23, 100
Rod and Staff Publishers curriculum, 115, 116
Romanelli, E., 56
Romanowski, M., 37, 142, 155
Ross, R. L., 68
Rousseau, J. -J., 33
Rudner, L. M., 17, 20, 21, 22, 23, 25, 26, 108, 111, 115, 118, 124, 136, 138, 139
Russo, C. J., 45
Rutherford Institute, 40, 47

Sanchez, A., 82
Saunders, M., 147
Savas, E. S., 63, 64, 66, 71, 73
Schemmer, B. A. S., 4, 136
School choice movement, 2, 48, 69, 72
Scientific management, 58
Secular humanism, 90, 91, 92, 96
Secularization process, 90–92
Self-concept/self-esteem, 145–147
Service learning activities, 43, 117, 119
Sheehan, M., 117
Sheffer, S., 4, 106, 116, 146
Shyers, L., 146
Sikkink, D., 72, 129
Sizer, T. R., 67
Slayton, J., 69
Slocum, S., 134
Smedley, T. C., 119, 127
Smith, C., 72, 129
Smith, M., 47
Social capital, 160
Social harm, 99
Social norms, 141
Social skill development, 146–147
Social structures, 2–3
    See also Context of homeschooling movement; Socialization
Socialization, 3, 39, 99, 118–119, 140–145, 150
Somerville, S., 45
Sorey, K., 148, 149
Spaulding, H. W., 77
Special needs children, 83, 87, 102–103, 136, 139
Standardized testing, 49, 82, 113, 119–120, 126, 135–137
    See also Achievement tests
Stanford Achievement Tests, 119, 120
Starr, P., 71

Stevens, M. L., 7, 19, 29, 32, 35, 37, 42, 53, 59, 70, 86, 97, 110, 112, 113, 124, 126, 132, 133
Success. See Academic achievement; Impact of homeschooling; Positive effects of homeschooling
Support group networks, 37, 39, 40–41
    Christian conservatives, support association goals of, 42, 43, 44
    collective action and, 43
    conventions/conferences and, 40, 43–44
    field trips and, 43
    ideological values/beliefs and, 40, 41, 42–43
    inclusive organizational system and, 42
    interconnected families and, 41–42
    legal information/support and, 40, 43
    liberal left vs. conservative right ideology and, 42, 43
    local support groups, 41, 44
    macro-level purposes of, 41–43
    membership in, 40, 47
    micro-level purposes of, 43–44
    national organizations, 40–41, 44
    parent needs and, 43–44
    polarization/homogeneity of, 42–43
    politicization of homeschooling and, 43
    public policy and, 44
    resource suppliers and, 40, 44
    service learning activities and, 43
    socialization opportunities, networking/satellite relationships and, 119
    statewide organizations, 41, 43, 44
    student needs and, 43
    support grid maturation, fracturing process and, 42–43
    See also Context of homeschooling movement; Legalization initiatives
Sureau, J., 44
Sutton, J. P., 137, 147, 148
Sutton, L., 19, 132, 149

Taylor, J., 4, 7, 116, 145
Taylor, J. W., 17, 18, 22, 24, 26, 27, 85, 90, 145, 146
Taylor-Hough, D., 29, 84, 95, 114
Television viewing habits, 118
Tillman, V. D., 140, 143
Toma, E., 82, 83
Tracking, 158
Tullock, G., 65
Tushman, M. L., 56
Tyack, D. B., 55, 57, 58, 66

Unschooling movement, 33–34
  child-centered learning and, 34, 35
  children's rights and, 34, 35
  child's own best interests and, 34
  Christian fundamentalism and, 35
  countercultural/humanistic orientations
    and, 33
  flexible learning environments and, 34
  inherent goodness and, 34, 35
  instructional programming and, 106,
    114–115
  See also Homeschooling origins; Liberal
    progressive ideology

Valle, J. P., 79, 129, 132
Van Galen, J., 64, 85, 90
Van Horn, C. E., 73
Vanourek, G., 67
Vasudeva, A., 69
Vaupel, C., 134
Veritas curriculum, 115
Virtual institutions, 51

Vouchers, 2, 129

Ward, D. L., 106, 136, 156, 159
Wartes, J., 15, 17, 18, 19, 22, 23, 40, 108,
    112, 119, 126, 129, 135, 139
Watson, T. G., 136
Webb, J., 148, 150
Weller, N., 131, 132
Wells, A. S., 69
Wenders, J., 131, 132
Wenger, J., 1, 10, 136, 150
Whitehead, J., 38, 44, 156
Wilhelm, G., 125
Williams, D., 85, 101, 116, 118, 133
Winstanley, C., 102
Wood, P., 148
Woodruff, S., 37, 44, 125
Wraga, W. G., 57

York-Barr, J., 39, 77, 108, 140

Zirkel, P., 66

CORWIN

A SAGE Company

The Corwin logo—a raven striding across an open book—represents the union of courage and learning. Corwin is committed to improving education for all learners by publishing books and other professional development resources for those serving the field of PreK–12 education. By providing practical, hands-on materials, Corwin continues to carry out the promise of its motto: **"Helping Educators Do Their Work Better."**

Printed in the United States
By Bookmasters